WOMEN AND STATE SOCIALISM

£38·00
2D90

WOMEN AND STATE SOCIALISM

Sex Inequality in the Soviet Union
and Czechoslovakia

ALENA HEITLINGER

First published 1979 by
THE MACMILLAN PRESS LTD
London and Basingstoke
Associated companies in Delhi
Dublin Hong Kong Johannesburg Lagos
Melbourne New York Singapore Tokyo

Printed in Great Britain
by W & J Mackay Limited, Chatham

British Library Cataloguing in Publication Data

Heitlinger, Alena
  Women and State Socialism
  1. Women – Russia – Social conditions
  2. Women – Czechoslovakia – Social conditions
  I. Title
  301.41′2′0947   HQ1662

  ISBN 0–333–26227–1

For
Hana and Ota in Prague
and
Suse and Arnold in London

Contents

viii   *Contents*

List of Tables

ix

Acknowledgements

This book is an updated and substantially revised version of my doctoral thesis, which, in turn, was inspired by the re-emergence of the women's movement in the 1960s. In undertaking and preparing the book for publication, I received assistance from a number of people and institutions. I am particularly indebted to Professor Olive Banks, under whose supervision I worked at the University of Leicester. I should also like to thank Dr Miriam Glucksmann, now of the Polytechnic of the South Bank in London, and Dr Anthony T. Jones, now of the University of North Carolina at Chapel Hill, who supervised my thesis in its earlier stages. I am also grateful for their generous support, advice and helpful comments to the late Mr Geoffrey Barker, Dr Philip Hanson and Ms Alex Holt, all of the Centre for Russian and East European Studies at the University of Birmingham; Dr Sara Delamont, formerly of the University of Leicester and now of the University of Wales at Cardiff; Dr Lorna Duffin of the University of Leicester; Dr David Hughes of the City of Leicester Polytechnic; Dr Pradeep Bandyopadhyay of Trent University; and my husband, Dr David Morrison, of Trent University. My husband also provided me with invaluable editorial assistance during the preparation of the final draft of this book and I should like to express to him my special gratitude. My thanks for making improvements to the grammatical and stylistic presentation of this work also go to the following friends from Leicester and London: Gary Bates, Anne Cesek, Shen Colman, Kathy Fitzgibbon, Nick Guy, Nick and Jane Hislam, Ruth Horwell, Mike Kelly, Cherrie Knowles, Liz Mercer, Robert Owen, Margaret Page and Julia Velacott.

I am grateful for the financial assistance from the United Kingdom Social Science Research Council that I received as a Ph.D. student. I should also like to thank the Research Committee of Trent University for a generous grant to defray some of the costs entailed in completing this study. Both Leicester University and Trent University provided secretarial assistance and duplicating facilities. Ms June Lee and Ms Audrey Craig of Leicester and Ms Mary Snack of Peterborough deserve special thanks for secretarial assistance and for typing earlier drafts of the manuscript; so too do Ms Marisa Haensel of Peterborough for typing the final version of the book and Ms Susan Wheeler for preparing the index.

Finally, it must be noted that I alone am responsible for any errors or deficiencies in this study.

A.H.

1 Introduction

There has been considerable recent interest among feminist scholars in the implication for sex equality of the ideology of egalitarianism, but much of the debate about the nature of, and strategies for, the social emancipation of women has been confined to Western capitalist societies. State-socialist societies in Eastern Europe have been largely ignored by feminist scholarship in the West,[1] despite the fact that these societies themselves have an ideology of egalitarianism that incorporates a concern for sex equality. This book attempts to remedy the deficiency.

Although the ideology of egalitarianism suffers from a number of ambiguities, we can identify two broad perspectives on the form sex equality can take: assimilation, so that women become more like men, or an enlargement of the common ground on which men and women share their lives together. The assimilation model of sex equality tends to take the present social structure and its values favouring hard work, individualism, competition, aggression and power for granted. In other words, it is a rather one-sided plea for women to seek careers in the political and occupational world in sufficient numbers eventually to show a 50-50 distribution.

There are, however, a number of practical difficulties involved in this type of equality. For instance, does equality suffer more when 75 per cent of Soviet doctors are women or when 'only' 40 per cent of Soviet engineers are women? Another, more important problem is that a predominantly masculinity-oriented equality may facilitate an increasing similarity between the sexes without a parallel change in, and restructuring of, social institutions, thus leading to a double burden rather than to equality for women. The assimilation model also ignores the need for social compensation during the period when the female is pregnant and an understanding of the consequences of traditional sex-role socialisation.

The hybrid model of equality rejects both traditional psychological assumptions and the institutional structures we have inherited. It looks for equality on the basis of a radically restructured society (both in terms of institutions and values):

> The *hybrid* model is a radical goal which rejects the present structure of society and seeks instead a new breed of men and women and a new vision of the future . . . With the hybrid model of equality one envisages a future in which family, community, and play are valued on a par with

politics and work for both sexes, for all the races, and for all social classes and nations which comprise the human family (Rossi, 1969: 353).

However, as I am interested in the reality of contemporary life rather than in an imaginative conception of what a future good society should be, I have adopted a modified version of the 'assimilation' model of equality. The ideology of sex equality examined in this book is defined in terms of *roles*. It refers to a

> socially androgynous conception of roles of men and women, in which they are equal and similar in such spheres as intellectual, artistic, occupational, domestic and child-care interests and participation; and complementary only in those spheres dictated by physiological differences between the sexes (Rossi, 1964: 308).

What does this definition imply in terms of my own position on sex equality? Provided that present social institutions remain by and large intact (and this now includes widespread availability of housekeeping and child-care facilities), it urges men and women to change the social definitions of approved characteristics and behaviour for both sexes. For instance, child care and housekeeping should be an equally shared parental rather than solely a maternal responsibility.

The demand for equality in the labour force is more complex, because one has to take into account biological differences between the sexes. It is necessary to take into consideration woman's reproductive function, and labour legislation must have special rules relating to childbirth. This, however, does not mean that women should avoid *all* physically strenuous or disagreeable occupations (if any are left after mechanisation) as a matter of principle. Given that pleasant occupations are still relatively scarce in present-day societies, sex equality implies that women must also share the less-agreeable aspects of work.

In the context of this orientation towards the central issue, the book addresses the following questions. (1) How successful have the state-socialist societies been in implementing their ideology of equality, what has hindered them and what can we learn from their experiences about the 'optimal' conditions to achieve ideological goals? (2) What do the case studies tell us, in comparative terms, about the implications of policies affecting the sexual division of labour for broader social processes? (3) What is the relevance of these cases for Western feminist ideology and practice? Thus, I am concerned with the social, not the individual level of analysis.[2] As a sociologist, I am interested in the *social* processes involved in sex-role differentiation, not in the biological and psychological processes (if any).[3] Whether *individual* women want equality or not is bound up with their *social* position because that decision is a consequence of socialisation.

Any number of state-socialist societies (China, Cuba, etc.) could have been used to explore these questions, but I have chosen two European countries, the Soviet Union and Czechoslovakia, which are more relevant to our situation in the West than, say, China. These are also countries of which I have personal experience, since I was born in Prague and Czech is my mother tongue. I also read Russian, since the study of the Russian language and literature is compulsory in all East European schools; thus, I have been able to study the USSR, and its evident political presence in Eastern Europe, from primary sources. In fact, of course, the Soviet Union has assumed a much more dominant political position in Eastern Europe than the United States has in the Western world.

This does not, of course, mean that we should see Eastern Europe as a monolithic bloc, as many people in the West tend to do. The Soviet-type countries of Central and Eastern Europe do not constitute a single entity. Considerable differences exist in their sizes, social and economic development, urbanisation, living standards, social habits, religion, political traditions, and other characteristics. For instance, the USSR is the largest and most powerful declared socialist country in the world, while Bulgaria, Hungary and Czechoslovakia are rather small. Furthermore, the Soviet state-socialist transformation preceded those elsewhere by some 30 years and we can perhaps learn more from its much longer history than from that of the 'younger' Soviet-type societies. Nevertheless, we have to realise that on the eve of the October Revolution and for at least a decade afterwards, the USSR was a backward society, with a predominantly peasant and largely illiterate population (this also applies to Bulgaria, but certainly not to East Germany (the German Democratic Republic) or Czechoslovakia). The sheer weight of Soviet history, as an explanatory factor of the 'old-fashioned' nature of Soviet attitudes about women, is perhaps not so relevant to our situation in the West, and in this respect we can perhaps learn more from the state-socialist history of Czechoslovakia.

Czechoslovakia arose in 1918 as one of the successor states of the Austro-Hungarian Empire. It was a democratic republic, the only Western-type liberal state in the whole of Eastern and Central Europe. It was also the richest and most economically advanced, as the Czech lands inherited two-thirds of the industrial base of the Austro-Hungarian Empire. (Slovakia, in contrast to the Czech lands, was an economically undeveloped area.) Thus, Czechoslovakia was already economically and culturally advanced *before* its state-socialist transformation, which began in 1948. Its experience of 20 years of parliamentary democracy in the period between the two world wars makes it perhaps also more relevant to the West than the history of the Soviet Union.

This book therefore attempts to be less an examination of the two countries in themselves than a study of two countries which separately and together help us to understand the forces working for and against the liberation of women. As we all know, the position of women in Eastern Europe is far from satisfactory, despite the commitment to their liberation at a policy level. How can we account for the failure to implement policy? Among other factors, we look at:

1. Economic necessity: shortage of investment resources, low level of economic development, economic requirements for female labour and higher birthrates.
2. The Soviet model of socialist economic growth, which has been extensive, aimed at increasing the volume of capital goods and the size of the labour force engaged, including many women. (The Soviet pattern of industrialisation, giving a marked priority to heavy industry, thus depressing the consumer sector, i.e., trade, services and housing, was also adopted by Czechoslovakia.)
3. The existence of traditional structural arrangements, namely the individual family, housework and child care.
4. The prevalence of sexist cultural norms, supported by 'male chauvinism' and advice from experts.
5. The failure to understand the vital need for personal changes in any socialist society.

Our arguments are supported by data from Soviet, Czech and Slovak statisticians, economists, lawyers, psychologists, sociologists, historians, politicians, journalists and ordinary citizens, whose letters have been published in the press. Because of official censorship in all East European countries, these data are often incomplete and insufficient. A great deal of information is simply not available at all, or only for certain years. For instance, the huge Soviet statistical yearbook, *Narodnoe Khoziastvo*, devotes only five out of its 800 pages to data on individual earnings, and these are not differentiated by sex.[4] Information about abortion rates is also not published, despite the fact that the Soviet Union is estimated to have one of the highest abortion rates in the world. Moreover, many Soviet social-science publications are rather vague and lack precision. There is more information available within Czechoslovakia than in the USSR, which accounts for the greater richness of data on Czechoslovakia than on the Soviet Union. However, the Czechoslovak material also has to be treated critically. Since many publications are nearer to government propaganda than to an accurate picture of social reality, 'reading between the lines' and checking of accuracy is often necessary.

The book is divided into four parts. The first evaluates critically three existing theoretical perspectives that analyse social relationships between males and females: the structural-functional sociological approach; the classical Marxist theory of women and the family; and the current Marxist theory of domestic labour and reproduction of labour power. The chief concern of the second part is to examine the relationship between socialist and feminist movements within the comparative framework of the theory and practice of the German Social Democratic Party at the turn of the century, the Russian Bolshevik Party (both before and after the October Revolution), the Second and Third International, and the Czechoslovak Communist Party (both before and after the state-socialist transformation). The effects of the state-socialist transformation on the productive and reproductive roles of women in the Soviet Union and Czechoslovakia are discussed in the third and fourth parts respectively.

Part I
Theoretical Approaches to the Study of Women

2 The Sociological Approach of Structural-Functionalism

Although the study of social stratification has been prominent in theoretical and empirical research in sociology, the criterion of sex has played a relatively minor part in such studies.[1] Sociological analysis of social stratification has concentrated on differences between such social groupings as classes, races, castes, age-groups, elites and masses; sex-role differentiation has been largely ignored or dismissed as irrelevant. As Parkin (1971: 15) put it:

> . . . if the wives and daughters of unskilled labourers have some things in common with the wives and daughters of wealthy landowners, there can be no doubt that the *differences* in their overall situation are far more striking and significant.

As sex lines cut across class lines and as many sociologists regard the family, rather than the individual, as the basic unit of the social system,[2] many scholars have concluded that the nature and quality of sex-role differentiation is not comparable to that of other social categories. Moreover, sociologists interested in differentiation of sex roles have tended to approach the subject only through the study of the family. As the literature on the sociology of the family has been heavily influenced by structural-functionalism, the main theoretical arguments about sex roles have been concentrated in this particular school of thought.

Empirical studies informed by structural-functionalism have been focused upon: (1) the description of the existing division of labour between the sexes; and (2) the functions of this division for the maintenance of the family itself and other social systems, such as those based on occupation and personality. However, what has been lacking is any linkage between this specific aspect of the division of labour and concepts of inequality or conflict. In other words, functionalist family sociology has tended to devalue the importance of stratified relationships *within* the family and, by extrapolation, between the sexes in general. While class inequality has been linked with subjective aspects of stratification and with such concepts as life chances, income differences, differences in status and honour, differences in power and authority, such themes have not been prominent in the traditional sociological study of sex-role differentiation. For

9

instance, Talcott Parsons, one of the leading proponents of the approach, has not considered the possibility that the 'instrumental' role of the male could mean more formal power, since the father is the head of the household.

However, sex inequality can be relatively easily conceptualised. As Rossi (1969: 344) put it:

A group may be said to suffer from inequality if its members are restricted in access to legitimate valued positions or rewards in a society for which their ascribed status is not a relevant criterion.

One form of inequality is to be found in statutory and civil law, yet others are embodied in corporate or organisational policies and regulations and covert social pressures that restrict the aspirations or depress the motivation of individuals, first because they are women or men. For example, a society or an educational system that uniformly applies pressure on girls to avoid choices in medicine, engineering or law exercises covert pressures which bolster sexual inequality. Forms of inequality therefore range from explicit legal statute to corporate discriminatory regulations to informal social pressures. We can also distinguish types of inequality in various areas of social life. One can find sex inequality in the public sector (in education, employment, income distribution, political participation) and in the private sector (especially in the family).

These dimensions of inequality are nowhere mentioned in the structural-functionalist analysis of the division of labour between the sexes. All existing sex-role differentiations are seen as 'functional' to society, the family and the personality structure.[3] The family is seen as a functioning unit, adequately providing the basis for child care, sexual security and emotional protection. The functions that women may lose by entering a family (economic, educational, etc.) are seen to be more than compensated for in the remaining areas of emotionality and primary socialisation.

Talcott Parsons regards the typical contemporary urban middle-class family, with conventional differentiation by sex and age, as functional both for society and for the individuals concerned. The female position within the family and in society at large is seen in terms of maintaining group solidarity by virtue of preserving emotional, expressive, ascriptive and particularistic values. It is claimed that the woman's position as wife and mother institutionally segregates this set of values, 'reserved' for the family, from universalistic and achievement values, 'reserved' for the economic sphere and the occupational role of the father. It is also claimed that this conventional, mutually exclusive, sex-role differentiation is the major factor in stabilising adult personalities. This particular social arrangement is then justified on biological grounds, by the fact that

the bearing and early nursing of children establishes a strong presumptive primacy of the relation of mother to the small child and this in turn establishes a presumption that the man, who is exempted from these biological functions, should specialise in the alternative instrumental direction (Parsons and Bales, 1955: 23).

It is questionable whether the existing sex-role differentiation is as 'functional' and as 'integrative' for the individual's emotional stability as structural-functionalists have suggested. Parsons is so concerned with the adaptive nature of social processes that he tends to ignore the ways in which changes can set up new tensions and strains. However, one could argue that rather than satisfying each other's emotional needs, this structural setting in many instances creates frustration and alienating experience for both spouses, but especially for the wife. Many authors have suggested that because of the roles they typically occupy, women are more likely than men to have emotional problems;[4] moreover, disproportionately more women than men are found to be mentally ill.[5] What is especially significant is the fact that the major sex-related differences in rates of mental illness are found among married people. For example, in the United States single white women report less psychological distress than married or separated white women (Chesler, 1971: 748). Some studies investigating the relationship between marital status and mental disorder have even found that it is quite common among unmarried persons for men to have slightly higher rates of mental illness (Gove, 1972).

Certain forms of emotional disturbance are also found in the present-day mother-child relationship. A number of studies have pointed out that many housebound mothers experience a sense of deprivation (Friedan, 1963; Gavron, 1966; Oakley, 1974a, 1974b). Let us briefly look at Gavron's study. Her sample was made up of white working-class and middle-class mothers, all young married women living in London with their husbands, with at least one child. Almost all of the mothers in the sample experienced feelings of isolation and felt burdened with responsibility. They all felt that their children in some way restrictd their freedom, although the middle-class mothers defined the restriction more in psychological terms and the working-class mothers expressed it more in physical terms. Both groups found it difficult to articulate their uneasiness with their status. Neither Gavron nor the mothers questioned the inevitability of the conflict between the motherhood role and other social roles outside the family.

Parsons explicitly (and Gavron in her essentially empirical study implicitly) argue that maternity is the female social 'destiny'. This assumption has led Parsons to regard alternative social roles of the woman (especially in the labour force) as conflicting with the basic biological 'root' function of reproduction. Moreover, his analysis is extended to account for the difference between the roles performed by men and women in the occupational sphere. He claims (1955: 15) that the distribution of women in the labour force clearly confirms this general view of the balance of the sex roles. Thus, on higher levels typical feminine occupations are those of teacher, social worker, nurse, private secretary and entertainer. Such roles tend to have a prominent expressive component, and often to be 'supportive' to masculine roles. Within the occupational organisation, they are analogous to the wife-mother role in the family.

While the empirical observation is correct, the explanation is insufficient, as the Bankses (1964a) have pointed out. They argue that it is the whole trend of industrialisation rather than innate sex-role differences that accounts for the feminisation of certain sectors of the economy and for the lack of marked occupational achievement on the part of women. Women worked as assistants to their husbands and fathers before the Industrial Revolution, and their subsidiary role was later perpetuated and reinforced in factories and offices by protective legislation. In fact, the whole trend of industrialisation has been in the direction of an increasingly hierarchical organisation of roles within the economy, and bureaucratisation has created a large number of subsidiary positions within the occupational system for both men and women. However, the division of labour between the sexes has not corresponded closely to what Parsons sees as innate differences between the sexes: some roles with a strong 'expressive' element, such as personnel work, have been largely male-dominated.

The Parsonian account of the occupational structure is therefore questionable and the deduction made from the biological function of the woman is overstated. Yet the intellectual implications of reproductive determinism go further than this, because they have been largely responsible for the relegation of the study of women to the 'sociology of the family'. As Oakley (1974b: 16–17, 18) put it:

> If women have no place of their own in much sociology, they are firmly in possession of one haven: the family. In the family, women 'come into their own'; they *are* the family. By far the largest segment of sociological literature concerning women is focused on their roles as wives, mothers and housewives . . . Possibly the family and marriage are areas in which sociological visibility exceeds social presence; certainly the presence of males as fathers is not matched by an equal visibility in the discipline.

This line of thinking does not, of course, imply that marriage and family life are not important to women today. Indeed, the evidence suggests that these areas of experience are still crucial. But do we know *how* crucial? What has been lacking is a sociological account of the relative importance these areas play in the totality of women's experience. Other aspects of women's lives have been wholly or partially neglected. For instance, the relations between work and family life, and their impact on the role of women, have seldom been studied in structural-functional sociology. Those few studies which have dealt with the subject have failed to relate the 'dual' role of the working mother in a systematic fashion.[6] The conflict between these two roles has been taken for granted, and the analysis of the nature and significance of housework in modern industrial societies neglected.

The traditional academic sociology of women is therefore unsatisfactory, but this specific criticism must be linked with a more general complaint about structural-functionalist theory. The unsatisfactory treatment of women in sociology has been at least partly related to an underlying premise of functionalist sociology as a whole, namely its emphasis on the *status quo*, on persistence, integration and pattern maintenance.[7] It is these general shortcomings of functionalism that have been largely responsible for the failure of the sociological argument about sex-roles to go much beyond the level of description of what exists, or appears to exist, in certain sectors of Western industrial societies.

Indeed, some authors have gone as far as suggesting that the functionalist account of sex-role differentiation within the household and in society at large is not a theory at all, but an ideology.[8] Middleton (1974: 182–3) is very precise on this point, and deserves to be quoted at some length:

> In the present century, changing assumptions about human behaviour and its relationship to the social world (as embodied in the expanding disciplines of the social sciences) made a reformulation of sexist ideology imperative. The new improved version (Freud, Bowlby, Parsons, and Spock are key figures in this respect) has stressed the socio-psychological importance of the woman's traditional wife-mother role for other members of the family; and as I shall show it is in this variant that sexist ideology has had such a pervasive and subtle influence even on those who would discredit it . . .
>
> The functionalist theory of structural differentiation may be the sociological heir to the nineteenth-century conservative philosophy of organic harmony, but *that* philosophy had perceived woman as an inferior and subordinate being, whereas modern functionalism manages to combine the theory of organic harmony with an ideology of familial democracy. In other words, functionalism discounts the existence of actually prevailing inequalities between the sexes which conservative philosophy had at least acknowledged – even if it had done so with approval.

Finally, it is important to bear in mind that this sort of specific critique has emerged within the wider context of the so-called 'crisis' of contemporary academic sociology. Not only the Parsonian theory of women and the family, but the whole structural-functionalist approach has come under attack. As Giddens (1973: 13) puts it:

> Now sociologists are chronically subject to self-doubt and we might ask whether there is indeed anything unusual about the present situation of controversy on sociological *accidie*. The answer is that there is. The 'crisis' – a trite and unsatisfactory term in itself – in contemporary sociology is symptomatic of the fact that we stand at an important phase of transition in social theory. In broad outline, the origins of the current situation are not at all difficult to discern. Two connected sets of factors are involved. One is to be found in the events which, in the past few years, have disrupted the pattern of 'consensus politics' in the capitalist societies: the increase in strike levels in certain countries, the struggles in France in 1968, and the eruption of student protest movements. To these may be added the conflicts which have arisen within the socialist world, culminating in the Soviet invasion of Czechoslovakia. The second factor is the manifest poverty of the dominant forms of theory in sociology in accounting for these events. In academic sociology, structural-functionalism, and its main interpretative support, theories of 'the end of ideology' appear blank and barren in the face of a new upsurge of social and political conflict in the West. But Marxism, especially as transmuted into the official ideology of state socialism, seems equally inept when confronted with the events of the recent past.

Giddens raises a number of points that are relevant to this study. Firstly, one could legitimately argue that his list of 'events which in the past few years have disrupted the pattern of "consensus politics" in the capitalist societies' should also have included the emergence of the Black Power Movement and the Women's Liberation Movement. Secondly, the structural-functionalist theory of women appears 'blank and barren' not only in the face of a new upsurge of feminism, but also in the face of such a 'non-militant' phenomenon as the growing entry of women into paid employment. If women are seen primarily as wives and mothers, and if these 'root' functions are considered as conflicting with their gainful employment, how do we account for the growing numbers of women entering paid employment – a trend characteristic of *all* industrial societies? Furthermore, if women are supposed to specialise in the 'expressive' direction, both within the family and in the occupational structure, how do we explain within the Parsonian framework the large numbers of Soviet women scientists and engineers? Surely, they cannot all be 'deviant'?

Thus, structural-functionalism is clearly unsatisfactory. What strategy should one then adopt at the level of sociological theory? Does the traditional Marxist theory of women offer a better alternative?

3 Classical Marxist Theory of Women's Oppression and Liberation

In liberal capitalist countries the influence of academic theory on social reality is rather limited and often unintentional, because the link between theory and practice is only implicit. However, in state-socialist societies Marxist theory is explicitly treated as a political ideology, as a guide to action for socialist revolution, socialist reconstruction and the transition to communism. Within this context, the Marxist theory of women's oppression and emancipation is a significant factor in our understanding of the position of women in state-socialist societies.

Marxists have been aware of the subordination of women largely in terms of the moral problematics for socialists, and all Marxist political movements have been explicitly committed to women's emancipation. However, such a commitment was not, on the whole, considered a political priority (as we shall see in Part II); moreover, the level of theoretical discussion on the issue never matched the degree of sophistication attained by Marxist analysis of class antagonisms. When one considers the volume of writing by Marxists, the amount of space devoted to the 'woman question' is indeed negligible. As a result, the one classical text that does deal with sexual inequality and female emancipation has assumed particular significance in defining the Marxist position on the question – Frederick Engels's *The Origin of the Family, Private Property and the State*, first published in 1884. (August Bebel's *Woman and Socialism*, published in 1875, never assumed the same degree of *theoretical* significance.) Engels's book laid the foundations both for a socialist theory of women's oppression and a strategy for women's emancipation. An evaluation of the strengths and weaknesses of Engels's analysis is therefore important in giving us one set of criteria for assessing the performance of Marxist parties and states in promoting and achieving sex equality.

Engels's analysis can be considered in three parts: (1) the reconstruction of the past; (2) the oppression of women under capitalism; and (3) women's emancipation under socialism. The first part is controversial and problematic, and in many places misleading and inadequate.[1] Far more evidence than Engels offers is needed to clarify the supposedly egalitarian status of women in primitive societies and the process of women's subjugation in relation to the rise of private property, class distinctions, commodity production, the economic isolation of the family and patrilineal kinship. The current archeological and anthropological data suggest that sex oppression pre-dates class oppression, though there is some evidence to support the argument that the position of women relative to men deteriorated with the advent of class societies and colonial conquest (Leacock, 1972).

ENGELS'S CONDITIONS FOR WOMEN'S SOCIAL EMANCIPATION

The argument that sexual liberation is impeded by the structures of class societies is quite uncontroversial. Engels correctly understood that female inequality in capitalist societies is due to the institution of private property, women's private service within the family, their inability to work outside the home and their material dependence on men. Sacks (1975: 216–17), in reviewing Engels, argues that

> with time, production by men specifically for exchange purposes developed, expanded, and came to overshadow the household's production for use . . . As production for exchange eclipsed production for use, it changed the nature of the household, the significance of women's work within it, and consequently women's position in society. Women worked for their husbands and families instead of for society as a whole. Private property made its owner the ruler of the household . . . Women became wards, wives and daughters instead of adult members of the society . . . Women's reproductive labour, like their productive work, also underwent a transformation from social to private. That is, women bore men's heirs – to both property and social position – whereas before they had borne new members of a social group that included men and women.

Sacks claims that, in fact, it is the exclusion of women from the growing public sphere of political and economic activities as much as their restriction to a domestic setting which is the critical factor in their infantilisation – a process which culminates in Western society in the dependent housewife, and in non-Western societies in the veiled and secluded women we associate with 'purdah'.

Social equality between the sexes, according to Engels, was to be achieved once the restrictions excluding women from the public sphere were eased. As this could be accomplished only through a socialist revolution, the emancipation of women was seen as an element in the proletarian struggle. In other words, the abolition of private property and its replacement by social ownership and control of the means of production were seen as the most fundamental *pre-conditions* for the emancipation of women. The realisation of sexual equality was thought to be brought about by two specific structural changes: the reintroduction of women into social production and the socialisation of private domestic work and care of children.

> . . . the first condition for the liberation of the wife is to bring the whole female sex back into public industry, and . . . this in turn demands that the characteristic of the monogamous family as the economic unit of society be abolished (1972: 137–8).

> With the transfer of the means of production into common ownership, the single family ceases to be the economic unit of society. Private housekeeping is transformed into a social industry. The care and education of the children becomes a public affair; society looks after all children alike, whether they are legitimate or not (ibid: 139).

Engels's successors further elaborated these strategic perspectives, seeing full entry of women into social production both as a means of escaping household drudgery and as a pre-condition of their emancipation in a wider context. As Lenin (1965: 64) put it:

> The *real emancipation of women*, real communism, will begin only where and when an all-out struggle begins (led by the proletariat wielding the state power) against this petty housekeeping, or rather when its *wholesale transformation* into a large-scale socialist economy begins. (Italics are Lenin's own.)

Lenin (ibid.: 64) was also quite explicit on why a socialist, rather than a capitalist, economy is required for the industrialisation of housework.

> Public catering establishments, nurseries, kindergartens – here we have examples of these shoots, here we have the simple, everyday means, involving nothing pompous, grandiloquent or ceremonial, which can *really emancipate women*, really lessen and abolish their inequality with men as regards their role in social production and public life. These means are not new, they (like all the material pre-requisites for socialism) were created by large-scale capitalism. But under capitalism, they remained, first, a rarity, and secondly – which is particularly important – either *profit-making* enterprises, with all the worst features of speculation, profiteering, cheating and fraud, or 'acrobatics of bourgeois charity', which the best workers rightly hated and despised. (Italics are Lenin's own.)

However, Lenin made a significant point when he suggested that the socialisation of domestic activity can be met, under certain circumstances, *within* capitalist society itself. Socialists should not find this so very surprising since it does not conflict with

> Marx's own analysis suggesting that the socialisation of production (and to this we now have to add the socialisation of domestic production and reproduction) was the historic task of capitalism – not of socialism. Indeed, it is this process that creates the contradictions in a society characterised by private appropriation (Middleton 1974: 199).

This argument, of course, does not preclude the possibility that a socialisation of domestic labour could be also implemented, perhaps even more effectively, in a socialist planned economy. State-socialist societies lack private property[2] and their resource ownership is centrally controlled. As a result, the substantial cost involved in unifying the processes of domestic labour and commodity production could be spread throughout the whole society.

However, in assessing these early Marxist writings, it is important to point out that the arguments were one-sided, that they underestimated the pressures that eventually did work *against* the socialisation of housework and child-care in the state-socialist societies. To Lenin, analysing the question in somewhat abstract terms, the savings in labour time resulting from socialising housework would substantially cheapen the process. This impression was mistaken, for savings in time represent only one outcome of socialisation. Another arises when previously unpaid domestic labour becomes wage work and it commands payment in accordance with what is generally expected in the labour market, thus actually becoming more expensive. As a result, *very* great savings in labour time are necessary for the socialisation of domestic labour to become a viable economic proposition. For instance, it has been argued that adequate socialised child care requires a minimum of one adult to five children, without taking into account administrative and ancillary staff. If one compares these numbers with an average family of two to three children to one woman, one arrives at a rough estimate suggesting that the saving of labour is no more than 50 per cent (Gardiner, 1975).

During the period of War Communism (1918–21), when the world revolution was still expected, the Bolsheviks were optimistic that rapid economic development would be achieved, thus making possible early progress towards socialising housework and childcare. As it became increasingly obvious that matters were not working out this way, no one in the Bolshevik party, except Alexandra Kollontai (a prominent Bolshevik feminist) and a few others in the women's department, was aware that another approach to women's liberation was necessary. As a result, the Soviets and, later, other state-socialist regimes by and large ignored Engels's second condition of women's emancipation, that traditional family responsibilities should be socialised. Housework has remained a private and largely female responsibility.

Meanwhile, all East European countries did act upon Engels's first condition, that women should be reintroduced to social production. There developed a nearly universal expectation that women would work and see work outside the home as a central continuing feature of their lives. In time, this change had profound psychological consequences in terms of women's confidence and their concern with intellectual and social problems and public affairs generally. However, the failure to achieve more than minimal restructuring of working and living arrangements has meant that, unlike working fathers, the majority of working mothers have had to undertake two jobs – one in the family and one outside the home. Because of this, women's participation in the economy has turned out to be something quite different from what Engels intended – gainful employment outside the home has been added to work in the home. As Firestone (1972: 248) writes, 'the roles of women were enlarged rather than redefined'. However, we cannot blame Engels or Lenin for this 'masculine equality', but rather East European practice, which has chosen to ignore one of the most vital conditions of women's emancipation.

What we can blame Engels for is his inadequate analysis of the nature of *individual* housework and its role in the reproduction of labour power under capitalism. The main fault lies in his too-narrow definition of production, which derives more from capitalist than Marxist ideology. He was probably struck by the new separation of home from work and by the visible exclusion of the wife and the family from the factory, and therefore did not consider domestic labour as production. We are, however, only speculating. Whatever the reason, the fact remains that Engels failed to apply the Marxist concepts of use-value, exchange-value and surplus-value to the analysis of domestic labour. He merely made a distinction between the material production of the means of subsistence and the biological reproduction of the human species, but said nothing about their interrelationship. We shall take up this question again in Chapter 4, in the context of more recent writings that apply Marxian categories of analysis to domestic labour and the reproduction of labour power.[3]

WOMEN'S PERSONAL LIBERATION UNDER SOCIALISM

Having briefly discussed sex equality on the policy level, we can now turn to the individual level. Engels is less helpful here, because his discussion of the ordering of sexual relationships under socialism (which he predicts will be monogamous and based on romantic love) is speculative and expresses only his personal opinion. He freely admits that future generations may think differently from him:

What we can now conjecture about the way in which sexual relations
will be ordered after the impending overthrow of capitalist production is
mainly of negative character, limited for the most part to what will
disappear. But what will there be new? That will be answered when a
new generation has grown up . . . When these people are in the world,
they will care precious little what anybody today thinks they ought to
do; they will make their own practice and their corresponding public
opinion about the practice of each individual . . . (1972: 145)

Thus, although Engels takes romantic love and monogamy as 'given' for
himself, he is reluctant to engage in utopian speculation and he leaves the
future open to the historical forces that will shape it.

Alexandra Kollontai was the only Russian social theorist of any
prominence who expanded on Engels's ideas about personal relationships.
She was also the only Bolshevik thinker who focused directly upon the
personal liberation and psychological self-transformation of both men and
women. She argued in her pamphlets and novels that, under socialism,
relationships between men and women would be based on complete
freedom, equality, genuine friendship and free love. She opposed the old
hypocritical philistine morality, characterised by the advocacy of monogamy on the one hand and the patronage of prostitution on the other.
(This contradiction had already been brought out by Engels.) Moreover,
she also criticised the oppressive nature of individual sex love, where each
partner possesses the other and both are jealous of each other.

Kollontai called for greater fluidity and experimentation in sexual
relationships, and this is where she not only radically diverged from
Engels, but also met disapproval from the Bolshevik leadership. The
Bolsheviks had some justification for their criticism: her pamphlet *Sexual
Relations and the Class Struggle* represented a development and expansion of
Engels's theory, but, as a foundation for social policy for the Soviet Union
of the 1920s, her ideas were unrealistic. Free love came to be used as an
expression and justification of social and moral disintegration under War
Communism (1918–21) and the New Economic Policy (1921–28),
characterised, among other things, by widespread sexual exploitation of
women rather than by personal freedom and social care. The unavailability of contraception only added to the difficulties experienced by
the majority of women in their lives during that period. Sexual freedom
therefore meant sexual freedom for men only. Rather than liberating
women, it burdened them with unwanted pregancies, children and
abortions.[4]

In terms of how people of peasant origin would respond to her analysis at
a personal level, Kollontai was thus out of touch with social reality. Given
the existing cultural level, it was inevitable that Soviet women and men
would misunderstand and distort such radical ideas as separation of
sexuality from love or sexual experimentation generally.[5] However, to do

Kollontai justice, we need to stress that the essay *Sexual Relations and the Class Struggle* was written about 1913 and was not, therefore, addressed specifically to the sexual problems of the Russian Revolution. Kollontai's championing of abortion, her stand on the question of prostitution, her work for the economic emancipation of women and her novels show, I think, that she was aware of the complexities of achieving sexual freedom.

Lenin was the primary mover behind the notion that the revolution demanded more discipline and less personal freedom. He argued that the nature of sexual morality was not a private and personal affair (as Engels had argued it would be under full communism), but a social matter – a duty towards the community. Although he did not advocate sexual abstinence, he did not formulate a positive concept of sexual life for youth either, thus playing down the role of sexuality in both private and social life.[6]

Lenin's successors moved much further in the direction of repressing freedom (including sexual freedom) in personal and social life. Wilhem Reich saw the new repressive measures of the 1930s (e.g. the reintroduction of legislation against homosexuality, emphasis on discipline and authority) as symbolising the 'betrayal' of the revolution. In the 1930s, Kollontai was no longer published and her public opponent, Professor Zaldkin, became the semi-official Soviet spokesman on sexuality. An inverse relationship was postulated between sexuality and the class struggle, between the heroic 'building of socialism' and the 'unhealthy' preoccupation with the realm of private pleasure. In other words, Soviet people were urged not to 'waste' time on socially 'unproductive' sexuality, but rather to engage in fulfilling the Five-Year Plans (Geiger, 1968: 84–8).

In the late 1930s, all references to sex were practically eliminated from fiction, cinema, theatre and education. Until the early 1960s, there was hardly any public discussion of matters relating to sex. This has now changed: sex is publicly discussed in mass media, but the discussion usually takes the form of attacking young people for deviating from the official sexual morality. Girls are taught to be inhibited, modest and passive in their sexual encounters. For example, Lidia Bogdanovich, a doctor of medicine, from the Laboratory for the Problems of Sex Education of the USSR Academy of Pedagogical Sciences' Research Institute for General Problems of Education, argues that

> girls should learn self-respect, then there won't be any need to pass a law prohibiting hugging and kissing on the street. Woman's modesty increases man's sexual energy but lack of it repels men and brings about total fiasco in their intimate relations (*Ogonyok*, no. 26, June 1972. Translated in *CDSP*, vol. xxiv, no. 45).

The official way of thinking about sex under socialism has therefore remained virtually unchanged since the 1930s. Monogamy for both sexes, heterosexuality and no sex outside marriage have remained the official doctrine. No social theorist of any importance has emerged in the Soviet Union to develop a critique of these views or to construct a new theory of the significance of sex under socialism.[7] Reich's claim that the theory of the sexual revolution was always lacking in general socialist theory and that there was no attempt made to change the 'antisexual, moralistic, inhibited, lascivious, jealous, possessive, generally neurotic psychic structure of men and women' is still relevant today. Moreover, the already existing contributions of Reich and Kollontai have been ignored, played down or even suppressed.[8]

There is, however, a great deal of evidence that many individuals are less puritanical than the tone of many official discussions would suggest. For example, S. I. Golod has studied attitudes towards premarital sex among students and professional people and found that the majority of his respondents approved of such relations (Hollander, 1973: 209–10). Taubman (1967: 216) in his report on MGU students, recalls instances when 'students lived together for weeks and months without being disturbed. Some ended up getting married, and others drifted apart.' In fact, if George Feifer's recent novel, *Moscow Farewell* (1976) is anything to go by, many Russians are sexually very free and uninhibited.

Why then have sexual relations and freedom been surrounded with so much silence or hostility in the communist countries? Hobsbawm (1969) has argued that, while there is no intrinsic connection between the degree of sexual permissiveness and the type of system of political rule (a statement which is certainly open to a debate), there is a definite affinity between revolution and puritanism. Although most revolutionary movements have been characterised by a strong element of personal libertarianism, puritanism has always prevailed. This pattern certainly applies to the course of Soviet history, but we are not offered any hypothesis why this had to happen.[9]

The fact that all communist-ruled countries are today authoritarian rather than revolutionary may account for some of the obstruction of sexual revolution there. It can be argued that sexual freedom is incompatible with a strict authoritarian rule and child-socialisation within an authoritarian family. While sexual freedom and permissiveness do not necessarily politicise people and make them revolt (permissive sexuality might even act as a 'retreat sphere', thus actively hindering radicalisation), they do represent independent thinking and deviation from accepted norms. People who experiment with their personal lives might not pose any real political threat, but they do not submit easily to rigid authority. Thus it could be argued that the anti-homosexual legislation in authoritarian Russia was a response to the potential political implications of homosexuality rather than simply to homosexuality as such. Stalin needed more soldiers and a higher birth rate, and homosexuals did not fit the existing role-stereotypes of masculine warriors versus feminine mothers.

I think it important to stress the underdevelopment of classical Marxism in the analysis of women and the family, but it should be pointed out that this is an historical rather than an inherent weakness. A certain level of female involvement in the labour force and a change in sex-role stereotypes are necessary before women of the working class become militant as a group, and certain social and political conditions are necessary for the development of women theoreticians. Though women do not have a monopoly over the understanding of their oppression, it is obvious that they will make the greatest contribution to its full understanding. Thus, the concluding points are not that Engels was wrong in believing that heterosexuality and monogamy are 'natural', or in saying that the family as an economic unit will disappear under socialism, but that, on the one hand, the transition to socialism has not taken place under the circumstances that Engels envisaged and that, on the other, he did not give a sufficiently detailed analysis of the family under capitalism for socialists to do more than build upon during the period of transition. Finally, as we shall see in the next chapter, we must recognise that Engels's approach remains the only one on which it has yet been possible for modern feminists to develop their theory and practice.

4 Marxist Theory of Domestic Labour and Reproduction of Labour Power

In Marxist analysis, labour power is defined as the capacity to work, as the quality of a living labourer, which is sold on the labour market and exchanged for a living wage. The concept is particularly applicable to the proletarian class which, being excluded from ownership of the means of production, is forced to sell its only commodity: labour power. In turn, its reproduction consists of two distinguishable processes: (1) the daily maintenance of the labour power of those members of the family who work in the market economy (they are fed, clothed, rested, able to resume work the following day); and (2) the continuing reproduction of new generations of living labourers (which involves both biological reproduction and the socialisation of a labour force of a certain kind). These reproductive tasks have, of course, been historically performed by women. Let us look at each process in turn.

DOMESTIC LABOUR

In Marxist theory, productive labour in the sphere of work creates exchange-value, that is to say, it can be sold on the market, and as such can be a source of surplus-value. However, as Marx made clear, this type of commodity production does not exhaust all the forms of socially necessary and useful labour. Because a given system of economic production is surrounded by historically-specific social relations, it is these which dictate whether or not any particular form of socially necessary labour is considered 'productive'. Under capitalism, characterised by commodity production and typically private appropriation of surplus, the main criterion for determining the productive character of labour is whether or not it creates a surplus as a source of profit. In this sense, the labour of self-employed people such as peasants (who produce for their own consumption but not for the market) is socially useful (that is, it has use-value);

24

however, from the capitalist standpoint, it is not productive as it does not involve commodity production or create a surplus.

Domestic labour performed by the unpaid housewife for the benefit of her family falls into the same category. Commodities which the housewife buys at the market are not in themselves in a finally consumable form. Food must be unpacked, cooked and served; clothes must be washed and mended. Housework therefore transfers and creates use-values, but, because it does not have exchange-value, it in itself cannot produce a surplus. Domestic work has and creates exchange-value only when domestic services are transferred to the social sphere of production outside the home, or are performed within it by a paid servant or a housekeeper instead of an unpaid wife. In other words, only housework that is transformed into commodity labour exchangeable on the market can be considered as economically productive from the capitalist standpoint.

But how does this theory apply to socialism? What criteria should we adopt to determine 'productive' labour, that is, labour that develops specifically socialist forms of production and appropriation? Among early Soviet economists S. G. Strumilin was the leading proponent of the view that the only relevant criterion that determines the productive character of labour in a socialist society is its social nature. All social forms of labour that promote the welfare of the whole society are seen as productive. The only unproductive labour in a socialist economy is work directed solely towards private satisfaction and enrichment. In fact, Strumilin went as far as to include individual housework in the category of productive labour. He argued that, owing to the temporary inability of the Soviety economy to devote sufficient resources to the socialisation of individual housework, Soviet housewives were performing socially necessary, and thus productive labour (Strumilin, 1926).

However, the theoretical position that came to prominence in the Soviet Union in the 1930s was not that of Strumilin. Soviet statistics since then have distinguished between social activities that directly create national income (i.e. labour that is eventually embodied in material products), and those that only share in its utilisation. In fact, the embodiment of labour in a material product was adopted as the only criterion for determining the productive character of labour. Labour involved in administration and public services (the latter including institutionalised forms of social reproduction of labour power) came to be regarded as socially necessary, but unproductive. Family-based housework was not even considered.

The analytical validity of this distinction need not concern us as much as its political implications. As the Soviet Union had only limited resources, these were primarily allocated to the sphere of the economy defined as the most productive – heavy industry. Czechoslovakia had a similar experience: public services were left short of both material resources and labour power. Since labour in public services was regarded as unproductive, their extensive development was seen as undesirable. The logical conclusion from this is the rather absurd position that reproduction of labour power is unproductive under *all* circumstances!

In recent years, labour involved in public services has been again accepted as productive. For example, the Czech political economist Kerner (1973) regards all services as directly contributing to the creation of national income, thus being productive. The argument has therefore come a full circle. Since public services are now seen as productive, domestic labour within the public sector is also seen as productive and as socialist in the ways Lenin envisaged more than 50 years ago. In fact, Kontšeková (1968: 15–21), a woman and a prominent Slovak political economist, views the gradual elimination of individual housework as leading to further development of a socialist form of production and its corresponding form of appropriation (which is not defined). However, this line of analysis has yet to be translated into state-socialist policy as we shall see in greater detail later.

To digress briefly, it is ironic that advanced capitalism has produced more significant changes in the nature of domestic labour than state-socialism. Semi-processed foods, expanded and rationalised shopping facilities, dry-cleaning and laundering services on the one hand, and specialised household appliances such as washing-machines, mixers, vacuum-cleaners, freezers and microwave ovens on the other, are much more developed in the West than in the East. Since these facilities complement and to some extent replace the labour of the housewife, the position of women in the advanced capitalist societies is better in this respect than that of their counterparts in the state-socialist countries.

However, one needs to point out that in the West modern household technology has entered the home only on the level of commodity consumption. As Coulson (1973) put it:

> . . . each home requires – ideally – cooker, refrigerator, vacuum-cleaner, washing-machine, iron, etc. so that each domestic labourer may utilise these machines in the most inefficient way, in the isolated conditions in which she works, for the benefit of two or three other people, while millions of other domestic labourers with a similar range of machines go through almost identical routines for the sake of their two or three other people. The immediate gain from this duplication being the maximum sale of household commodities.

Thus, the main drawback of individual household appliances is their low productivity. Because they are so specialised, they are used within each household only once or twice a day. Public household services could make more effective use of them, but this would contradict the notion of 'personal freedom'. Moreover, an important aspect of domestic labour is the creation of a direct emotional relationship within the family, and there are, so far, few ways in which individual emotional needs can be satisfied outside the family. Families with sufficient means to purchase commodity substitutes for housework might well feel immeasurably worse off and indeed highly discontented if they were *forced* to take full advantage of their gadgets.

In the state-socialist countries, the dilemma has not been whether to use public household services or individual household appliances, but whether to use some form of domestic mechanisation or to do everything manually. Research undertaken in Czechoslovakia in 1959 revealed that only 8 per cent of households used the services of laundries for washing large items of clothing. Forty-four per cent of households washed such items in their own washing-machines and more than 30 per cent washed them by hand (Fukalová, 1967). Within this context, the overall effect of individual household gadgets is positive. Regardless of its social or individual form, modern household technology provides substitutes for the heaviest work and shortens the time for its execution.

However, in both West and East, when compared with the great technological and organisational advances in the social sphere of production, the labour process in the home has remained extremely primitive and inefficient, since its organisation has remained completely static. In other words, although the productivity of domestic labour has increased in absolute terms, it has fallen significantly behind the productivity of industrial labour. Because of this, more and more married women are working outside the home rather than within it. At the same time, the advance of technology and the rising productivity of labour in the industrial sector have lowered the cost of many consumer goods. Their lower cost has put them almost within reach of the majority of people.

To maintain what is now considered a reasonable standard of living, families must purchase a growing number of goods and services which are rapidly coming to be regarded as indispensable both in the capitalist and the state-socialist countries. In order to be in a financial position to purchase them, many wives must work outside the home. The existence of these goods and services is in turn a pre-requisite for women taking outside employment. It is the production of these goods and services that women themselves produced once in the home which has led to the expansion of 'female' occupations, certainly in the Western countries and to a large extent in the state-socialist societies as well. In Czechoslovakia, many women work because their husbands' wages cannot buy what seems necessary to maintain the family at a reasonable standard of living, although a higher proportion than in the West also work for other reasons.

Staying at home and trying to stretch their husbands' wages further (by mending rather than buying new things, shopping more carefully, cooking more – that is, using fewer costly prepared foods) is no longer a viable alternative for the majority of married women today. As industrialisation develops, the housewife has to work more hours in the home to equal work done in any given hour spent in factories producing wage goods. The money she can earn more than offsets the extra cost of maintaining the family. That housewives have a portion of their wage left after meeting the costs of baby-sitting, prepared foods and household gadgets, etc. is not because women's wages have risen; on the contrary, women's wages in the West as well as in the East have either remained the same or declined relative to male wages. Rather, the reason is to be found in the relatively high productivity in the industrial sector compared to the low productivity of domestic labour.

Thus, the central feature of women's position today is not their role simply as domestic workers, but rather the fact that they are both domestic and wage labourers. It is this dual and contradictory role, actualised or only latent, that generates their specific social situation, and that forms the basis of their inequality *vis-à-vis* men. Because of this dual position, housewives have been compelled to sell their labour more cheaply than their male counterparts. A number of reasons account for this.

First, women themselves have been inclined to accept lower wages or part-time employment. After all, given the pervasive and subtle influence of the sexual division of labour, the idea of women's primary responsibility and fulfilment in the family, rather than at work outside the home, is easily accepted and taken for granted. Secondly, women's work productivity has indeed, on the whole, been lower than that of men. Given the degree of physical and mental exhaustion produced by two jobs, one in the home and one at work, female productivity is unlikely to be as high as that of men. As I shall show in greater detail later, this relationship between the social sphere of 'work' and the private sphere of 'home' is the ultimate cause of women's oppressive labour conditions in modern industrial societies, both capitalist and state-socialist.

GENERATIONAL REPRODUCTION

Having examined the day-to-day reproduction of labour power and its relationship to commodity production, we can now turn to the analysis of generational reproduction. The Marxist theory of domestic labour is not very helpful here as it has paid insufficient attention to changing social perceptions of the family. All changes have been explained in terms of the productive processes of capitalism itself. The emergence of childhood as a social category pre-dating capitalism has been largely ignored, though this theme has played a prominent part in the radical feminist analysis.[1] As Firestone (1973: 85), its chief representative put it (and her analysis in this respect is based almost entirely on Phillipe Ariès's now widely acclaimed book *Centuries of Childhood*):

> . . . the development of the modern family meant the breakdown of a large, integrated society into small, self-centred units. The child within

these conjugal units now became important, for he was the *product of that unit*, the reason for its maintenance. (My italics.)

To put it differently, parents in modern industrial societies seek to reproduce not their society or lineage but themselves through their children. Hence, the modern child-centred nuclear family is not merely an agent of consumption, and of reproduction of labour power, but also a means of private reproduction of children, a means of the reproduction of individuals into which society decomposes (Harris, 1975). The emotional and ideological content of the present-day family is qualitatively different from its pre-industrial predecessor.[2] Needless to say that this historical transformation has led to some new contradictions for the family as well as for society as a whole. The most serious contradiction arises from the private and public nature of children: agents such as the state, along with their parents, have an interest in them. Hence, the emergence of the family as a closed household centred around child-rearing has coincided with attempts on the part of the state to interfere in the private production of children (Harris, 1975).

This interference has been much greater in the state-socialist societies than in the capitalist ones, largely because strategies for economic growth in the former have required population policies that have clearly conflicted with reproductive behaviour among individuals. By and large, these strategies have been aimed at a rapid growth of capital stocks, rather than on immediate improvement in labour productivity. This pattern of economic growth, based as it has been on a quantitative rather than qualitative improvement in the labour force, has required a substantial increase in the employment of women – the reserve army of labour. This in turn has led, among other outcomes, to the exhaustion of the labour supply and a rapid decline in fertility. As the possibility of importing labour from non-socialist countries is limited for ideological and political reasons, further extensive growth depends upon increased levels of natural replacement in the labour force.

Policy-makers in these societies are therefore faced with the task of finding material, psychological and emotional incentives that will per-suade individual families to produce more children. Although external support to larger families and the protection of employment rights for females on maternity leave have been in existence since the early days of the state-socialist transformation, motivations for a large family have been obviously weak and insufficient. The private procreation of children in child-centred families means that parents are primarily producing children for themselves and not for society as a whole. If the birth of additional children is seen as causing financial hardship and/or a shortage of living space, or if maternity is considered to compete with female economic roles, women are likely to decide to limit the size of their families, regardless of the economic needs of society as a whole. An individual decision to have an additional child must therefore be the result of strong pressures, both in terms of economic and psychological motivation. Hence, we have recently seen the emergence of extensive pro-natalist incentives in the East European countries.

The current fiscal measures (systems of family allowances and tax deductions, assistance with childbirth, rent rebates depending on the number of children, relatively cheap children's products, etc.) were originally introduced to produce greater social justice and opportunity, and to affirm the responsibility of the state for the welfare of the family, especially families with larger numbers of children. However, in the 1960s, following a decade of substantially declining birth rates, demographic objectives seem to have become the principal reason for extending these measures. The most important pro-natalist innovation, the so-called maternity allowance, has to be seen in this context. Introduced for the first time in Hungary and since adopted by Czechoslovakia and Bulgaria, this allowance permits mothers (it is not offered to fathers) to stay at home to look after their small children for up to three years without losing their jobs or seniority. In one sense, then, this measure represents an attempt to transform maternity into paid social labour. In other words, it transforms the private, but unpaid, procreation of children for use-value into a still private, but paid, production of children for exchange-value.

This transformation has important implications for the social meaning and significance of maternity. Because of their merit in upholding the level of reproduction, mothers have become much more useful for society than was traditionally admitted in socialist theory and practice. On the other hand, by acquiring this new social recognition and prestige, maternity also reinforces the confines of the female biological situation and the traditional sexual division of labour. In this sense, the production of children has a paradoxical effect on the position of women in the state-socialist countries.

However, this paradox, arising from the contradiction between the private nature and collective consequences of biological reproduction, also has important implications for the Marxist theory of domestic labour. The position of women has to be understood in terms of the historically-specific nuclear family centred around the private procreation of children, and Harris (1975) has argued that it is this aspect of the family which requires its isolation and the immersion of the housewife within it. He has also claimed that the 'collectivisation' of household tasks is in contradiction to the nature of the family as a means of private reproduction.

This argument is questionable. While collective production of children is more difficult to imagine than centralised domestic labour, it is by no means impossible. In fact, all societies intervene in procreation, up to a point. For instance, many primitive societies adopted *social* procedures of birth control, namely infanticide. Female infanticide was usually practised where women were considered to be economic liabilities, as in the patriarchal societies of ancient Greece and Rome, as well as India and

China. Small-scale societies such as the early *kibbutzim* used to make collective decisions about the procreation of children on the basis of the economic needs and resources of the whole group. Chinese communes are also attempting to decide collectively about the number of children produced in any particular year; parents are urged to adopt social rather than individual criteria – the needs of China as a whole are to come before individual parental wishes for male offspring.

In a market economy the social procedures of controlling the procreation of children will normally take the form of financial incentives or disincentives, although ideological, nationalistic or eugenic factors might also have some importance. Control does not always work, but the processes of giving birth and raising children are too important for societies to leave uncontrolled. Nevertheless, as far as the future is concerned, it is likely that biological reproduction of future generations will remain private and rooted within the child-centred nuclear family. However, given the rising rate of divorce and the expansion of child-care facilities, other people besides the natural parents are likely to be increasingly involved in the process of socialisation.

Once an analysis of the relationship between biological reproduction and the wider social formation is incorporated in the Marxist theory of reproduction of labour power, this perspective does seem to offer a better alternative for the analysis of the social relationships between men and women than either structural-functionalism or classical Marxism. In Middleton's view (1974: 201), Marxist feminists have

> produced a theory that meets the demand for an analysis of the material basis of those oppressions that are specific to women; that escapes from the hegemony of sexist ideology by recognizing women as historical subjects, as well as passive objects of the historical process; that structurally integrates the relationship between the sexes; and finally that need not commit the fallacy of assuming that all women share essentially identical conditions of material and social existence.

The Marxist theory of reproduction of labour power treats males and females as being neither antagonistic nor complementary, but in different social locations. While men are seen as being only wage labourers, women are considered to be both domestic and wage labourers. It is further hypothesised that these two aspects of female existence, productive and reproductive, are harmoniously related neither in capitalist nor in state-socialist societies. In turn, the theory suggests that full sexual equality will be brought about by the unification of reproduction of labour power with social production, and by the abolition of the sexual division of labour. Bearing this theoretical orientation in mind, let us now turn to an examination of the ways in which sexual equality has been promoted, achieved and/or retarded in Marxist parties and states.

Part II
Socialism and the
Women's Movement

5 The Historical Development of Socialist Women's Movements[1]

In assessing the relevance of the socialist experience for the contemporary Women's Liberation Movement in the West, one has to be careful not to commit the mistake of transposing the situation and demands of the present back in time. When we evaluate the performance of the socialist parties in promoting sex equality, it is not sufficient to say that because we make a certain demand, the German Social Democratic Party (hereafter SPD) or the Bolsheviks could or should have done so as well. One cannot compose a list of prioritised feminist demands suitable for every time and place, since what is feasible in a particular situation will be determined by a multitude of factors, by a particular historical conjuncture. To be able to judge what is the most that is possible in a given situation, we have to place conflicts in their overall political context and take into account inhibiting factors (Holt, 1976*b*). If we then try to achieve an analysis that is both historically and politically sensitive, what evaluations emerge?

The major themes examined in this chapter are: (1) the changes that have occurred in the initial Marxist assumptions about women workers and their revolutionary potential; (2) the types of Marxist revolutionary organisations and the place of women within these; and (3) the question of a separate women's organisation within a single revolutionary party of the working class. We shall trace the process of clarifying attitudes towards women workers and women's emancipation within the SPD from the initial opposition of one of its sections to female labour outside the home to its acceptance, and successive attempts to incorporate proletarian women into the various working-class organisations. We shall discuss the birth of the socialist theory of women's emancipation, its central thesis and its ideological counter-position to the theory and practice of bourgeois feminism.[2] Finally, we shall review the ways in which the SPD organised women workers and dealt with their demands. Similar analyses will be undertaken for the other working-class organisations: the Russian Bolshevik Party, the Second and Third Internationals, and the Czechoslovak Communist Party.

THE GERMAN SOCIAL DEMOCRATIC PARTY AND ITS WOMEN'S MOVEMENT[3]

Rejection, acknowledgement and emergence. Three successive phases in the SPD's attitude towards women workers and their movement can be identified. The first, between 1863 and 1868,[4] was marked by the rejection of female participation in the labour force. The second, between 1868 and 1898, was characterised by the acknowledgement of women's right to work and by the development of a socialist theory of women's emancipation. The third witnessed the rise of the political organisation of women workers within the framework of the SPD.

The discussion document of the German section of the First International,[5] published in 1866, and the resolution of the Sixth General Meeting of the General German Workers' Association in 1867, not only rejected female labour under the harsh conditions of the time, but favoured the limitation of women to the 'female sphere' in principle. The followers of Ferdinand Lassalle apparently demanded remunerative work for women at home instead of in the factory.[6] They urged that men go on defensive strikes to combat women workers, and, through the exclusion of women from industrial production, the Lassalleans hoped to increase male employment, reduce unemployment and raise men's wages. They did not reject every type of female labour, but only that in occupations 'outside the female sphere'. They planned to counter attempts to introduce more women into industrial production by stepping up agitation among men, who, with higher wages, would be able to marry early and thus preserve women from the constraint and the attraction of earning money themselves (Thönnessen, 1973: 16). Only very few women of bourgeois origin and even fewer workers found intellectual access to socialism and made contact with social democracy during this period (ibid.: 154).

The Lassallean attitudes reflect the oppressive working conditions and the increasing misery of the working-class family, as well as the failure to understand the basis of the increase in female labour. The workers' anti-feminist attitude was determined by the traditional ideal of the family and customary sexual division of labour. They saw women as their competitors on the labour market and attempted to eliminate this competition by prohibiting women from working. They were unable to see beyond outright rejection of the new social development.

This initial phase of 'proletarian anti-feminism' was succeeded by 'the acknowledgement of women's right to work' and 'the birth of the theory of women's emancipation' (ibid.: 8). These developments resulted from the recognition that female labour under capitalism would inevitably increase. While in 1875 the number of female workers in Germany amounted to 1 million, by 1882, only 7 years later, this had increased by almost 400 per cent to $5\frac{1}{2}$ million. By 1895, $6\frac{1}{2}$ million women had entered the industrial labour force and, by 1907, the number of women employed reached 9½ million (ibid.: 57). German male workers were thereby forced by circumstance to come to terms with women workers, their rivals and low-wage competitors on the labour market.

Rather than eliminating female competition by prohibiting women from working, which proved to be an impossible task in any case, the male labour movement was forced to try to reduce this competition by organising women into trade associations. It was assumed that organised women were less likely to undercut male wages than unorganised women workers. The question of the best form of trade-union organisation for women workers had long been a matter of controversy. In the course of time, exclusively female trades unions and mixed organisations of men and women both developed, and finally there were women's alliances which were affiliated corporately to the male trades unions. Socialist women campaigned against the formation of exclusively female trade associations on the grounds that such unions spoke for 'women' rather than for 'women proletarians'. The image of the 'lady' or the 'woman' which was cultivated in female trade associations was derided by the socialists as bourgeois ideology; moreover, the socialists also feared competition from bourgeois women's organisations, which supported separate female trades unions (ibid.: 29–30). However, the Combination Laws[7] forced upon the socialists the form of separate women's associations. This situation lasted until 1908.

The attempt to eliminate the detrimental effect that female competition had on male workers, by incorporating women workers in the proletarian struggle, clarified the SPD's attitudes towards women's emancipation. It also gave a specific direction to Bebel's, Engels's and Zetkin's work on the theory of women's emancipation. August Bebel's book, *Woman in the Past, Present and Future* (later renamed *Woman and Socialism*), was, when it was published in 1875, the first attempt to investigate the whole 'woman question' from a socialist viewpoint. The second attempt was Engels's *The Origin of the Family, Private Property and the State*, published, as we have noted, in 1884. Both authors saw the root of the oppression of both the proletariat and women in the institution of private property and the economic isolation of the nuclear family. As private property could be abolished only by a socialist revolution, the emancipation of women was seen as an element in the proletarian struggle. The socialist theorists explicitly stated that women's liberation was impossible in isolation and within the framework of class society – their fundamental point of disagreement with the bourgeois feminists.[8]

Thus, orthodox Marxism has considered gender differentiation less important than the division between social classes, as defined by their relationship to the means of production. This has meant that on the level of strategy the class struggle and the exploitation of the industrial worker have been seen as being politically more significant than the specific oppression experienced by women. The industrial proletariat has been regarded as the main revolutionary force which would bring about the overthrow of capitalism (an assumption that today perhaps also needs critical review).

The socialist parties saw women as potential historical subjects only when they entered the industrial labour force. This attitude was reflected at the organisational level, for few attempts were made by the socialist and communist parties to mobilise the wives of industrial workers. The socialist parties did not organise women simply on the basis of their gender. Rather, the SPD approached female workers as a specific segment of the working class, the most politically backward and unorganised segment, requiring special attention to bring them up to the level of men. This task fell to the women members of the party. As Ottilie Baader, a prominent woman member of the SPD, put it:

> If they [the women comrades] wanted to bring socialism to the mass of proletarian women, they had to take into account these women's political backwardness, their emotional pecularities, their two-fold burden at home and in the factory, in short, all the special features of their existence, actions, feelings and thoughts. Accordingly, they had in part to adopt different ways and means in their work, and seek other points of contact, than the male comrades did in their educational work among the male proletariat.[9]

Bebel's book played an important role in the SPD's agitational work among women workers. The fact that Bebel was the acknowledged leader of the party, and its most popular figure, gave the book and its intended cause more prestige. Although Bebel's contributions made little theoretical impact in the long run, numerous personal testimonies give evidence to the practical effect that his book had in drawing women into the proletarian struggle. Clara Zetkin evaluated the effect of the book in these terms:

> As dynamite shatters the hardest rocks, so its ideas pulverised the old prejudices which blocked women's path to the battleground of the proletariat and their complete liberation. They stimulated the self-confidence, the desire for self-realisation, the efforts on behalf of justice, the class-consciousness of oppressed and intimidated women.[10]

This pioneering work, she said, closed the first period of the revolutionary women's movement, the period of search and clarification.

The book went through 58 impressions in the German, of which 50 appeared between 1879 and 1909 (Thönnessen, 1973: 36). It was also translated into many foreign languages. The effect of the book abroad was similar to that in Germany. A Czech communist historian, recalling his own youth, wrote in the preface to a new edition published in Prague in

1962 a moving testimony to the book's importance in the Czech working-class movement:

> We remembered the time when the young workers brought it as a gift to their loved ones, and when socialist workers read it to their wives to awaken interest in their activities and win those closest to them for work in the movement. We experienced the passionate debates on questions of love, on the relationships between men and women, girls and boys, in the revolutionary communist youth movement between the two world wars. We can truthfully say that Bebel's book gained not only thousands and thousands of women for socialism, but men as well, and strongly influenced the education of a whole generation.[11]

Building on Bebel and Engels, Clara Zetkin was instrumental in developing a political strategy to mobilise women workers. In her pamphlet, *The Question of Women Workers and Women at the Present Time*, Zetkin summarised all the ideas on the 'woman question' that had evolved in the SPD up to that time. Zetkin argued that full emancipation of women could come only with labour's complete victory over capital. She described female labour as a pre-condition for the emancipation of women and emphasised the need to organise the industrial woman worker, to educate her politically and economically and to bring her into solidarity with men of her social class. She drew a distinction between bourgeois feminism (a few privileged women struggling *against* the men of their class) and socialist feminism (women struggling *together* with men of the working class against the capitalist class as a whole).[12] The two were incompatible, and the possibility of co-operation was excluded. However, Zetkin glossed over the deep antagonism that had existed between male and female workers on the labour market, male prejudices against women and the fact that women workers generally proved more difficult to recruit into trades unions and the party than male workers.

The line of argument outlined in the pamphlet was made more explicit at the 1896 Gotha party conference when the two wings of the German workers' movement, Lassallean and semi-Marxist, united and adopted a common programme. Zetkin presented a report on the 'woman question' and laid the organisational foundation for a socialist women's movement. She also specified the tasks of these separate women's associations. In addition to working for the general aims of the party, they were to concentrate on a whole range of issues of special concern to women workers: political equality, maternity insurance, protective legislation, education and security of children and the political education of women workers.[13]

In Zetkin's view, agitation among women workers and recruitment of new female members had to be achieved by pamphlets and organisational spadework and not by the SPD's women's journal, *Die Gleichheit* (Equality). The magazine, Zetkin argued, existed for the 'more advanced

women comrades', the organisers of the women's movement. Its main role
was 'to provide an educational and promotional influence within the
movement' and its theoretical and organisational quality ought not to be
sacrificed for some alleged mass attraction (Thönnessen, 1973: 49–50).
The Bolsheviks thought differently on this issue and their women's journal
became an aspect of their agitation among women workers both within
and outside the party.

Agitation and organisation. Having reviewed the debates over political
strategy, we can now turn to the question of agitation and organisation
among women workers in the period 1893–1913. Initially, German socialist
women were separately organised. This was not only because of legal
requirements, but also because of the assumed political backwardness of
women. In all her writings, Zetkin called for separate working-class
women's organisations on the basis of the special demands and needs of
women, their isolation within the family, their fear of speaking with men
around, and the need to develop the leadership capacities of women. After
the expiry of the anti-socialist laws, women were legally able to join the
SPD directly and those in the special SPD women's organisations did so.
They received proportional representation on all standing committees of
the party, and the women members of the committees were elected at
meetings of the women themselves.

Zetkin was thus suggesting that the idea of separatism had certain
positive values *vis-à-vis* the party's strategy towards women workers.
Separate working-class women's groups were seen as having some positive
input not only for the development of certain strategies that would
enhance women's support for social democracy, but also for women
themselves, increasing their confidence and developing their leadership
capacities. This particular organisational model was, however, adopted
neither by the Second International nor by the Bolsheviks.

The women's movement of the SPD also held a number of conferences.
The first conference was held in Mainz in 1900. On the agenda was the
extension of the system of women's representatives,[14] agitation among
women workers and the attitude to be taken by proletarian women to their
bourgeois counterparts. The special methods of agitation and organisation
of women workers were to be discontinued at the point where they
disturbed the unity of the working-class movement – a good illustration of
the assumption of the priority of the class struggle over the women's
struggle. Protection for women workers and children and the women's
movement were the major themes arising at subsequent conferences
(Thönnessen, 1973: 62–5).

For the purposes of political mobilisation it was necessary to concentrate
on the particular sufferings of proletarian women, but this in turn meant
that the achievement of such reformist goals gradually took the place of the
socialist transformation of society. Given its broad character and par-

liamentary orientation, the women's movement, like the working-class movement as a whole, was unable to confine itself to a generalised condemnation of existing conditions. It had to go beyond mere assertion that women's emancipation was impossible under capitalism and to make concrete suggestions. Electoral assistance to the party gradually became the most important task for the women's movement.

The continuous electoral success and numerical growth of the entire working-class movement seemed to open up bright prospects for the future. By 1913, approximately 190,000 women were members of trades unions, 140,000 were members of the SPD, the circulation of *Die Gleichheit* had reached 112,000 and there had been considerable improvements in the protection of women workers (Thönnessen, 1973: 66). Progress in these fields, however, was offset by the internal party struggle between orthodox socialists and revisionists, into which women increasingly became drawn. The great consistency and decisiveness with which Rosa Luxemburg and Clara Zetkin criticised revisionist tendencies frequently induced those leaders under attack to 'put women in their place' by means of malicious witticisms and sexist joking. At the Stuttgart party conference in 1898, Ignaz Auer in his reply to Zetkin's strong attack on the party executive, said jokingly, amidst the sought-for laughter of the audience: 'If that is the oppressed sex, then what on earth will happen when they are free and enjoy equal rights?', thus ridiculing the seriousness of women's criticisms. Another way of blunting women's criticism of the leadership's reformism was to attack personally the women leaders and point out the weakness of their movement. Auer adopted this condescending strategy at the Mainz party conference in 1900:

> Of course the nervous excitement of our women is, regrettably, easy enough to understand if we remember that despite years of exhausting work they have only had minimal success . . . The trouble is that there are too few women comrades in the party. I wish there were many more. The few who have to do all the work are overloaded and thus prone to become bad-tempered. So it comes about that they sometimes make life miserable for us, even though we are not to blame.

Such joking was extended to the whole question of sex equality. As a Ms Kähler pointed out at the Gotha party conference in 1896, 'many comrades make such a joke of the woman question that we really have to ask ourselves: Are those really party comrades who advocate equal rights?'[15] Deliberate discrimination was also practised against Rosa Luxemburg (Balabanoff, 1938: 22).

The issues that arose then are still relevant today, as many women who have had the experience of working with men in left-wing groups would testify. Paying lip-service to specific women's needs, but at the same time deliberately discriminating against women by symbolic, patronising and sexist attitudes, is just as effective today as it was 100 years ago. The settling of an uncomfortable debate with a woman comrade by a sexist joke or attack seems to be an easy and tempting way out.

To come back to the SPD, we have reached the turning point in its history – the First World War. By the time the war broke out, the SPD was no longer a revolutionary Marxist party. Reformism had triumphed over other political tendencies and the European revolutionary initiative had passed to the Bolshevik Party. It is to this party, and its experience of women's organisation, that we now turn our attention.

THE BOLSHEVIK PARTY

Theoretical readiness. As far as the question of women's emancipation was concerned, the Bolsheviks had a major historical advantage over the SPD – their theory of women's emancipation was ready-made, worked out by their German predecessors. Bebel's book (still popular in the Soviet Union today) had appeared in many Russian editions since the 1890s, although at first it was banned by the censor; the Bolsheviks added only very little to Engels's and Bebel's analysis. The first major Russian work on the 'woman question' was written by Nadezhda Krupskaya, Lenin's wife, in 1900.

Drawing upon her experiences of agitation among the workers of St Petersburg in the 1890s, as well as upon the existing Marxist theory of women's emancipation, Krupskaya produced a simple and effective illustration of women's life in factory, dwelling heavily upon the sorry lot of the working mother – perpetually pregnant and without maternity benefits – whose children either died or were nursed by strangers and raised on the streets. In contrast, she evoked the image of a bright future under socialism, where people would work in clean, spacious, well-ventilated factories; where society would care for the old, the sick and the weak, so that no one would be forced to seek charity; and where society would be responsible for the care and education of all children (Stites, 1973). Krupskaya also acknowledged existing male prejudices and criticised those workers who argued that politics should remain a 'male affair'.

Little else was written by Russian Marxists on the 'woman question' until 1908, when Alexandra Kollontai published a major work on the subject, *The Social Basis of the Woman Question.* Her early interest in the ideas of Bjorn Björnsen and Ibsen, which had swept through the intellectual life of Russia in the 1880s, her marital experience (she left her officer husband in order to lead an independent life), and, most importantly, her encounter with the works of Engels, Bebel and Zetkin, led Kollontai to undertake a lengthy study of the whole 'woman question' from a socialist viewpoint. The 400 pages of the book are largely polemical in nature. She attacks the bourgeois feminists, both Russian and foreign, who, she claimed, were more interested in winning voting rights for women of the privileged class than in any general emancipation of women. She warned against the efforts of 'bourgeois ladies' to enlist working women in a useless pan-female campaign for women's rights and appealed to working-class women to join the common socialist cause (Stites, 1973: 466–7).

Kollontai was probably the Bolsheviks' most ardent and powerful advocate for the separate organisation of women, but her ideas were continually dismissed as a harmful 'right deviation towards feminism', an unjustified attack in view of her continuous polemics with the bourgeois feminists of the time.[16] In her autobiography, Kollontai relates how for years she fought both Bolsheviks and Mensheviks on this issue (between 1905 and 1917, she changed several times from one to the other). She states that after 1906 the party did not forbid her activity among women, but gave her no help whatsoever (Kollontai, 1972*b*). In 1907, she 'infiltrated' one of the working-women's political clubs in St Petersburg, established by the bourgeois feminists, and gathered around herself a nucleus of working women. This club was frequented by 200–300 working women from various industries (Bobroff, 1973: 543).

In 1908, the Central Committee of the party agreed to send a small delegation of working-class women to the First All-Russian Women's Congress, organised by the bourgeois feminists. Official accounts of the Bolshevik attitude towards this conference claimed wholehearted support, and differ considerably from Kollontai's account. One source reports that the Central Committee adopted Lenin's view of the tactical advantage of using both legal and illegal means for the propagation of Bolshevik ideas, and charged P. F. Kudelliova with the task of organising a group of women to attend the congress.

Kollontai claims in her autobiography that the St Petersburg Committee of the party, especially Vera Slutskaya, opposed any form of Bolshevik participation in the congress, both on grounds of separatism and of collaborating with a bourgeois group, and that the eventual preparation for the congress fell to her, not to Kudelliova. Thinking that it would be a good educational and political experience for women workers, Kollontai went ahead with preparations for the conference despite the opposition. She worked among textile, cardboard, rubber, tobacco, footwear and domestic workers. She also obtained the support of the Union of Textile Workers and of the Central Bureau of Trades Unions in St Petersburg. Only then, shortly before the conference took place, did the St Petersburg Party Committee suddenly decide to participate and to delegate Slutskaya as their representative.[17]

In the end, 45 socialist women, 30 of whom were factory workers, attended this congress which totalled 750 women of bourgeois origin – professionals and wives of high-ranking officials. Kollontai gave the main speech for the working-class delegation. She raised the questions of high infant mortality, protection of women workers and maternity insurance.

The other delegates read reports which they had prepared on such topics as women workers and the trades unions, the position of female artisans, the budget of working-class women and maternity insurance. These issues were not on the original agenda because the feminists ignored class divisions among women and they were not too pleased to hear about them. Kollontai was obliged to flee from the police before the proceedings were over and the congress ended inconclusively.

It would be misleading to argue, as Bobroff does, that there was an official Bolshevik hostility to the 'woman question' or women's organisations, although undoubtedly there was individual prejudice. It is possible, even probable, that individual social democrats were unenthusiastic over the idea of a separate women's organisation, since they were still under the influence of a patriarchal ideology and did not understand the importance of women for the revolution. The position of the party was different. The Bolsheviks inherited the social-democratic tradition of organising women separately, both within political groups (such as women's study circles) and in production,[18] although in practice attempts were localised and sporadic. In 1909, the party passed a resolution approving separate women's organisations but there was little opportunity of taking action in the context of Russia at that time (Holt, personal communication). The extent of these activities contradicts Bobroff's argument that, aside from fighting the bourgeois feminists, the Bolsheviks paid little attention to organising women separately prior to 1913.

However, Bobroff's thesis that a rapid increase in women's employment[19] was a necessary, but in itself insufficient, condition to compel the Bolsheviks to integrate women's issues at the party level seems quite plausible. What was needed in addition was independent, highly visible and successful activism among women workers.

Women's strikes. Militant activity by working women had been absent before 1910, and the few strikes that did take place ended mostly in defeat. The majority of women workers were afraid to attend meetings or enrol in the trades unions, intimidated as they were not only by their employers, but also by their husbands and fathers (Bobroff, 1973: 550). However, this was beginning to change by 1910. Women workers became aware of their needs as workers and women, grew more militant and started to back their demands by strikes and demonstrations. Specific demands were formulated, ranging from wage increases to the improvement of working conditions, paid pregnancy leave and the use of the factory owners' bath and laundry facilities. After ensuring that no one would be subject to victimisation, the militants would present a copy of their demands to the factory management. Only after a refusal to accede to these demands would the workers strike. Sometimes they would issue an appeal to the factory inspector of the area to substantiate their complaints (Bobroff, 1973: 550).

What is particularly interesting in this period is the spontaneous growth of feminist consciousness among working-class women. For instance, they were no longer prepared to tolerate the widespread rudeness and sexual abuse of the foremen. At the Grisov factory in Moscow in 1913 a strike began because 'the attitude of the factory administration is revolting. There is no other word for it than prostitution.' Among the demands was one for the polite treatment of working women, in particular, the prohibition of swearing. One of the causes of discontent at a plywood factory in Riga was that several foremen 'were not ashamed to curse in the most obscene words even to women' (Bobroff, 1973: 554–5).

Other specifically feminist demands related to the problems of pregnant women and nursing mothers in industry. At the Bek textile factory the strikers demanded pregnancy leaves of 6 weeks and an end to the practice of dismissing pregnant women. These demands were met. The striking Mal'tseva weavers made the same demands, adding that women should receive half-pay during the period when they were not working. The pregnancy-leave demand was granted, but without pay. Workers at a Moscow factory in 1913 demanded that pregnant women be relieved of having to lift or carry heavy weights. They also called for two one-hour breaks each day for mothers to nurse their babies. At another Moscow factory, where 1,000 women were on strike, a demand was made that the management end its policy of not engaging married women. These demands were not apparently extended to equal pay – women workers pressed for an undifferentiated, overall pay increase, thus retaining discriminatory clauses.

The demonstration of women's independent power forced the Bolsheviks to reassess their earlier unenthusiastic attitude towards women workers as a separate segment of the proletariat. Women workers were now seen as an active, potentially revolutionary force, and the party was compelled to find effective ways of relating to them in order not to lose their support. The independent growth of women's militancy also suggested a critique of existing Marxist theory, which did not recognise women's struggle as a separate issue because it was subordinate to that of socialism and the working-class struggle. However, women's determination to organise themselves around issues specific to their sex brought its own political strength, forcing the Bolsheviks to question their initial opposition to the idea of the women's movement as a separate entity. Far from hindering the proletarian struggle and undermining party unity, the independent women's movement made a positive contribution. The Bolsheviks were compelled to recognise this and undergo a self-examination of their theory and practice.

Part of this effort at re-evaluation was the decision to organise the first celebration of International Women's Day on Russian soil. Kollontai (1920a) describes how they organised an illegal morning teach-in on the 'woman question' in St Petersburg in 1913, at the end of which almost all the party speakers were arrested. Towards the end of that same year, the Bolsheviks decided to approach women workers in a more systematic and permanent way, by bringing out a journal specifically designed for working women. The first issue of *Rabotnica* (The Woman Worker) was published on International Women's Day in 1914, despite great difficulties.

Rabotnica was an official organ of the Central Committee, appearing once a fortnight, like *Die Gleichheit* in the SPD. However, its orientation was different. It was directed specifically at women workers, not just at the 'politically more advanced women comrades within the party', and it opposed a separate autonomous organisation of women workers. Its message reflected the general Bolshevik strategy towards women workers: they should not form groups separate from men, but should join mixed organisations and fight for socialism 'hand in hand with men'. As Armand's editorial put in in the first issue:

> The 'women's question' for working men and women – this question is about how to involve the backward masses of working women in organisation, how better to make clear to them their interests, how to make them comrades in the common struggle quickly. The solidarity between working men and women, the common cause, the common goals, and the common path to those goals, such is the settlement of the 'women's question' in the workers midst. Politically conscious women see that contemporary society is divided into classes . . . The bourgeoisie is one, the working class the other. Their interests are counterposed. The division into men and women in their eyes has no great significance (quoted in Bobroff, 1973: 546).

In Bobroff's view, this analysis does not correspond to what was happening in practice. Rather than being backward and needing special attention (which was Zetkin's argument for a separate body operating among women workers), a significant fraction of Russian women workers was militant and relatively well organised.[20] It was their activism rather than their backwardness which compelled the Bolsheviks to recognise the 'woman question' as an important socialist issue and incorporate specific women's demands into their agitation in a significant way. *Rabotnica* dealt with a wide range of women's issues: maternity insurance, female labour, child-care centres, the problems of working women and the family, children's stories, Women's Day, female suffrage and the attack on bourgeois feminism (Bobroff, 1973; Artiuchina, 1964). The latter was particularly important for tactical reasons. As Popova (1949: 30) put it:

> The Bolshevik Party's struggle against bourgeois feminism was a struggle to free women from the influence of the bourgeoisie, to reveal the harmfulness of bourgeois feminist ideas and illusions, to expose the

efforts of the bourgeois feminist organisations to keep working women out of the class war waged by the proletariat.

The beginning of the war in 1914 brought to an end publication of the paper as well as the annual celebration of International Women's Day. However, the latter was again celebrated in 1917 and a spontaneous women's demonstration on that day, which was unrelated to earlier Bolshevik efforts to attract women's support, sparked off the February revolution. In fact, the Bolsheviks opposed the demonstration on the grounds that it was premature and that it might lead to the defeat of the working-class movement. But the women's determination prevailed. By March 1917 reports came from all over the country of women being elected to various representative bodies. Soldiers' wives, the majority of them of working-class origin, organised a highly disciplined anti-war demonstration, joined by 100,000 women to back their six carefully worked out demands (Bobroff, 1973: 559–60).

Competition for working women. These incidents again demonstrated the independent power of women workers and called into question the assumption that a separate women's organisation was necessarily undesirable. What was even more threatening to the Bolsheviks was the increasing support that working-class women were giving to the efforts of the bourgeois feminists. The liberal League for the Equal Rights of Women organised a massive demonstration of 35,000 women from all spheres of life, including the working class, to demand women's suffrage and full women's participation in the Constituent Assembly. On 8 March (in the old Russian calendar International Women's Day was on 25 February), a suffrage demonstration was organised that represented solely working women (Bobroff, 1973: 543).

As the Bolsheviks were rivals for the support of the same group, they could not afford to ignore the special concerns with women's issues, which were clearly effective in appealing to them. In other words, fear of losing to their competitors finally forced the Bolsheviks to put their 1909 resolution into practice. On 10 March, only sixteen days after the February revolution and two days after the working-class suffrage demonstration, the St Petersburg Party Committee gave one of its women members responsibility for drafting plans for agitational work among women. Within three days, on March 13, she recommended the formation of a Women's Bureau as part of the St Petersburg Committee and the revival of *Rabotnica*. At the end of April, some Bolshevik women leaders met Lenin and discussed with him political work among women. Lenin's advice to call a conference of women workers was taken up, and shortly before the October Revolution, 500 delegates, representing 80,000 women workers, met in St Petersburg.

This conference was tactically crucial for the Bolsheviks, because it was also attended by the Mensheviks and by bourgeois feminists who were all competing for the political support of women workers. Bourgeois feminists argued for a geographical basis of female organisation, which was taken by the Bolsheviks as an attempt to break up working collectives and to loosen the ties of women workers to their own factory organisations. Therefore, the proposal was firmly rejected. One Bolshevik feminist advocated that all work among women in factories should be conducted under the leadership of the party organisation. This was rejected by Menshevik women who argued that the women's movement must be independent and must not be subjected to party influence (Tarasova, 1959: 129). Of course, the October revolution ended this speculation about the form and character of the women's movement and the Bolsheviks' view prevailed.

German and Russian movements compared. When we now compare the German and Russian women's movements, we can see that the Russian one was much weaker. Although the Bolsheviks compromised with their original position on the 'woman question' as time went on, and some of their activities among women workers were similar to those of their German predecessors, a specific women's section within the Bolshevik Party was not established until the eve of the October revolution, and then only in St Petersburg. This was largely due to the Leninist concept of the party, which differed radically from that which characterised broad-based, social democratic parties elsewhere in Europe. In Germany, the women's movement, or even the party itself, could not confine itself to a general attack on existing social conditions. It had to go beyond the mere assertion that women's emancipation was impossible under capitalism. As parliamentary reformism gained ground, electoral assistance to the party became the most important political task of the women's movement – hence again its auxiliary and secondary role.

However, this sort of development was not possible in Russia. Because of the oppressive conditions existing, the Bolshevik Party could not be organised as a 'broad democracy', but had to be governed by the principle of democratic centralism (although the party was not as disciplined as Lenin would have liked). Discussion and publicity were impossible because, above all, secrecy was necessary. The need for secrecy also meant that numbers had to be small. Thus, there was no room for a separate women's organisation in Lenin's concept of the party, which was viewed essentially as an organisational tool for overthrowing the existing social system. He felt that directing particular attention to one segment of the working class would create unnecessary divisions within it. In other words, the Leninist theory of the party precludes the absolute autonomy of any sector or group within it – it is a party, not a federation.

This attitude was expressed explicitly in Lenin's position on separate national minority organisations, for instance the Jewish *Bund*. The Jewish labour movement, represented by the *Bund*, played a crucial role in the foundation of Russian social democracy, and initially constituted the strongest organised force within it. Lenin admitted specific oppression of the Jews under the Tsarist regime and supported their specific demands. However, he argued that under socialism, such a situation would not arise, for all forms of racial and national oppression would cease to exist. In an article entitled 'The Position of the *Bund* in the Party', published in *Iskra* on 22 October 1903, he applied this eventual renunciation of the special demands of the Jews to the right of their separate group existence, i.e. to the *Bund* itself (Mishkinsky, 1971).

Lenin's position on a separate feminist section within the party, although not explicit, may well have been similar. Female oppression would cease under socialism, and women's duty was therefore to join the party that sought to overthrow capitalism and establish socialism. The Bolshevik Party, as a small vanguard of the proletariat, operating under difficult political conditions, needed the unanimous support of workers; whether they were Jews or women was of secondary importance. However, this type of approach ignored the existing contradictions and antagonisms within the working class. Experience proved that they could not be solved by simply avoiding them.

Having examined the similarities and differences between the socialist women's movement in Germany and Russia, we turn to an examination of what had been happening on the international level. After all, the women's section of the Second International had influenced both SPD and Bolshevik strategy towards women by focusing their activities on specific occasions such as International Women's Day.

THE INTERNATIONAL SOCIALIST AND COMMUNIST WOMEN'S MOVEMENT

Beginnings. The foundations of the international socialist women's movement were laid at the same time as those of the German movement. On the occasion of the International Socialist Conference in London in 1896, the same year as the congress at Gotha, a private meeting of thirty socialist women delegates took place. Discussion centred around the distinction between bourgeois feminism and the socialist women's movement. The First International Women's Conference took place in Stuttgart in 1907, in connection with the general International Socialist Congress. A separate International Women's Bureau was set up, and Zetkin became its secretary. *Die Gleichheit*, under her editorship, became an international socialist women's paper in addition to its function in the German socialist women's movement.

At the request of Zetkin and others, the general congress debated the question of the struggle for suffrage conducted by the Austrian social democrats. In clerical Austria, male workers were still fighting for a direct and secret vote, and they hesitated to 'prejudice' their case by a struggle for universal suffrage. They suggested a compromise which would have postponed that struggle until after male suffrage was won. This viewpoint, of which many Austrian women approved, was vigorously criticised by Zetkin and the majority of the delegates, and the general congress passed a resolution advocating women's suffrage. This resolution said, among other things, that women workers should campaign for their franchise in conjunction with the working-class parties and not co-operate with the bourgeois supporters of women's equal rights. The period 1908–11 was thus characterised by extensive participation by women workers in the election campaigns of their respective parties in Germany, Holland, Denmark, Sweden, England, Austria, the United States and elsewhere. The socialist women's movement was beginning to take root in most European countries.

The Second International Women's Socialist Conference took place in Copenhagen in 1910. On the suggestion of Zetkin, this conference called for an international day of action to demand universal female suffrage – later to be called International Women's Day – on 8 March 1910. Zetkin chose this particular day in order to express solidarity with New York seamstresses who had called a strike. By choosing the beginning of the strike for International Women's Day, the conference supported the garment-workers' struggle for higher wages and better working conditions, and emphasised the relationship of the struggle for female suffrage to the wider social struggles of the working class against capitalism. By 1911, International Women's Day was being celebrated in Germany, Austria (including Bohemia), Denmark, Switzerland, and the United States. Social democratic movements in other countries followed later – for example, the occasion was celebrated in Russia in 1913.

The Third International Socialist Women's Conference was scheduled for August 1914 in Vienna, but was not convened because of the outbreak of the First World War. Another conference was organised in Bern in 1915, upon the initiative of Zetkin. However, Zetkin took the initiative upon herself, and the conference did not have the approval of the German SPD as such. The resolutions of the conference expressed the dedication to peace and socialism of working-class women, despite their governments' and social-democratic leaders' support for the war. The causes and consequences of wars were explained, as well as the ways in which they could be abolished.

Bolshevik women played a prominent part in this conference. Working under Lenin's direction, they introduced a resolution calling for the formation of a new Socialist International. The majority of the delegates opposed this resolution, not because it was too radical or because they approved of the Second International, but because they could not sign it. Most of them wished to remain members of their respective parties at this time in order to influence the rank and file. Nor would they make decisions which committed their parties to a specific action of such far-reaching consequences. But the Bolshevik delegates refused to alter their position, thus threatening to break up the desired unified stand. The Bolshevik women withdrew the resolution only after Zetkin negotiated separately with Lenin and he agreed to compromise (Balabanoff, 1938: 151–2). This is a good example of Lenin's control of the women's movement within the Bolshevik Party.

A new International was launched in Moscow in 1919. In July 1920, the First International Congress of Women Workers took place in Moscow, in conjunction with the Second Congress of the Third International.[21] Seventeen foreign delegates participated, and presented a resolution calling for the establishment of the International Secretariat for Work among Women.[22] This women's section of the Comintern, modelled on the organisational form of the Bolshevik Party at that period, was established on 15 November 1920. Clara Zetkin became its head and thereby a representative of the women's movement on the Executive Committee of the Comintern. She thus provided continuity between the social democratic and communist women's movements at the international level. With co-operation from an appointed committee, Zetkin prepared a thesis on the women's communist movement which was approved at the next congress of the Communist International.

The adopted resolution on the women's communist movement reflected the Bolshevik tradition of the socialist women's movement. Separate organisations for women were opposed, but special methods of work among women workers were favoured and encouraged. The resolution was concerned with reaching women (who were in the mass neither militant nor political) and with integrating women's issues at the party level. The resolution recognised the specific social position of women in terms of (1) their biological function of child-bearing and the resulting need for special protection, and (2) their political ignorance and conservatism, the result of their isolation within the family and other factors.[23]

Basic propositions reaffirmed. These attitudes held by communists must be understood within the context of the overall Bolshevik strategy. Following the tradition of Marxism and orthodox social democracy, that is to say rejecting reformism within the capitalist system, the Third Congress of the Comintern reaffirmed the basic Marxist proposition that there is no 'specific woman question' and no 'specific women's movement' (*Decisions*, 1921: 102). Women were therefore urged to concentrate on the general struggle for socialism, which supposedly included the struggle for women's liberation. Cultural, psychological and other similar components of female oppression were not mentioned in the communist resolutions dealing with women. Any statement of the need for self-transformation of personal relationships was also lacking. The main task of the women's section of the Communist Party was to awaken the class consciousness of women workers and then recruit them to the party, the agent of the forthcoming revolution. It was assumed, rather naively, that women's emancipation would follow automatically after the socialist revolution.

Thus, the origin of the socialist women's movement, both within social democracy and within communism, is best understood as a short-term political need to win the support of women workers, a specific social group of potential followers. The communists were much more explicit on this subject than their social democratic predecessors. For example, the Third Congress of the Comintern in 1921 (mentioned above) was devoted to a discussion of revolutionary tactics. One session dealt exclusively with the methods of work among women. The debate centred around the tactical problem of how to win the support of the mass of women workers for the common struggle of the proletariat. The creation of a specific political organisation of proletarian and semi-proletarian women was the only answer to the political danger that unorganised women workers posed to the communists. The resolution (1921: 98) said specifically:

> Whenever the question of the taking of power arises, the communist parties must consider the great danger to the revolution represented by the inert, uninformed masses of women workers, housewives, employees, peasant women, not liberated from the influence of the bourgeois superstitions, and not connected in some way or other with the great liberating movement of communism. Unless the masses of women of the East and the West are drawn into this movement, they inevitably become the stronghold of the bourgeoisie and the object of counter-revolutionary propaganda.

Thus, the Third Congress made clear the conviction that the Comintern and communist parties had to win the support of women through the party's special organs for work among women or else lose women to the political enemies of the communists.

While warning women workers against entering any form of alliance or co-operation with bourgeois feminists, the Third Congress of the Comintern also singled out another 'enemy' – the opportunistic social democratic parties and the Second International. The Comintern criticised the opportunism and lack of concern with female emancipation of the rival International, pointing out that women socialists had neither representation nor a decisive vote within it. While the situation within the communist movement was not that much better, I would not see the early communist movement as merely opportunistic. It wanted the support of men and women for a revolution that would give people a chance to refashion their lives. The main problems of both the social democrats and the communists seem to have been the integration of issues concerning women with the class struggle at the party level on the one hand, and reaching 'backward' women on the other.

THE CZECHOSLOVAK COMMUNIST PARTY

Praxis. Having examined the communist theory of the socialist women's movement, we turn now to look at what has happened in practice. The Czechoslovak Communist Party (hereafter CCP) is a good example for discussion purposes because, of all the parties represented in the Communist International, it had the highest percentage of women among its members. In fact, the Czech communist women's congress actually preceded the founding congress of the Communist Party – another demonstration of the separatist power of women socialists. Anna Křenová and Marie Strnadová, leaders of the social democratic women's movement[24] and members of the left wing of the Social Democratic Party, left the party and organised a communist women's conference on 12–13 March 1921. The foundation congress of the Czech Communist Party took place two months later on May 14–17.

The women's conference was attended by 180 delegates. The most important items on the agenda were the nature and implications of the defeat of the working-class movement in that period. The congress criticised the reformist leadership of the Social Democratic Party and argued the necessity of establishing another working-class party which would be revolutionary in nature. It then aligned itself with the new Communist International and accepted its 21 principles. The women's conference also discussed some of the immediate problems facing working-class women, namely poverty, unemployment, persecution of strikers, high prices of food and low wages. Women delegates demanded day-care centres, playgrounds and public dining rooms for their children.

The First Congress of the Czech Communist Party decided, on the recommendation of the resolution of the Third Congress of the Comintern, to set up agitation committees for work among women at all levels of the party hierarchy. These committees were established with the explicit aim of recruiting as many women as possible to the working-class movement. In 1936, the executive committee of the women's section charged women's sections at all levels of the party hierarchy with the responsibility of finding 1,500 new members for the CCP to honour its Seventh Congress – a rather opportunistic strategy, but the target was more than met (Vaníčková, 1971: 54).

On the whole, women in the Czechoslovak Communist Party were more numerous and better organised than their social democratic predecessors, but the areas of their activities were similar. The women's journal, *Ženský list* (Women's Gazette), founded by the Social Democratic Party, was replaced in 1923 by *Komunistka* (The Woman Communist).[25] In 1926 the party instructed the women's movement and its journal to expand the party's influence among the female masses, rather than concentrate on party members. An open discussion on the new character of the women's movement took place in the pages of *Komunistka* – shortly to be replaced by another journal, *Rozsévačka* (Dissemination) as a symbol of the change in political tactics.

Because of a legal ban and competition from general women's magazines, *Rozsévačka* could not be sold commercially in shops. As a result, the paper's distributors played a significant agitational and political role. Through personal contact, they attempted to recruit women to the party. *Rozsévačka* also published letters from readers and women's agitational groups which served as a forum for an exchange of political experiences. In addition to this agitational role, the journal and its editors initiated various socialist campaigns which uncovered the real character of bourgeois society and the equality that it offered. It campaigned against rising prices, unemployment and discrimination against women in teaching, banking, the civil service and industry.

The communists did not concentrate all their activities in the 'female sphere' on the women's press. Again in the tradition of social democracy, they celebrated International Women's Day. However, its content had changed, because the struggle for female suffrage was no longer an issue. The 1918 constitution had granted women legal equality, including the right to vote. The Communist Party also no longer needed to fight against bourgeois feminism, because it was politically no longer threatening.[26] The idea that the struggle for female suffrage was only a limited part of the social struggle for female equality also became obsolete. Instead, the March 8 celebration became an active demonstration against unemployment, economic depression (which had hit Czechoslovakia very severely), hunger and poverty. For instance, on 8 March 1935, working-class women filled Prague's largest hall shouting 'We want work! We want bread!' As such, International Women's Day had a similar function to the celebration of 1 May.

International Women's Day was also used as a platform for various solidarity campaigns, both within the Czechoslovak working-class movement, and internationally. For example, its celebration in 1929 was characterised by support for the demands of striking textile workers, 70 per cent of whom were women. The 1936 celebration was used as a mobilisation against fascism. In 1937 the Central women's section called for action with the slogan 'We shall clothe 1,000 children of the dead Spanish heroes.' The figure was later raised to 2,000, but, in the end, 3,200 Spanish children were sent some clothing by women who themselves were quite poor (Brejchová, 1960: 95).

The Nazi occupation of Bohemia and Moravia and the creation of a separate Slovak state in 1939 drastically interrupted all forms of political activity, including that among women. These were resumed only after the war. Then, with the communist seizure of state power in February 1948, the history of the socialist women's movement, as defined by its relationship to the proletarian struggle for socialism, ended. Czechoslovakia declared itself socialist, and the socialist women's movement, along with the party as a whole, had to find a new role for itself in a society where the party was the ruling political force. As we shall see in the next two chapters, women's movements in state-socialist societies are fundamentally different from socialist women's movements in capitalist societies.

6 The Women's Movement in the Soviet Union

In an ideal situation, a women's movement in a socialist society should be in a position to influence directly the formation and implementation of state policy on issues that are either of specific concern to women (such as abortion or the appointment of more women to positions of authority) or to women and men alike (such as the availability of day-care facilities, household appliances and services, or the safeguarding of personal freedom). The women's movement also has to ensure that socialist planning and the allocation of resources do not sacrifice women's interests (especially day-care and the industrialisation of the domestic economy) to 'more important' male concerns, such as higher wages in the 'preferred' sectors of the economy.

However, the situation in the Soviet Union after the October revolution was far from ideal.The Soviet Union was an economically backward country and its women, in the mass, were neither militant nor educated nor political. Thus, the main initial task facing Bolshevik feminists was how to reach the women masses, win their active support for the October revolution and mobilise them behind official Bolshevik policy. Kollontai, Samoilova, Armand and other Bolshevik women were the prime movers behind the formation of the First Congress of Peasant and Working Women which took place as early as November 1918. Although only 300 delegates had been expected, 1,147 in fact appeared. The congress had seven main items on the agenda: the question of women workers in Soviet Russia, the relationship between the family and the Bolshevik government, the social security of women, the international proletarian revolution and the woman worker, the organisational question, the struggle against prostitution, the struggle against child labour, and the housing question (Artiuchina 1959: 31).

Speakers at the congress urged more politically conscious women to tell other women what the October revolution meant to women workers and peasants, and sought to teach them how to make use of the new laws which freed women from their traditional subjugation. The congress also aimed at mobilisation of women for the defence of the Soviet state and the restoration of the national economy. The latter was important because most men were fighting in the civil war and against foreign intervention; it was therefore crucial for women to continue production in villages and factories. A distinction had to be made between 'socialist reconstruction' and 'bourgeois work', which certainly was not an easy task, since the daily conditions of Soviet Russia during the civil war were probably harder than under the Tsarist regime.

Some of these themes were also expressed in the general party propaganda of that period. The Bolshevik appeals concentrated first on women workers; only later, after their initial mobilisation, did the focus shift to peasant women. Bukharin's pamphlet appealing to working-class women to support the new Soviet government was published early in 1919. In it, he describes the difficult conditions of the time, such as famine and the civil war, and blames these on the enemies of the working class. He then lists a number of improvements in the position of women under the Soviet government: equal rights with men, a protective labour code, protection of motherhood, child-care facilities. These reforms are contrasted with the situation under Tsarist rule, which, he claims, the White counter-revolutionaries were seeking to restore. Bukharin then urges women workers, as an integral part of the working class, to support 'their government', particularly the Red Army.

Many women workers responded positively to this and similar appeals. For example, in Samara, women workers gave up their only free day, Sunday, and organised a 'work-in', where they sewed, unpaid, underwear and warm clothing for the Red Army soldiers. Women workers also took an active part in the military defence of Leningrad, Lugansk, Tula and other places. In Tula, women workers even passed a resolution declaring that the Whites would get through to Moscow only over their dead bodies (Samoilova, 1920*b*).

A pamphlet similar in spirit, written by Samoilova in 1921, was directed towards peasant women. It begins by contrasting the slave-like conditions of peasant women under the Tsarist regime with the Soviet improvements: equal rights, representation in soviets, free education in reading and writing, free village clubs and reading rooms, and the protection of motherhood and youth. As agricultural production had declined drastically during the civil war and as many parts of Russia were experiencing famine, peasant women were urged to step up agricultural output, to plan and work systematically and to struggle against the profiteering middle peasants, the *kulaks*.

In accordance with the attempt to mobilise women behind official Bolshevik policy, the congress of 1918 also addressed itself to organisational questions. As a result of resolutions passed there, the Central Committee of the Bolshevik Party established in September 1919 a women's section, known as *Zhenotdel*.

Zhenotdel – its principles. The clearest and most coherent account of the role and tasks of *Zhenotdel* is to be found in the writings of its first leaders, Armand and Samoilova. Armand prepared a report for the First

International Conference of Women Communists, which took place in Moscow in July 1920 (*Otchet . . . 1921*: 92–4). In it, she listed ten guiding principles for the party's work among women:

1. *Zhenotdel* should increasingly and urgently draw women workers and peasants into all Soviet institutions – executive committees of soviets or sections of soviets, the party, professional and technical schools, etc. It was emphasised that women should be drawn into such work in order to liberate them from domestic and family servitude.
2. Delegates from meetings of women workers and peasants should be elected to attend general meetings in factories and villages. Delegates' conferences should take place periodically and they should promote the party's communist propaganda.
3. Through the delegates' meetings, the party should exercise influence on the women masses. In villages, delegates' meetings should help to differentiate bourgeois elements from proletarian ones.
4. Elected delegates should enlist the services of Soviet departments not only for the inspection and control of nurseries, orphanages, public dining rooms, hospitals and other institutions, but also for the delegates' meetings themselves.
5. *Zhenotdel* should nominate probationers, instructors and organisers to play an active part in various Soviet departments, and to guide the work of women delegates in the control and inspection of the institutions of that particular department.
6. Women delegates should account for their work both to the delegates' meetings and to general meetings at their factories.
7. The Communist Party should pay great attention to cultural and educational work in order to increase the cultural standard of the women masses.
8. The Communist Party should lead propaganda campaigns to enlighten the masses on questions of prejudice in attitudes towards women, and of their roles in the family and in social production.
9. The party should give greater attention to the struggle against religious prejudices among women workers and women peasants.
10. Special work should be undertaken among women of the east and Muslim areas.

Zhenotdel's practice. As the central organ of the party for work among women, *Zhenotdel* assisted and co-ordinated the women delegates' meetings. It provided them with documents, bulletins and various women's journals for discussion. *Kommunistka*, the organ and mouthpiece of the executive of the women's section, was concerned with the general tasks of agitation and propaganda and as such was designed for the party cadres, who were involved in the women's movement. *Rabotnica*, the original Bolshevik women's journal, re-appeared in January 1923, and was aimed at women workers irrespective of their party affiliation. *Delegatka* (The Woman Delegate), published in the period 1927–31, reported various delegates' meetings in towns and villages, and thus served as a means of exchanging experiences among hitherto unorganised, non-party women (as *Rozsévačka* was later to serve in the Czechoslovak Communist Party). However, owing to the difficult economic circumstances, the circulation of these journals was very limited. For example, in 1921, each of the ten numbers of the monthly journal *Kommunistka* had an edition of only 30,000, which certainly was not enough for the whole of Soviet Russia.

Zhenotděl also organised various summer schools and other courses for women workers and peasants. Some women delegates were sent on political courses at the Academy of Social Education in Moscow or at Sverdlov University. Kollontai gave a course of 14 lectures at the latter on the role of women's work in the development of the economy. These were later published in book form (Kollontai, 1923).

Thus *Zhenotdel* functioned rather like modern women's centres, organising campaigns, exhibitions, meetings, consciousness-raising, etc. Its various bodies catered for the nucleus of active party women who, as representatives of the women's sections on various party committees at all levels of the hierarchy, had a permanent place in the party apparatus. At the same time, through the delegates' meetings, the Bolshevik feminists reached the mass of women previously outside politics. The delegates' meetings were set up in factories, villages or workers' settlements in the towns. An American feminist, Jessica Smith (1928: 48), directly observed their initiation:

> One out of every ten workers and one out of every hundred housewives and peasants are each elected by as large a number of women as can be got to participate in the elections. The women thus elected meet twice a month under the leadership of a trained party worker and are given a political course.

However, in the rural areas, especially in Muslim Central Asia,[1] illiteracy had to be combated before political education could begin. In 1920, 67 per cent of the whole population was still illiterate, of whom more than 77 per cent were women (Serebrennikov, 1937: 192). Consequently, party cadres and delegates' meetings first arranged reading classes and circles and then attempted to combine literacy education with political agitation. These meetings and lectures tried to bring women out of their individual isolation within the family and teach them something about the life of others. Peasant women were encouraged to speak out at these meetings so that they would be able to take part without any inhibitions in larger meetings with men.[2] Journals of the period portray women as aggressive, active, interested in politics and generally ready for new things.[3]

Apart from their political role, the delegates' meetings also performed an economic role, by teaching women new skills. Delegates' meetings trained women for public work in day nurseries, canteens, children's playgrounds and medical institutions, and guided them when they first took up such employment (which, however, was not generally available until the First Five-Year Plan, 1928–33).

The high rate of unemployment in the Soviet Union in the 1920s is an important limiting historical factor which has to be taken into account when we evaluate Bolshevik failure to challenge the sexual division of labour. It is true that *Zhenotdel* concentrated on bringing women into education, catering and child care, but, given the fact that opportunities for teaching and practising new skills in the 1920s were practically non-existent, this priority was correct. The main problems were at the level of economic policy (discussed in Part III) and individual male prejudice in official Soviet institutions, not at the level of the party's policy towards women.

Male prejudice. As Lenin said in his conversation with Clara Zetkin in the autumn of 1920, most male communists regarded agitation and propaganda work among women as of secondary importance. Samoilova (1920a: 3) identified two main categories of male party members who were unsympathetic towards a separate women's organisation: those who considered specific women's sections unnecessary because their work, it seemed, could be divided among organisational-instructional and agitational sections of various party committees; and those who viewed *Zhenotdel* as a separate, independent organisation, which was doing some special women's work that had nothing to do with general party work.

These attitudes stemmed from the fundamental Bolshevik distrust of all specialised mediating networks standing between the population and the party-state unless those networks were totally subject to central surveillance, manipulation and control. It was feared that feminist voluntary associations (such as women's clubs) would tend to approach and attract women as women, irrespective of their social background. This would lead to an organisational bias towards 'mass' rather than 'class', which would undermine the class struggle waged by the party. Many male party members (and some female too) therefore opposed women's clubs on the grounds of deviation towards bourgeois feminism. It was also feared that specifically female problems, and feminism generally, would distort the overall Bolshevik thrust, dilute women's revolutionary concern, and sidetrack them into narrow feminist pursuits.

In some parts of the country, *Zhenotdel* was actually abolished soon after it was set up and submerged with the department of *Agitprop* (agitation and propaganda). Cases like that of Comrade Pamysov in Permskaya *gubernia* (district), who actually took all the documents of the women's section and burned them, were not uncommon or extreme. Samoilova (1920a: 11) asserts that most of the local and district party cadres openly expressed prejudiced, even scornful attitudes towards *Zhenotdel*. As in the German SPD, sexist satire and ridicule were used as an effective means of silencing women and their just criticism. *Zhenotdel* and women's delegates meetings were maliciously called '*centro-baba*' and '*babkomy*' (old hags' committees).

The weak co-operation between the women's section and other party committees and sections and most state institutions was also due to male prejudice. The report of *Zhenotdel* on its work in 1920 complained about the unsympathetic, unhelpful and unco-operative attitudes within most Soviet institutions. In fact, the only satisfactory contact and co-operation that existed was with the 'female' Department for the Protection of Motherhood and Childhood. The report concluded that 'the success of the work of *Zhenotdel* ultimately depends on the positive attitude and co-operation of the party and state organisations'. Samoilova (1920a: 29) urged *Zhenotdel* and the party to lead agitation and propaganda not only among women, but also among men, to combat their prejudices and teach them to appreciate the importance of women's participation in the building of a new socialist society.

Despite the widespread anti-feminist prejudice within the party and among the population at large,[4] a solid base of organised women was created during the 1920s. While in 1920 only 853 village women delegates' meetings took place, and out of 500 general meetings only 300 women were chosen to work in district soviets, by 1924 the number of women peasant delegates had risen to 58,000 and this figure apparently doubled during the following year (Samoilova, 1921: 11–12; Zueva, 1925: 61). The women delegates were greatly assisted by a decree signed by Lenin authorising that they be paid, albeit on the barest subsistence level. Thus, when judged within the specific historical context, the Soviet women's liberation movement in the early post-revolutionary period was successful and it is hard to fault the Bolsheviks on this point.

End of Zhenotdel. With the advent of Stalinism and the 'building of socialism in one country', the permanent place of *Zhenotdel* in the party apparatus was gradually undermined until it was eliminated altogether. In 1929, the Central Committee of the party adopted a new policy regarding its work among women. As for the rest of Soviet society, rapid industrialisation now became the chief social concern and the party accordingly appealed to women to show strength of will and proletarian heroism in the struggle to fulfil the First Five-Year Plan (Artiuchina, 1964: 148). Instead of women's liberation *per se*, the women delegates' meetings were to concentrate on increasing productivity, the leading role of the party and the intensification of the class struggle.

These tendencies were clearly expressed by *Zhenotdel's* leader of that period in a speech given at the Delegates' Congress of Moscow District at the end of 1929.[5] The criterion of productivity was emphasised more than once in the course of Artiuchina's speech: 'The main thing in the work of women delegates has to be the question of productivity', or, more dramatically but also more firmly: 'The work of a delegates' meeting will be satisfactory only if it succeeds in educating the woman delegate in such a way that, when she finishes her work, she says to herself: the interests of productivity are my own interests.' Since *Zhenotdel* always attempted to draw women to social production, the emphasis on increased productivity represents a change in policy emphasis rather than policy as such. The new Five-Year Plan created a demand for female labour and *Zhenotdel* continued in its original task, although with a new one-sided emphasis.

Another shift in emphasis concerned the link between the party and the delegates' meetings. While previously women delegates were free to choose whether to join the party, by the end of 1920s this had changed.

> Each delegates' meeting, working this year, must address itself seriously to the question of the preparation of women delegates for entry to the party . . . Delegates' meetings have to prepare strong, self-assertive women party members, who steadily hold the general party line (Artiuchina, 1929: 4).

Party discipline and support for Stalinist economic policies rather than commitment to women's liberation were now required of women activists.

In this context, *Zhenotdel* was becoming increasingly unnecessary from the party's standpoint. The Five-Year Plan, a massive project in sublimation, self-denial, sacrifice and discipline, did not differentiate between men and women and, from this point of view, a specific women's section of the party was indeed unnecessary. From the women's point of view, a separate women's organisation was essential, since women needed an organisational medium through which they could defend their interests and put forward new demands. For instance, during the discussions on family and abortion legislation in the mid-1930s (discussed in Part III), there was no way women could express themselves collectively as women on issues which were of direct relevance to them.

Thus the final dissolution of *Zhenotdel* is directly related to the victory of the Stalinist faction and its policies within the party. The Stalinists were determined to suppress all spontaneous, potentially autonomous, pluralistic forces (including a separate feminist organisation) as intrinsically intolerable in a tightly centralised, organisationally and culturally homogeneous, monolithic party-state. At some time in the mid-1930s,[6] *Zhenotdel* was abolished as a distinct component of the secretariat of the Central Committee of the Communist Party. Work with women throughout the USSR was designated as merely one of the many (and relatively minor) responsibilities of the secretariat's newly constituted Department for Agitation and Mass Campaigns. The resolution of the Central

Committee to set up women's sections of soviets was passed on 10 July 1932 (Zagumennykh and Gaidukov, 1932).

This fairly abrupt designation of the soviets rather than the party as the main organiser of the female masses meant that many of the day-to-day concerns for women's welfare were relegated to what was politically a distinctly inferior domain. Given the soviets' largely ceremonial functions and increasingly evident subordination to the party in all matters, female emancipation was being relegated to relatively low-key priorities and activities.

The Soviet Women's Committee. The women's liberation process did not, of course, end with the elimination of the *Zhenotdel* organisation.[7] Its functions were merely dispersed. Party work among women has continued to the present day through special organisations, congresses and journals devoted to women's affairs. Moreover, a new women's organisation, the Anti-Fascist Soviet Women's Committee, was formed in September 1941. Its main objective was self-evident: women's struggle against fascism. After the war, the emphasis was broadened to the struggle for the preservation of world peace. The International Democratic Federation of Women, founded upon the initiative of the Soviet Women's Committee in December 1945, embodied this concept in its constitution. Not surprisingly, the federation, as well as the Soviet Women's Committee, took an active part in the Campaign for Nuclear Disarmament movement initiated by the Stockholm Peace Congress in 1950. The Soviet Women's Committee (the word 'anti-fascist' was dropped in 1956) also took part in the World Congress for Peace in Moscow in 1962 and in Helsinki in 1965. The Committee also participates in the UN Commission on the Status of Women and has played host to several UN seminars on the equality of women. The emphasis is clearly on international rather than on home affairs.

Although the Soviet Women's Committee claims that it co-operates closely with women's sections of local soviets and the trades unions (*Zhenshchiny mira* . . . , 1972), there has been some criticism of its lack of co-operation with local groups (Yankova, 1970*b*). Yankova (a Soviet sociologist) believes that co-operation could be improved in the future with the formation of local women's councils and clubs. While women's clubs would primarily serve as leisure centres, women's councils are assigned a more active political role in Yankova's scheme: 'Under a skilful leadership of party and *Komsomol* cadres, sociologists, doctors and educationalists, these councils could exert significant influence on the formation of women's communist way of life.'

The very fact that this proposal is an anticipation of the future suggests that at present the women's movement is politically inactive. It is of some significance that the mass-circulation women's magazines, *Sovetskaya Zhenshchina* and *Rabotnica*, contain very little information about political events in general and a Soviet women's organisation in particular. This contrasts with the 1920s and early 1930s, when the women's press reflected an active women's movement. Soviet women tend to express their grievances through the trades unions or through the opinion-forming mass media rather than directly through a women's organisation. Given the monolithic political domination of the party, it is quite inconceivable to imagine that autonomous feminism could legally flourish in the Soviet Union today. This state of affairs is common to all communist countries, including Czechoslovakia, as we shall see in the next chapter.

7 The Women's Movement in State-Socialist Czechoslovakia[1]

As we noted in Chapter 5, the Czechoslovak Communist Party had an active women's movement before the state-socialist transformation, unlike the Soviet Union, where the communist women's movement became prominent only after the October revolution. However, lacking a sufficiently strong and autonomous power-base, the Czech movement did not long survive the transformation, and the objective situation that emerged was not unlike that in the USSR – in 1952, the women's section was abolished. The establishment of socialism legitimised the abolition of separate women's organisations, and responsibilities for women's issues were assigned to trades unions in the case of employed women, and to sub-committees of 'national committees' (similar to soviets) in that of full-time housewives.

TRADES UNIONS AND WOMEN'S SUB-COMMITTEES BEFORE 1966

The trades unions. The transfer of responsibility for women's matters to the trades unions occurred slowly. The resolution of the Presidium of the Central Council of Trades Unions, which laid down the principles of trade-union activities among women, was passed only in 1957. It argued that all problems concerning employed women should be fully discussed with their direct participation. The Central Council also decided that an auxiliary body, a Women's Commission of the Works Committee,[2] with the same status as other commissions of the Works Committee, should be set up in enterprises which employed a low percentage of women. These bodies were considered unnecessary in enterprises where women were in the majority, because it was assumed that in these the trades unions were of necessity forced to deal with women's problems. However, despite these formal changes, it was another two years before specific women's demands appeared on the list of trade-union priorities – more than a decade after the communist victory and during a period in which women's employment had increased from 38 to 43 per cent.

What were the problems that the trades unions were supposed to solve for employed women? First of all, they were to create the material conditions necessary for the full realisation of the equality of women. This meant the improvement in quantity and quality of various social institutions and services and the raising of women's qualifications. However, data on day-care centres and kindergartens (presented in Chapter 16) indicate that very few trade-union branches devoted their resources to the construction of these facilities, which were mostly built by the local authorities. The task of political education that is necessary if men and women are to change their self-perceptions and prejudices was also largely ignored.[3]

As we have noted, the trades unions acknowledged women's concerns only in 1959 when the difficulties encountered by women in industry were on the agenda of the Fourth Trades Union Congress held in that year. One of the issues raised by Bedřich Kozelka, Secretary of the Central Council of Trades Unions, was that most women were unskilled or semi-skilled, while only a fraction were highly skilled. So while women received equal pay for equal work, they were not actually doing equal work and earned on average one-third less than men.[4] The solution suggested at the congress was more factory schools for raising workers' qualifications, with courses arranged at hours convenient for housewives. Unions were to 'insist' that such schools should feature in every annual collective agreement signed with the management. The trade-union bodies were also to 'insist upon' mechanisation of minor operations and organisational changes so that women would not have to lift heavy weights or stand when they could just as well sit. The unions were also 'finally' to solve the question of what to do about small children kept at home from school with minor illnesses, and thus reduce the absenteeism of employed mothers – one cause of employers' prejudice against women workers. It was suggested that local Red Cross branches seek out older women who would like occasional employment as baby-sitters (Scott, 1974: 102–3).[5]

The National Trades Union Conference in May 1965 put forward more concrete proposals for the solution of the problems of employed women. The basic problem was, and incidentally still is, that of the discrepancy between the high rate of female employment and the slow growth of household services and child-care facilities. The conference called for an extension of such services as laundries, cleaning and repair shops, and house-cleaning, together with an improvement in their quality and speed of service. It also recommended establishing shops close to enterprises employing women in large numbers and giving priority to shops carrying a wide range of foodstuffs and basic manufactured goods, both in the centre and in the outer districts of cities (Brejchová, 1967: 27–33).

As the traditional sexual division of labour, an important component of female inequality, was not challenged in these trade-union proposals (it was simply taken for granted that women do the shopping and housework, even if both spouses are engaged in full-time jobs), these recommendations certainly did not represent a complete programme for the realisation of sex equality.

The Women's Sub-Committees. Oversight of political activity among housewives was transferred from the party's women's section to women's sub-committees of national committees, established by the local authorities at all levels of the hierarchy. Modelled on the Soviet experience with delegates' meetings, it was assumed that by involving women in the activities of local authorities, they would be drawn into public administration and effective participation in social life. As housewives could be approached only in matters within their experience, namely the care of children, housekeeping and nursing, women's committees served in an advisory capacity only in those areas. The directives for the elections to the committees of women, published by the Cabinet Office in 1954, stated five main tasks and functions of the women's committees:

1. They should help employed women to solve the problems of *care of their families and children* [my italics], by demanding the establishment of day-care centres, kindergartens, children's messrooms, shops with semi-finished foodstuffs, etc., in their particular localities.
2. They should put forward able candidates for positions responsible for consumer control of the quality of food in shops and public canteens.
3. They should take a general interest in health and social services, for example, they should take care of the aged and disabled, and control hygiene in children's institutions and within their localities.
4. They should keep under review female participation in employment and help women to raise their professional qualifications.
5. They should mobilise women for various seasonal activities, such as the harvest.

It is clear that only the fourth principle is a specifically feminist demand. The first three directly reinforce the traditional sexual division of labour by accepting activities such as housework, childcare, shopping, cooking and hygiene as feminine rather than social concerns. Rather than challenging the sexist ideology which makes women responsible for their husbands' and children's well-being, the party only altered the form of this responsibility. Women were now supposed to look after their husbands and children not only within the context of the family, but also by co-operating with public institutions. For example, the traditional female housekeeping role was upheld by assigning to women the task of controlling the quality of consumer commodities. Another consequence of these activities was that they confined women only to local problems. Only the first two principles have wider societal application, yet the primary function of the women's

committees was to draw women from their narrow family circle into a
wider social sphere!

Thus, after 1952, for a period of 15 years, women had no democratic
representation in the political system of Czechoslovak society, because
their organisation did not really exist. Women were supposed to work
politically, as women, either in the trades unions or on the women's
committees. The latter, however, served only in an advisory capacity to the
national committees. In fact, women's committees were more under the
influence and control of local authorities, at the corresponding level of the
bureaucratic hierarchy, than of the hierarchical structure of their own
organisation. As a result, these sub-committees were more concerned with
helping local authorities to fulfil their economic assignments than with the
specific problems of women.

In 1963, the women's committees attached to local authorities in towns
had been dissolved, although they survived at the district and regional
levels and in the farm villages and the smallest communities. Again, the
reasons given were that there was no separate 'woman question' and that
there were enough other organisations through which women could
express themselves. A Central Committee of Czechoslovak Women
(appointed by the party) also had no political existence of its own, its role
being of a symbolic nature. Its main functions were to represent
Czechoslovakia at international women's meetings, to play host to foreign
delegations, to hold special seminars and conferences from time to time
and to publish two women's magazines, *Vlasta* (in Czech) and *Slovenka* (in
Slovak). Its recommendations on domestic issues were either ignored
by the authorities or politely received but rarely implemented
(Scott, 1974:101). For example, a government-sponsored research
project on the problems of employed mothers with small children,
undertaken in the early 1960s, at no stage consulted the Central
Committee of Czechoslovak Women, not even after the research had been
completed (Háková, 1967). Yet these issues were of direct relevance to
women, and should have been of some concern to 'their' representative
organisation.

THE PERIOD FROM 1966 TO 1968

In the mid-1960s, within the context of 'economic reform' and public
debates on the 'effectiveness' of women's employment,[6] some women
communists in the Central Committee of the Communist Party and in the
trades unions began to press for a new women's organisation. In 1965, the
Central Committee of Czechoslovak Women put forward a document for
public discussion at the Thirteenth Party Congress proposing that a firmer
organisational basis was necessary if the activity of women in economic,
political and cultural life was to be intensified (Scott, 1974: 112–13). The

congress agreed to the creation of a new mass women's organisation. The resolution of the congress read:

> In accordance with the results of the pre-congress discussion, the Thirteenth Congress charges the Central Committee with the task of elaboration of suggestions for the consolidation of the organisational basis of the women's movement and enhancing the co-operative role of the Czechoslovak Committee of Women (*Vlasta*, no. 27, 6 July 1967).

It took only six months to begin the construction of a new women's organisation. Public meetings elected local and town committees of the new Czechoslovak Union of Women (hereafter CUW) during the period from November to March. The founding congress of the Slovak section of the CUW met in Bratislava on 30–31 May 1967. It discussed employment opportunities for women (which are fewer in Slovakia than in Bohemia), problems facing peasant and gypsy women and the difficulties involved in finding employment for 15-year-old girls unwilling to continue their education. The congress rejected a suggestion that mothers in low-paid jobs should stay at home and that society should either pay them directly for bringing up their children or increase their husbands' salaries (*Vlasta*, no. 24, 11 June 1967).

Then, on 5 July 1967, 656 delegates attended the national founding congress of the CUW. Helena Leflerová, Chairwoman of the former Czechoslovak Committee of Women gave the main report, in which she criticised the previous state of affairs and explained why the new women's movement had been created:

> The Czechoslovak Union of Women was created to overcome, by its activities, the hitherto fragmentary, unco-ordinated and accidental character of approaches by other institutions to the solution of women's problems, to unite these institutions in a common course of action . . . The task of the women's organisation is also to check what is happening to our proposals, and how various institutions deal with them. It is necessary to elicit from them concrete proposals which contribute to the solution of the problem (*Vlasta*, no. 29, 19 July 1967).

Although the CUW formally became autonomous (it no longer formed a section of the party, but became a regular member of the National Front, the body to which all political and social organisations are affiliated), it could not escape from the political rigidity which characterised the whole political-bureaucratic system. In other words, most political and administrative institutions did not take much notice of the new organisation. It was a radical innovation that the CUW had the right to give its opinions on issues concerning women, but in practice the party and government organisations were not obliged to consult the Union or take much notice of its proposals and suggestions.

The newly elected Central Committee of the CUW assembled various comments and suggestions that had been expressed at the congress and forwarded them to the main political and administrative institutions. In response, several ministries at least expressed interest in seeking solutions to the social problems of women, but the commitment was in most cases insufficient and nominal. For example, the Ministry of Justice replied that certain problems could be solved by appropriate legislation, without adding that laws often become distorted and abused in their application. Protective legislation frequently achieves the opposite from what is intended because it is used against women in a discriminatory way: women are assigned work below their qualifications, with worse pay, and protective legislation is conveniently used as justification.[7] The trade-union reply, signed by the Chairman of the Central Committee of the Trades Unions, was vague and inconclusive. It did not even mention that the obligations of the trades unions towards employed women are not always fulfilled in practice. The Chairman of the National Assembly, B. Laštovička, did not even bother to answer the CUW letter (*Vlasta*, no. 21, 22 May 1968).

Thus the CUW was autonomous only formally – the leading role of the Czechoslovak Communist Party had to be uncritically and obediently accepted. The party could choose to take notice of the organisation or to ignore it. The organisational structure and the scope of activities of the women's movement were also defined by the party. For example, women could join the CUW only by virtue of their membership of local committees; individual membership was not allowed. As late as April 1968 (the 'Prague Spring' started in January 1968), the Central Committee of the CUW complained to the party and the government about the prejudiced attitudes prevailing towards women and their organisation:

> . . . we are expressing our dissatisfaction with the fact that now, as in the past, the state and the party bodies do not take into account the complex and difficult situation in which Czechoslovak women are living . . . It is no longer possible to contemplate in silence discrimination against women in the matter of financial reward, particularly in the shifts towards the lower-limits of wage categories and in the current tax system. The condition of women is further aggravated by the low standard of services and trade. Only a few women occupy leading positions, even in such obviously feminised sectors as the educational system, health service, textile and food industries, from factories to ministries . . . (*Vlasta*, no. 17, 24 April 1968).

THE PRAGUE SPRING

On 10–11 April 1968, at the plenary session of the Central Committee of the CUW, the old leadership resigned. Some women, who had worked in the women's movement before the war and who had not been allowed to do so after 1948, were co-opted to the Central Committee. Then, at the plenary session of the Central Committee, held on 26–27 June 1968, the *Action Programme of the Women's Movement* was adopted. It had seven sections:

1. Women in the public and political life
2. Women and the family
3. Position of employed women
4. Women in agriculture
5. Development of the woman's personality
6. Women for peace and international co-operation
7. The mission and construction of the Czechoslovak Union of Women.

The last section is of particular importance to the present discussion. The CUW saw itself as an independent organisation, as a pressure group within a pluralist political system, and as an equivalent to political parties and other social organisations. Feminist consciousness was considered to be the most important issue and the chief concern of the organisation: indeed, the CUW thought that feminist issues should be its exclusive responsibility. The action programme stated explicitly:

Through the medium of its organisation, women must have a direct influence on state policy, its formation and realisation. [The CUW] puts forward proposals to parliament, government and other accountable organs from the central to the local ones, and demands their realisation. It participates in the formation of laws connected with the position and problems of women, families and children. And the condition for the Czechoslovak Union of Women to carry such weight in our political system is the fostering of voluntary membership and activities by the largest possible number of women of all ages, professions, positions and opinions.[8]

The action programme was widely accepted and membership of the CUW began to grow. The principle of collective membership previously forced upon the CUW by the party, was abolished in June 1968. By January 1969, the organisation had 300,000 individual members, almost double the total of the previous year. Feminist institutions such as CUW clubs, which were social centres for women, were also in their formative stages. The Soviet invasion in August 1968 did not put an immediate end

to these activities, as the organisation continued for another year. The
Chairwoman of the Czech Union of Women[9] could claim as late as May
1969:

> The Czechoslovak Union of Women became the equal partner of other
> members of the National Front. Following on from the former formal
> organisation, the Czechoslovak Union of Women became an inde-
> pendent organisation, equivalent to political parties and other social
> organisations . . . In practical terms, it intends to express openly
> women's demands, exploiting individual approaches and arguments to
> the full, to put forward proposals, to demand that the National Front
> discuss the legitimate demands of women, and to insist on their
> fulfilment.[10]

However, by September 1969, any suggestions of political pluralism or
independent feminism were denounced as 'reactionary' or 'counter-
revolutionary'.

THE CUW AND THE TRADES UNIONS AFTER 1969

The CUW. In September 1969, the leadership of the CUW was forced
collectively to resign and the movement was brought back under the
complete control of the party. As an internal discussion document of the
secretariat of the present-day CUW indicates,[11] the leading role of the
Communist Party is the guiding principle for women's activities in
Czechoslovakia today:

> The Czechoslovak Union of Women enlists the support of its members
> and other women for the policy of the Communist Party of
> Czechoslovakia . . . It develops mass-based, politico-educational and
> organisational work among women in the spirit of resolutions of the
> congresses of the Communist Party of Czechoslovakia . . . The
> Czechoslovak Union of Women participates in the management and
> administration of the state, co-operates with state bodies, above all local
> authorities, and takes the initiative in submitting proposals for the
> solution of questions concerning the position of women under socialism.
> It helps to train women for active participation in public life and
> proposes the best of them for election to representative bodies and to
> other functions.

Thus, while the organisation has some autonomy and scope for intiative, in
the final analysis its overall political status is subordinate.

The party now determines the orientation of the women's movement
rather than women themselves. For example, at the moment the chief

concern of the party is with population policy; therefore, the women's movement is also preoccupied with that issue. A government resolution of 1 September 1971, about the solution of the population problem, specifically urged the CUW to 'orient its activity to the systematic education of young women for parenthood' (*Děti, naše budoucnost*, 1972: 50). The CUW readily complied with that resolution. The discussion document mentioned above includes a whole section devoted to the 'enhancement of the social significance of motherhood'. The pamphlet emphasises that the CUW will support the pro-natalist policy of the government, popularise the ideal of a multi-membered socialist family and educate women towards conscious motherhood. Thus, the traditional female child-bearing and socialising function within the family is now uncritically reinforced by women's own organisation!

The failure to challenge the existing division of labour within the family and in society is also evident elsewhere in the document. The CUW does not challenge and does not seek to alter the existing female responsibility for housework; it only seeks to ease its burden. The CUW attempts to 'help women to extend their leisure by organising special-interest activities; to teach them to use all types of labour-saving services and facilities and how to organise housework more easily and rationally.' There is not even a suggestion that housework should be the equal responsibility of both spouses.

This sort of attitude has also found its expression in some of the activities of the Czechoslovak youth organisation. In 1969, Young Pioneer Houses at district and regional levels founded the first so-called 'Girl's Clubs'. These clubs provide facilities for those girls attending elementary schools

> who have realised the importance and true meaning of the old Czech saying that 'love passes through the stomach', preferably full stomach, we might add . . . the clubs enable young girls to learn to cook well and quickly, shop economically, and to know their way around the stores. Also to sew, embroider and make lace . . . the clubs turn out modern, able and prudent housewives who will retain their typically female qualities and talents even though they will actively participate in the building of our socialist homeland (Štětinová, 1974).

One must add that the author wrote the article for a propaganda journal intended for readership abroad, which might account for some of its conservative and un-Marxist leanings, but the reactionary character of these views is nonetheless quite startling. Neither the author, nor the clubs themselves, advance the goals of good and fast cooking, economical shopping and rational housekeeping as in any sense applicable to boys!

Thus, the most publicised activities of the women's and youth organisations occur in the traditional female domain – the family. The Slovak Union of Women has taken the task of educating young people for marriage and parenthood very seriously and has worked out a project called the 'Little Family School'. The project is in two parts: theoretical and practical. The theoretical part consists of ten lectures, seminars and discussions, with films and slides, covering such topics as: the drive for a better life for women and children, spearheaded by the party; the position of women in socialist society; knowledge of oneself as a woman, and of the opposite sex; the care of the mother and the child by the socialist health service; the physical and mental development of the child in the first year of its life; infectious diseases and the struggle against them; the position of women in the family and in society; inter-human relationships, friendship and love, woman and marriage; woman as mother-educator. The practical part consists of courses in cooking, knitting and household management (Hinnerová, 1973: 27–8). During the academic year 1971/72, forty-two such 'Little Family Schools' were held throughout Slovakia, with an average participation of 25–30 young people. The main Slovak women's magazine, *Slovenka*, has a regular column under the same title and thus helps to popularise the whole project. While local committees have some autonomy in working out their particular projects, it is clear that the Slovak Union of Women is promoting the strengthening of the family.

Thus far, the project has been heavily biased towards women and the traditional sexual division of labour, but, as distinct from their policy on girls' clubs, the Central Committee of the Slovak Union of Women has suggested that similar schools should also be arranged for boys and young men. It has also emphasised that the theoretical part of the project should be more important than the practical part. As quite a few topics of the theoretical part cover interpersonal relationships, an area which has been neglected by socialist theory and practice, the 'Little Family Schools' project can be regarded in this sense as a step forward.

These developments should not lead us to the conclusion that the Communist Party and the CUW are advocating some kind of 'feminine mystique'. What has happened is a change in emphasis and priority rather than a fundamental reorientation of policy. Although the women's organisation has taken various measures over the last few years to make maternity more attractive to women, it has not ignored women's productive roles in the economy. The different bodies of the CUW have special commissions not only for the family and education for parenthood, but also for political education and employed women in industry, agriculture and public services.

The commissions for political education concentrate mainly on political and cultural work among women. They arrange meetings to discuss important current issues, give lectures, hold debates, seminars, etc. The agricultural commissions help to raise the cultural level of women's life and work in the villages and to improve qualifications. For example, the commissions organise excursions to particularly successful agricultural co-operatives (there is no private agriculture in Czechoslovakia) to promote exchanges of experience, arrange discussion evenings and meetings of women doing different jobs in agriculture, and assist in improving the range of products supplied to village shops. The commissions for employed women give their attention to places where the majority of workers are women and check whether the legal regulations issued in the interest of women are consistently observed. However, as in the mid-1950s and early 1960s, the political activities of employed women are concentrated in the trades unions rather than in the women's organisation.

The trades unions. In April 1974, 3,652 women's commissions with a total membership of 18,000 existed within trade-union organisations at the local and district levels. Of these committees, 2,594 were at local branch level (Růžičková, 1974). Their specific tasks were defined as follows:

1. Politico-educational work – foundation of collectivities competing for the title of socialist work, deepening of relations of comradely co-operation, mutual support and help at the place of work, enlisting women for higher participation in public and political life.
2. Improvement of hygiene and working conditions and of the standard of care of working women by employing enterprises.
3. Persuading women to use works or office canteens (because women frequently refuse cooked meals on the grounds that they have them later at home after finishing work).
4. In co-operation with other commissions, to check that enterprises make full use of women's qualifications and the principles of the existing wage policy in rewarding women, including provisions for various forms of further education.
5. To assist other committees responsible for children and workers' recreation.
6. To check the distribution and capacity of day-care centres and kindergartens, with regard to present as well as future needs, and to exert pressure on their enterprises to establish day-care centres and kindergartens either by themselves or in conjunction with other enterprises.

We can see that these activities are extensive and beneficial to women, but also rather localised and non-political. Women's commissions and other women officials of the trades unions can be credited with the establishment of women's rest corners in various enterprises, the introduction of refrigerators and buffets selling beverages at places of work, the installation of adequate air-conditioning, the provision of cloakrooms and showers, as well as hairdressing and pedicure centres, the provision of electric massage equipment for women, etc. – all politically non-controversial matters. Women's commissions in many cases have also been responsible for the introduction of such services as the dispatch of clothes for dry-cleaning and laundering (*Working Women in Czechoslovakia*, 1975: 75–6).

Marie Růžičková, the Secretary of the Czech Trades Union Council and one of the most highly placed women within the trade-union hierarchy, concludes an article (1974) on working women and the trades unions with the following words:

> The solution of the problems faced by working women is the task of the whole of society. They cannot be solved in isolation from the overall problems of our socialist construction. On the other hand, it cannot be assumed that the problems of women will be solved automatically with the development of socialist society. They also cannot be a matter for women alone – the whole of society must pay attention to them, but they cannot be solved without women.

What Růžičková does not mention is how the 'overall problems of our socialist construction' can be solved within the existing repressive party-state framework. No opposition political parties are allowed in the communist countries and labour unions only rarely involve themselves in autonomous politics. Their primary concern is with day-to-day welfare issues and the mobilisation of workers behind the official policy to stimulate higher productivity and ensure fulfilment of the production plan. The women's organisations are expected to play a similar role. As in other state-socialist societies, the Communist Party retains a monopoly of power and doctrine, and a potentially autonomous political force would be regarded as a threat to this monopoly. An independent feminist movement of the current Western type therefore cannot legally emerge in the communist countries to campaign against male domination or for fundamental changes in the sexual division of labour.

Part III
Women in the Soviet Union

Introductory Note

There are different ways of assessing the position of women in any country. One can compare the present with the past; one can compare practice with claims; one can make comparisons with other countries; one can develop a model as a focus of comparison; or one can use some combination of these approaches, as I do in the pages that follow. In this context, I also argue that an understanding of the history of women's liberation in the Soviet Union requires knowledge of the prevailing strategy for industrial development, which has had contradictory implications for sex equality. On the one hand, the pattern of economic growth in Eastern Europe, based as it has been on a quantitative expansion of the labour force, has required heavy involvement of women in the labour force. On the other, the strong emphasis placed upon increasing stocks of capital goods has led to the wage disparities between 'preferred' industrial occupations, largely dominated by men, and the 'non-preferred' occupations in the basically feminised service sector. Moreover, this emphasis has meant that rather low priority has been given to easing women's domestic responsibilities. If the Soviet leadership had been less preoccupied with rapid economic growth and more with human welfare, more attention would have been paid to providing sufficient housing space, adequate child-care facilities, cafeterias and household durables, and less to investment in other commodities. As a result, Soviet women have won equal opportunity in the industrial sphere, but this equality in the workplace has actually led to a broader form of inequality, because women continue to bear the burden of domestic and family responsibilities.

The conflict between work and family has had important consequences for the productivity, fertility and self-realisation of women, especially in the more demanding occupations with higher levels of responsibility. In turn, a declining birthrate has produced serious problems for the state-socialist societies because they cannot easily import labour from elsewhere. The following analysis of the role of women in the USSR is focused upon five areas in which these conflicts have been apparent: the family, housework, gainful employment and politics, child-rearing and birth-control.

8 The Family versus the House-commune

LEGAL CHANGES

Revolutionary legislation directly affecting the status of women, the family and the Church was introduced soon after the October Revolution. The new government granted women suffrage, passed divorce and civil-marriage laws that made marriage a voluntary alliance and eliminated the distinction between legitimate and illegitimate children, enacted employment rights equal to those of men, gave women equal pay for equal work and introduced universal paid late-pregnancy and early-maternity leave. The 1926 family code went even further, for it sanctioned both marriage and divorce without the necessity of registration. Divorce was permitted at the request of one or both parties without a requirement to give reasons, and registered and non-registered marriages were made equal before the law. It should be noted, however, that the code was not introduced into the polygamous Muslim republics of Central Asia, where enforcement of marriage registration was seen as an essential step in the attack on religious and tribal cultures.

Thus, with respect to family law, this was the period of the 'postcard' divorce, when a dissatisfied spouse could simply inform the authorities that he or she wished to discontinue the marriage; if the other party were not physically present, he or she would simply be informed by postcard of the change in marital status. The prime intent of the law was to free millions of women who had been married against their will under traditional patriarchal procedures. However, these laws proved catastrophically counter-productive, because women lost the protection that they and their children had previously had against desertion.

The principle of marriage as a free and dissoluble institution rather than a life-long union reflects the ambiguous Marxist theory of the 'withering-away' of the family. The influence of this thesis can also be traced in the writings of Alexandra Kollontai, who, as we have noted, was an influential feminist and the first Soviet commissar (minister) for social welfare. She prophesied the following:

Family households will inevitably die a natural death with the growth in number of communal houses of different types to suit different tastes:

and as the individual household which is enclosed within the limits of a separate flat dies out, the fundamental clamps of the contemporary bourgeois family will be wrenched looser. Once it has ceased to be a unit of consumption, the family will be unable to exist in its present form – it will fall asunder, be liquidated (Schlesinger, 1949: 51).

A. M. Sabsovich, an architect, was also known as a supporter of this 'left tendency' in social relations. He claimed that the provision of communal services and facilities of recreation and leisure-time pursuits would 'dispense with any need or reason for the separate life of separate families in isolated flats and little houses designed with an eye on the "family hearth"' (Schlesinger, 1949: 171). While the Bolshevik Party programme of 1919 advocated communes as *supplementary* institutions freeing women from the burden of the 'outmoded' household economy, Kollontai and Sabsovich went further and considered communes as *alternatives* to the family.

HOUSE-COMMUNES

The idea of the commune as a means of sharing production, consumption and recreation among the same group of people had been prominent in the theory and practice of early utopian socialists, especially Robert Owen and Charles Fourier. However, the Bolshevik Party, as an urban-oriented political movement, had no room for a romantic and idyllic appreciation of rural Russia and the communal living of the Russian *mir*.[1] Its idea of a city commune was more limited: it was viewed as a residential urban complex which would provide a framework for co-operative social interaction and shared services, but without a formal link to productive enterprises. As the evidence concerning youth communes is rather flimsy,[2] and as this chapter investigates the official Bolshevik policy on women and the family, we shall deal here only with the government-sponsored house-communes. When evaluating these communes, we have to differentiate between ideological aspirations and the virtue made out of necessity, that is to say, the widespread scarcity and ruin of the civil war. During the first few years of the revolution, the fate of Soviet Russia was in the balance and in the conditions of civil war and economic chaos, little could be done about communes.

A number of urban communes were organised in the large cities in the early 1920s once the fighting was over. At first, existing houses were converted into co-operative residential and service dwellings; the first architectural experiments in this direction were undertaken a decade later. The converted communes were usually managed by elected committees, which not only looked after housing needs, but in some cases also organised food-stores, bakeries, laundries and recreational facilities. Some of the communes were composed only of students, who shared their slim resources in a manner familiar to poor students of other places and times (Wesson, 1963: 84). The greatest difficulties were experienced by house-communes composed of families. The communes soon became small and overcrowded, both because of the scarcity of housing and the women's unwillingness to share their cooking with other families.[3] The central kitchen was often used by each woman separately to prepare meals for her own family, 'the women jostling each other for places at the stove, the air thick with smoke and quarrelling' (Smith, 1928: 149).

As we noted earlier in Chapter 3, the Soviet masses in the 1920s were evidently psychologically unprepared for life-style experimentation. But what about political agitation for communes? In the period following 1921, when the fighting was over and it became clear that world revolution was unlikely in the immediate future, the question of the place and importance of women's issues and communal facilities in the transitional period should have come up for party discussion.[4] What was needed from the very beginning was a commissariat (ministry) to co-ordinate attempts at providing communal facilities, conduct theoretical research, work out practical proposals for a change in the position of women and fight for economic backing in these areas. As it was, the party lacked a proper conception of the relationship between women's struggle for liberation and the struggle for socialism in the transitional period. (Some members of the party had a better understanding than others.) The party saw itself primarily as the defender of women's rights but it failed to grasp the implication of this role for its politics. Propaganda and the organisation of women through *Zhenotdel* was not enough. In a period when the economic situation prevented any change in women's productive role, a campaign to change women's reproductive role – through the encouragement of nursery groups and house-communes – was essential. But no such campaign was begun, despite support from some party leaders (Holt, 1976*b*).

For example, Trotsky (1924) argued that it was the task of the revolutionary party, the vanguard of the working class, to make workers aware of the contradictions in their home life. He urged the party to make it clear to the masses that communal housekeeping was more practical and beneficial than separate housekeeping for individual families. To solve the political and cultural lag between the aspirations of the party and the masses, he put forward a number of proposals. For instance, he urged the more progressive and enterprising families to group themselves into collective housekeeping units or family-group communities and thus set an example of a model community. He also advocated the formation of voluntary associations, as a link between the state and the initiative of the masses. Trotsky (1924: 94) was convinced that the initiative for communes must come from the masses rather than simply from the state:

> People cannot be made to move into new habits of life – they must grow into them gradually, as they had grown into their old ways of living. Or

they must deliberately and consciously create a new life. It would be pointless for the Soviet government to create communes with all sorts of comforts and simply invite the proletariat to live in those places.

But this is precisely what initially happened.

> Many houses which have been allotted to families living in communes got into filthy conditions and became uninhabitable. People looked upon their dwellings as upon barracks prvided by the state (Trotsky, 1924: 90).

The initiative of the masses, namely voluntary associations, was then seen as essential if the idea of the house-commune was to gain popularity among the people. A decree of 19 August 1924 gave the population the right to organise voluntarily into housing co-operatives. Smith (1928: 160–1) claims that by 1928, 15 per cent of the urban population lived in housing rented by the Housing Co-operative. These housing co-operatives also had a political character. The cultural departments of the co-operatives were concerned with political work among women not reached through the factory or some other means. The head of such a department in Moscow advocated communal houses, but was cautious about their chances of success, as Trotsky had been. She proposed houses that would demand a minimum of household drudgery for women,[5] that is, small houses for individual families, with separate kitchens which could possibly be later used for some other purpose when communal dining rooms were established (Smith, 1924: 160–1).

The newly constructed house-communes were, in fact, modest in their communal arrangements. Soviet architects organised a number of design competitions for the *dom-communa*, but only some ten commune-type houses were actually built during the period before the Second World War. The first experimental building was opened in 1929. Some of its residential units were without kitchens and served by a communal dining room, but even these were abandoned after only two years and the dining room and other communal facilities subdivided to make further flats for individual families. A dormitory for university students built at about the same time suffered a similar fate (Osborn, 1970: 235).

The modest scale of such efforts was hardly surprising, for this was a period of massive drift to towns, with very little additional housing provided to meet the heavy demand for living space. Stalin's decision to build 'socialism in one country' at all costs relegated housing to a low position on the list of investment priorities, the limited resources that were available being poured mainly into heavy industry.[6] Moreover, in the early 1930s, Stalin sharply attacked all those who were trying to introduce the communist future piecemeal into the present, whether by levelling wages or by organising urban communes. The design and construction of commune-type dwellings were therefore abandoned, in line with a series of other policies that did away with the last vestiges of political autonomy and experiment. Workers became liable to labour conscription; factories witnessed the re-introduction of piece-work; women were deprived of their right to abortion; the women's section of the party was abolished; motherhood became glorified; divorce was made extremely difficult; and, along with the idea of the commune as an alternative to the family, theories about the 'withering away' of the state and the family under socialism were themselves discarded.[7]

STRENGTHENING THE FAMILY

Since the 1930s the 'family collective' (extended or nuclear) has been the only form of intergenerational living arrangement considered acceptable in the Soviet Union. Advocates of other arrangements have been attacked, and the works of authors who supported communal living in the 1920s have been condemned and not re-published. The family has been seen as the primary social unit, and its 'strengthening' has been an important policy goal.

This policy of 'strengthening the family' has been seen in the West as another manifestation of the traditionalism of Soviet policies and of the similarity of Soviet social institutions to those of the Western countries, but this perspective is misleading. For one thing, it ignores the very different views about strengthening the family in the 1930s and today. In the 1930s, strengthening the family meant tightening the divorce and abortion laws, while current policy is coming more and more to mean the creation of the 'ideal socialist family', about which some sociologists have been theorising for many years and which was already envisaged by Engels. The ideal Soviet family is supposed to be held together by love and not by economic necessity and to function along lines of absolute equality. This concept is promoted in every possible way by the state (Holt, 1976a).

How does this ideal correspond to practice? The high divorce rates suggest that Soviet marriages and families are unstable and emotionally unsatisfying, especially for women. In the period after the revolution it was the men who took advantage of the relaxed divorce laws, because women were financial dependents. In the more recent post-war period, although financially independent, women were 'emotional' dependents. Men were so scarce that a woman had to think twice before divorcing a husband, even if he were far from ideal. (After the Second World War there were over 20 million more women than men.) This state of affairs is now changing. Over the last 15 years the divorce rate has been steadily rising – from 1.3 per thousand marriages in 1960 to 2.6 per thousand in 1970 (Holt, 1976a).[8] What is significant is that the majority of divorce proceedings are now begun by women. In over half of these cases the women cite drunkenness as the reason for their decision. Previously a woman would have learned to live with an alcoholic husband; now she is more likely to divorce him. More than half the women seeking divorce have a child; until recently, the inadequate pay women received and the inefficiency of the alimony system acted as a restraint, but these problems seem now to have been resolved. Women have become more confident, self-assured and eager to organise their own lives.

In the past it has always been the woman who has held the family together. The family has serviced the men but men have remained largely on the outside, with outside friendships and activities. There is some indication that this is now changing and that the Soviet family is beginning to retreat into itself. As the standard of living has improved and as internal and international tensions have relaxed, an opportunity to develop a richer personal life has been created. Moreover, society has had to find its members new purposes in life. Men in particular, who have not had such a firm base in the family unit, have needed new values. There is the danger that unless new interests and hobbies are found within the framework of the family, more time and more money might be expended on 'anti-social activity', namely drink and vandalism (Holt, 1976a). The frequent complaints in the media about drunkenness, hooliganism and 'loose' morals indicate that these tendencies have already begun to develop.   The policy of strengthening the family is therefore very useful in this context. Indeed, it kills two birds with one stone. By persuading men to become more active members of their families, the government provides an outlet for their energies. By providing women with assistance in the performance of their domestic duties, the government satisfies their long-standing demands, for the fundamental factors inhibiting the development of women's equality in the Soviet Union have been related to the household economy. These are examined in some detail in the next chapter.

9 Housework

The time and labour taken up by private housework have remained high in the USSR, despite the Marxist commitment to socialisation. Soviet sociologists have calculated that housework takes up to 100 billion hours every year and that its abolition would be equivalent to freeing another 45–50 million persons for production (Andryushchkyavichene, 1970).[1] The amount of domestic labour required in individual Soviet families is especially high because shopping takes a long time, convenience foods are in their infancy, amenity services are still very underdeveloped, housing is cramped and facilities such as kitchens, lavatories and bathrooms often have to be shared (although less so today than in the past), modern household technology has only recently become fairly common and there is a general shortage of consumer goods.

HOUSEHOLD SERVICES

One has to hunt for things in the Soviet Union (as in the rest of Eastern Europe!) because of shortages of goods and retail outlets. Many shops use an old-fashioned trading system whereby the customer first has to identify and order the goods required, then must go elsewhere to pay, and finally return with a receipt to claim the goods. Supermarkets with pre-wrapped and pre-weighted goods have been introduced only recently (Czechoslovakia is well ahead of the Soviet Union in this respect). Home deliveries or shopping by order are common neither in the Soviet Union nor in the other East European countries.

Shopping is generally extremely time-consuming, irritating and energy-draining, since it often involves going from one store to another in the hope of finding the desired product, frequently with little success. Existing Soviet stores are too small and too crowded, with queues stretching out into the streets. This daily queueing and hunting for goods, the exhausting struggle over trivialities, is virtually unknown to people in the West.

As far as daily preparation of meals is concerned, public catering plays little part in easing the burden. In 1960 there was one catering establishment for every 1,469 people and in 1970 one for every 1,208 people, compared with one for every 411 people in Britain in 1961. In 1962 only about 4 per cent of meals appear to have been eaten out and the average Soviet citizen ate in a public catering establishment (canteen or a restaurant) only 11–12 times a year.[2] As the number of public catering establishments increased from 147,000 in 1960 to 280,000 in 1976, this figure would now certainly be higher; indeed, about 16 per cent of retail trade turnover is now through the public catering system. The quality of public food is often no more satisfactory than its quantity. In the Leningrad survey carried out by Kharchev and Golod (1971), 211 of the 1,230 women questioned complained that meals were poorly cooked, while 256 considered the expense of canteen food the main drawback. However, judging from my personal experience of British and Canadian universities, canteen food in the West is also pretty bad and far from cheap!

Amenity services, another form of socialised domestic labour, are still very underdeveloped in the USSR and there are many complaints about inferior quality and tardy delivery. In Leningrad, as many as 29 per cent of working women use dry-cleaning facilities, but only 10 per cent use laundries and many complain about the poor quality of the service and of the long wait: 10–12 days (ibid.). Again, it is quantity as well as quality that needs improving. The queues in laundries suggest that demand is high but that the services at present cannot cope with more than 2 per cent of domestic washing requirements. In all, Soviet household services cover only 5 per cent of the domestic labour requirements (Yankova, 1970a: 45). With a population of 244 million, there were in 1970 only 42,300 hairdressers and barbers, 40,100 dressmakers, 33,500 shoe-repair shops, 3,300 laundries and 1,100 dry-cleaners. The United Kingdom, with a population of 55 million, had 8,769 boot and shoe repairers, 1,205 laundries, 2,554 launderettes and 1,834 dry-cleaners (*Board of Trade Report on the Census of Distribution and Other Services, 1966*: 125, 129).

HOUSEHOLD TECHNOLOGY

Modern domestic gadgets that save time and energy in food preparation, house-cleaning and so on, have only in recent years become more commonly available in the USSR (see Table 9.1).

Table 9.1 Holdings of items of domestic equipment by the public (per hundred households)

Item	1965	1970	1974
Sewing-machines	52	56	60
Washing-machines	21	52	62
Refrigerators	11	32	56
Vacuum-cleaners	7	12	16
Radio sets	59	72	77
Television sets	24	51	71

Source: SSSR v cifrakh v 1974g: 191; Zhenshchiny v SSSR, 1975: 101.

These commodities are more easily obtainable in the West. For instance, in 1974, 67 per cent of all British households had a washing machine and 78 per cent had a refrigerator. Seventy-two per cent of Canadian households had a vacuum-cleaner (1963), 97 per cent a refrigerator, 84 per cent a washing-machine, 37 per cent a clothes-dryer, 29 per cent a home-freezer and 5 per cent a dish-washer (1968). Clothes-dryers and dish-washers are virtually unknown in the Soviet Union and refrigerators and washing-machines are relatively expensive. As such, they are often sacrificed to the more 'desirable' television set, which is in the same price range. In other words, there appears to be a deliberate choice of home entertainment first, and easing the woman's physical lot second. Nevertheless, in 1974, more than half of Soviet families had a television set as well as a washing-machine and a refrigerator. Home-freezers are not on sale at all – except perhaps to members of the Politburo!

Young and working-class families are typically less likely to have washing-machines than the average urban family. One survey indicates that in working-class families, only 15 per cent have washing-machines, 37 per cent refrigerators and 20 per cent vacuum-cleaners (Yankova, 1970a: 45). Another survey reveals the discrepancy between the generations (see Table 9.2).

Table 9.2 Holdings of items of domestic equipment by age (%)

	Age category	
	up to 30	31–40
Sewing-machines	18	38
Washing-machines	31	62
Refrigerators	2	19

Source: Andryushchkyavichene, 1970: 79.

A washing-machine has been reckoned to save Soviet families 500 hours of work every year. It has been further calculated that 'full electrification' of the home could increase leisure by 2 hours a day and time spent on 'socially useful activity' by 40 per cent (Andryushchkyavichene, 1970: 79). Thus, the 'real goal' of the October revolution of 'putting the home on a social basis' still has far to go, although more rapid progress is now taking place than for many years. Table 9.3 shows the savings envisaged for the future, both in terms of socialisation of housework and of updating modern household technology within the individual family.

These estimates should be treated with caution as they tend to rely too heavily on technological determinism, ignoring Western experience of the

Table 9.3 Estimated time expenditure if housework socialised and mechanized (hours per week)

Activity	1963	Outlook	
		If housework mechanised	If housework socialised
Preparation of meals	12	6	0·5
Provisions-buying	5	2·5	0·6
Care of dresses, shoes, linen	5	3·5	2·4

Source: Artemov *et al*, 1967: 169.

domestic equivalent of Parkinson's law. Better organisation and equipment make it possible for the housewife to do the same work faster, but she often raises her standards and uses the increased efficiency to do more work at the same time. As Betty Friedan (1963: 231) put it, 'every labour-saving appliance brings a labour-demanding elaboration of housework.' Furthermore, extensive use of specialised household gadgets increases the element of co-ordination required. Today's housewife has more to organise than in the past. Since the home is now dependent on outside agencies for many supplies and services, she must keep in touch with them, doing everything from shopping to telephoning and waiting for the plumber, the electrician or the television repairman. The inefficiency and unreliability of these services in Eastern Europe is notorious!

In the case of shopping, the housewife must either write a list, since she alone knows all the extra things needed in the house, or she has to check what has been bought (by her husband or children) so that she can buy the additional items herself. Long-term shopping for pickling, fruit-preserving, jam-making, dressmaking and so on (these are very popular hobbies in many Soviet families), also requires specialised organisational domestic skills, planning and budgeting. The modern housewife must decide not only how to organise the various domestic tasks (and most women tend to be more efficient in this than men, having learned from their mothers and through long experience how to do many things at once), but also what activities should be carried out in the home. For example, is the time saved by using pre-cooked food worth the extra expense?

Improved shopping facilities and household technology, as well as more help given by other members of the family, relieve the housewife of some of the burden of housework, but they do not really solve the problem of co-ordination. Admittedly, this is a very difficult problem to solve. Who, for instance, instead of the housewife, would co-ordinate socialised housework? An authority able to impose a timetable on several different households? For such arrangements to be made voluntarily, changes in values and attitudes would be required that are not in sight for most of the population, anywhere.

SHARING HOUSEWORK WITHIN THE FAMILY

Having looked at the amount of housework carried out in Soviet society, we must now examine in more detail who does it. Soviet ideals of child-rearing require that all children should participate in family chores, but this, of course, only applies to older children. A fact that emerges from all sources is that it is invariably the woman who carries by far the heaviest part of the burden. This was remarked upon by Lenin (1965: 115) as far back as 1920:

> Could there be any more palpable proof than the common sight of a man watching a woman wear herself out with trivial, monotonous, strength- and time-consuming work, such as her housework, and watching her spirit shrinking, her mind growing dull, her heartbeat growing faint, and her will growing slack.

The fact of men's unwillingness to undertake an equal share of housework emerges from all surveys and discussions in the mass media. The monthly journal *Krasnaya Zvezda* (Red Star) published the following letter (from an anonymous woman) in its December 1966 issue:

> I come back from work. The house is cold, untidy, there is no water, there is nothing. I do not know where to start: to prepare food, to put the house in order, to light the stove. My husband is lying on a bedstead, on fur pillows, and is reading a newspaper. He is cross, does not talk. I ask him, what has happened? He answers: Why didn't you light the stove? I say: Why didn't you make the fire? Isn't it true that you came home from work earlier? – I did not get married in order to light the stove.

Similar attitudes are revealed in a report of a divorce case published in *Izvestiya* (the main government newspaper) on November 17 1967:

> She is guilty! One day she sends me to the shops, the next to the market. I am a doctor, I could meet my patients anywhere. What would people think? A doctor with potatoes, a doctor doing the job of a housewife? And anyway it's not my place to think about bread, which she's forgotten to buy . . . What am I, her servant?

Such views do not represent isolated or extreme cases of 'male chauvinism'. In 1967, *Literaturnaya gazeta* (an influential weekly) published a number of articles and readers' letters concerning women's place in life, the family and paid employment. Many male readers expressed views such as: 'the way to a man's heart is through his stomach'; 'woman is supposed to adorn the family hearth just as flowers adorn the meadows'; ' . . . why separate a woman from the kitchen? Why deprive her of additional opportunities to manifest love and consideration for her husband?' and so on. One man complained quite bitterly that

> a woman earns almost as much as a man. She considers herself independent and equal. The man's prestige in the family has been thoroughly shaken and is determined only by his prestige at his job. The woman has already stopped thinking of how to surprise her husband with a tasty dinner, and more often she surprises him by cooking nothing at all.

However, many women writers criticised the axiomatic, unquestioned premise that everyday concerns are the woman's concerns, and advocated the elimination of the tradition of the man's privileged status in everyday life on justifiable grounds. For example, the findings of a sample survey of 280 women in two Vilnius plants (Vilnius is the capital of Latvia) revealed that men's contributions to domestic work were limited to minor repairs, bill-paying, and helping with dishes and tidying. The contributions of husbands to the preparation of food and general child care were but a fraction of those of their wives (see Table 9.4).

One needs to point out that the situation in the West is not all that different in this respect. For instance, the results of a sample survey of 340 couples (103 of whom were two-job couples) in eight areas of Greater Vancouver in Canada are very similar to those in the Vilnius survey (see Table 9.5). Daily cooking and house-cleaning, the two largest items in proportion as well as average time, take up about half of the time of women's regular and irregular housework and over one-fifth of men's. The contributions of husbands to these essential tasks and other routine chores were always but a fraction of their wives'. Only 39 per cent of the husbands did any regular housework on a working day and 51 per cent at weekends, compared with 97 per cent of their wives. Only a small proportion of husbands with a child under 10 helped with its care. Only seven of the 340 husbands did any washing, in comparison with nearly half of their wives: men's bent for technology does not extend to the washing-machine! As in Vilnius, help from husbands came mainly in two items of irregular domestic work whose characteristics often approximate a state of leisure and where discretion is greater: repair and maintenance, and sundry services such as animal care, small errands, and work related to leisure activities.[3]

The husbands' conception of willingness to 'help' their wives is often very limited and token. An anonymous woman who wrote to the

Table 9.4 Carrying-out of domestic tasks by performer(%)

| | Performed by | | | |
Task	Wife alone	Husband alone	Husband and wife together	Other members of family
Housework:				
Food-buying	64	3	18	16
Making breakfast	61	10	20	10
Preparing lunch	69	2	14	15
Clearing and dish-washing	19	12	32	36
General tidying	45	9	32	14
Small repairs	24	68	2	6
Paying bills	49	30	15	6
Washing and ironing	67	2	19	12
Child care:				
Washing, dressing and feeding	81	1	12	6
Taking to nursery or kindergarten and bringing home	78	6	12	4
Visiting school	75	12	12	1
Help with homework	73	14	9	4

Source: Andryushchkyavichene, 1970: 82. Results of a survey of 280 women in two Vilnius plants.

newspaper *Sovetskaya Rossiya* claimed that help with shopping usually meant queueing at liquor stores, while buying meat, eggs, bread and milk remained a woman's task. A woman from Siberia complained that modern facilities such as central heating and gas freed the men (they no longer have to chop the wood for the fire), but did not really solve the problems of women. Thus, women do most of the housework either unaided by their husbands, or their husbands contribute only in minor ways.

The less well-off a family is, the longer a wife is likely to have to spend on housework, because she is likely to have fewer gadgets to help her. Unskilled women in the USSR spend $3\frac{1}{2}$ hours a day on housework, compared with the $2\frac{1}{2}$–$3\frac{1}{2}$ hours of skilled women (Yankova, 1970a: 44). Much greater discrepancies between poorer and richer women with regard to the time spent on washing clothes, cleaning and shopping, were revealed in a survey undertaken in a number of Moscow factories in the early 1960s. It showed that less well-off women spent twice as much time on household duties as the better-off ones. Women in families with a *per capita* family income of 50 roubles or less, spent more than 32 hours a week on housework, those in the 51–75 rouble income range spent more than 28 hours on housework and those in families whose *per capita* income exceeded

Table 9.5 *Percentage of time and hours spent on housework in Vancouver*

Activities	Working day		Day off		Either day		Estimated Weekly hours	
	Wife	Husband	Wife	Husband	Wife	Husband	Wife	Husband
	%	%	%	%	%	%	%	%
Regular housework								
Daily cooking	86	13	77	18	93	27	8·0	0·7
House-cleaning	74	8	61	20	86	26	7·8	1·1
Washing-up	47	4	41	8	64	11	2·1	0·2
Regular shopping	54	15	14	11	61	24	3·9	1·2
Laundry	36	1	21	1	48	2	2·9	0·0
Child care	36	7	33	18	43	21	3·3	0·9
All reg. housework	97	39	95	51	99	69	28·0	4·1
Irregular housework								
Irr. food/clothes	25	0	23	1	38	2	3·3	0·0
Irr. purchases	8	4	7	8	14	11	0·7	0·2
Sundry services	31	22	21	28	42	43	1·4	1·1
Repair, maintenance	5	11	6	22	10	28	0·2	2·2
Building	0	3	1	5	1	6	0·0	0·4
All irr. housework	54	36	46	52	70	65	5·6	3·9

Notes: Estimated weekly hours are the sum of five times the average workday hours and twice the average weekend-day hours; N = 340 couples, excluding those with wife or husband off the job on the time-budget working day.

Source: Meissner, Humphreys, Meiss and Schew, 1975: 432

75 roubles spent 22 hours. Men in the same income categories devoted only 13, 12 and 9½ hours respectively to housework each week (Matthews, 1972: 104).

Differences between the sexes in this sphere thus override differences between income groups. In fact, women's heavy burden of housework and family responsibility, together with men's unwillingness to undertake an equal share, provide a large part of the explanation of why women have failed to achieve the equal status the leaders of the revolution believed it would bring. Most surveys on the patterns of leisure distribution have yielded similar findings – women's relative poistions *vis-à-vis* men have hardly changed at all and in some instances have even worsened. In 1924, women spent 1 hour a week on education and men 1 hour 50 minutes. In 1961, women had increased time spent this way to 2 hours 13 minutes, but men had increased it to 6 hours 36 minutes (Yankova, 1970a: 43). Women's relative positions have therefore *worsened*. On average, men tend to have twice as much leisure as women and more time for their hobby-pursuits – sport, self-education, touring and voluntary work.

Women's leisure and hours of sleep tend to decrease with the number of children in the family (see Table 9.6).

Table 9.6 Use of working women's week, according to number of children (in hrs)

Time Use	Women With:					
	No child-ren	1 child	2 child-ren	3 child-ren	4 child-ren	5 or more children
Total time	168·0	168·0	168·0	168·0	168·0	168·0
Work and work-related	49·1	49·0	48·9	49·5	50·2	47·5
Physiological needs:	62·8	60·2	59·1	58·1	58·0	59·1
sleeping	50·0	47·0	45·0	44·3	44·5	45·4
eating, etc.	12·8	13·2	14·1	13·8	13·5	13·7
Housework and personal care	28·1	43·8	46·7	48·5	51·9	52·0
Relaxation	11·4	5·6	5·0	3·9	3·5	4·3
Study and cultural pursuits	16·6	9·4	8·4	8·0	4·6	4·7

Source: Slesarev, 1965: 159. Survey of 8,468 women in a large enterprise in the city of Gorki.

The disruption caused by the arrival of the first child is self-evident. The working mother's sleep drops by 3 hours, her relaxation, study and cultural pursuits are practically halved, her housework substantially increased. This gets worse with more children.[4] Not surprisingly, many Soviet women postpone their second child, often indefinitely, and almost never have a third.

We therefore find that Soviet working mothers spend substantially more time on housework, sleep fewer hours and have less time for study and cultural pursuits than their husbands. We find, too, that this situation also exists in the West,[5] but then capitalism has not officially committed itself to the liberation of women and the abolition of private domestic work. The failure to develop sophisticated domestic equipment and support services on a scale large enough to free women to pursue their self-development rather than merely become part of the labour force is largely explicable by the relative poverty of the USSR and the overriding priorities of industrialisation. At present, with society's greater affluence, these aids are developing faster than ever before and plans envisage their further extension. For instance, the 22nd Party Congress in 1961 called not only for an expansion of the network of communal dining rooms in factories, offices and houses, but it also envisaged a free communal dining service within the next 10–15 years (*Programma i ustav KPSSSR*, 1964: 164–5). Although this goal is too optimistic, recent developments suggest that the gap between the ideology of socialised domestic work and its practical implementation will be reduced. It is quite likely that the volume of required domestic work in the Soviet Union will eventually approximate Western levels.

In contrast to questions relating to housework, it is less easy to ascribe the continuation of traditional sex-roles to objective obstacles. Sex-role stereotyping is being eroded by increasing urbanisation and education, but only partially and rather slowly. A significant proportion of Soviet men tends to hold 'male chauvinist' views on sex-roles in marriage and consequently refuses to participate in the more arduous and unpleasant domestic tasks. Attitudes such as that woman's place is in the home and that housework is beneath a man's dignity are still fairly widespread, even among the educated and the young. Surveys conducted in rural areas near Moscow between 1964 and 1967 revealed that 25 per cent of those questioned, including the young and the intelligentsia, believed it was 'permissible to punish one's wife' (which presumably meant physical maltreatment, although this was not clear). Of those questioned, 20–30 per cent held that, if possible, it was 'better for women to concern themselves only with housework and child-rearing' (of the intelligentsia group, only 9 per cent agreed with this) (Arutyunyan, 1968: 129–30).

Until recently, many Soviet women have been prepared to tolerate this situation, but there are signs of change. Surveys have been showing for several years that only a minority of women (15 per cent) actually thinks that husbands ought not to help with housework. Moreover, women are beginning to make their dissatisfaction felt and decision-makers are beginning to respond. For example, the February 1976 issue of the youth newspaper, *Komsomolskaya pravda*, criticised the tendency of the media to idealise women's role in domestic work; men were called upon to do 'at least' half the housework.

It is therefore not true to say that, while Soviet women have achieved equality in the sphere of production (the subject-matter of the next chapter), their position in the family is the same as before. Although women's independence as wage-earners initially brought neither immediate changes in domestic roles nor any rapid progress towards the elimination of domestic work, the latter burden has decreased over the years. The dependence of the wife upon her husband has been gradually undermined, and new relationships between family members have been established. In view of these developments, we can expect further pressure from women to change work-relations within the family. Women are now willing to answer alcoholism with divorce; perhaps the un-cooperative, 'male chauvinist' husband will soon be given the same treatment! The threat of divorce would undoubtedly be an effective way of changing men's attitudes.

In a not-too-distant future, one can envisage a situation in the USSR in which both partners will be more equally involved in domestic work, with the result that women will be freer to participate in social activities. Let us now examine the role of women in the Soviet economy and politics in greater detail.

10 Employment and Politics

The persistence and continuity in the priority assigned to women's employment can be understood in the light of (1) ideological factors – the Marxist theory of women's emancipation; (2) economic factors – industrialisation in the 1930s and the accompanying demand for female labour; and (3) specific demographic circumstances – a significant excess of females in the population as a consequence of wars and civil troubles. Engels's advocacy of 'the re-introduction of the entire female sex into public industry' has been put into practice almost completely. There is now nearly universal employment of women in the USSR. Women constitute 51 per cent of the labour force in the state sector (see Table 10.1) and 52 per cent of those working on collective farms. They also do most of the work performed on the private plots of farm households (Matthews, 1972: 175–6).

Table 10.1 Employment of women in the USSR

Year	Numbers	Percentage of labour force
1922	1,560,000	25
1928	2,795,000	24
1940	13,190,000	39
1945	15,920,000	56
1950	19,180,000	47
1955	23,040,000	46
1960	29,250,000	47
1965	37,680,000	49
1970	45,800,000	51
1971	47,313,000	51
1972	48,707,000	51
1973	49,959,000	51
1974	51,297,000	51
1975	52,539,000	51
1976	53,632,000	51
1977 (estimate)	54,700,000	51.5

Source: Vestnik statistiki, 1976/1: 84; 1978/1: 86; Narodnoe Khoziastvo SSSR za 60 let, 1977: 469.

While the percentage of gainfully employed women in Eastern Europe (with the exception of Poland) is well above 40 per cent, the proportion of women in the work force in Western capitalist countries is much lower, ranging from 27 to 38 per cent. However, the West is 'catching up' and the trend towards a larger female component within the labour force is both clear and accelerating. With the exceptions of France (where the female labour has remained numerically stable) and Italy (where it has actually declined from 30 per cent in 1962 to less than 27 per cent in 1972), women's employment in the West has also been growing rapidly, especially during the 1960s. For instance, less than 21 per cent of all Canadian women worked for pay in 1941. By 1971, the female participation rate had increased to 40 per cent. (The participation rate of a particular group in the labour force is the percentage of the group aged 15 and over which is working.)

However, these figures conceal the dramatic rise and fall of female labour participation during and immediately after the Second World War. The participation rate of Canadian women rose steadily from 21 per cent in 1941 to about 34 per cent in 1944, then dropped slightly to 33 per cent in 1945 and plummeted to 25 per cent in 1946. In 1954, it sank to a post-war low of 24 per cent and it did not reach the 1945 level again until 1966 (H. and P. Armstrong, 1975: 371). Similar use had been made of women as a reserve army of labour during the First World War, while, in the context of the present economic crisis in the West and the substantial cuts in public expenditure, we are likely to see yet another downturn in women's participation rates.

Numbers, however, do not tell the whole story. The real significance of women's employment is grasped only if we look at its distribution. The substantial increase in the number of employed women in the West did not result from a widening of job opportunities, as it did in Eastern Europe. It merely increased the tendency for women to work in very few sectors of the economy. For instance, about a quarter of all employed women in the United States in 1969 were in five occupations – those of secretary, shorthand-typist, domestic worker, book-keeper, elementary school-teacher, and waitress. Secretarial and shorthand-typing jobs alone accounted for one in every ten women workers. There are more than 250 distinct occupations listed in the Bureau of Census tabulation, but half of all women workers were employed in only 21 of them, while 50 per cent of male workers were employed in 65 such occupations (Hedges, 1970).

TYPES OF WORK UNDERTAKEN BY SOVIET WOMEN

Women are much more widely (although far from evenly) distributed in the Soviet economy. Obviously, the profile of the female labour force is at least partly determined by the legacies of economic backwardness. Despite the substantial increase in the role of women in industry, agriculture still remains the main sector of the economy in which women are employed. Indeed, women still perform much of the 'physical' agricultural work, and a comparison of the proportion of men and women among those engaged in primarily 'physical' agricultural occupations (excluding those in the private subsidiary economy) for the years 1926, 1939, 1959 and 1970 reveals little or no improvement in the position of women in this respect. The proportion in 1926 was 50 per cent and in both 1939 and 1959 it stood at 58 per cent. By 1970 it had declined only to 56 per cent. Ninety-eight per cent of milkmaids, 74 per cent of workers in livestock feeding and 72 per cent of orchard, vineyard, vegetable and melon workers in 1970 were women (Dodge, 1975). However, the absolute number of women in work of these sorts has declined to approximately 35 per cent of the 1926 level, corresponding, of course, to the overall decline in the number of persons employed in agriculture.

While older unskilled women are estimated to do most of the work on private plots, many young women in rural areas enter industry, construction, trade and the professions. The wide range of women's employment is an indication of its economic importance. Indeed, without the drawing into the economy of large numbers of women, the staffing of low-priority sectors, such as services, would have been virtually impossible. Over 90 per cent of trade and public-catering workers (sales assistants, managers of sales stands and buffets, and cooks) are women, and almost 85 per cent of postal workers (Dodge, 1975).

Women are also concentrated in these service jobs in the West. For instance, no less than 75 per cent of all women in paid employment in the United Kingdom in 1971 were in the service occupations; 29 per cent were clerical workers, 23 per cent service, sports and recreation workers (cleaners, canteen cooks, etc.), 12 per cent professional and technical workers (75 per cent of these were nurses and teachers in primary and secondary schools) and 10 per cent sales workers. Unlike the situation in the Soviet Union, women were for many years debarred from joining the postal service. After the Second World War the recruitment of postwomen was stopped and resumed only because basic wages were low and staffing shortages became severe. The Union of Post Office Workers agreed to women's recruitment, after much resistance. Women were classed as 'temporary unestablished' and repeatedly told: 'You have been recruited solely against a male vacancy. We consider a postman's job to be an all-male establishment' (while it is an all-female establishment in the Soviet Union) (*Crisis*, CIS Anti-Report no. 15, 1976: 9, 14).

Soviet women are also extensively employed as manual workers in productive industry, making up nearly half of the manual industrial labour force and constituting an absolute majority in such industries as textiles, garments, fur, leather, footwear and food (which are also dominated numerically by women in the West). A significant proportion of

women is employed in industries producing materials not traditionally
handled by women. For example, more than 40 per cent of those engaged
in engineering and metal-working are women. (See Table 10.2 for more
detailed statistics.)

Table 10.2 Women manual workers in manufacturing industry (%)

Industry	1932 (1st July)	1940 (1st Nov.)	1950 (5th May)	1960 (1st Jan.)	1967 (1st Jan.)	1969 (1st Jan.)	1974 (1st Jan.)
Engineering and metal-working	21	32	40	39	40	41	42
Cellulose and paper	29	49	50	43	47	49	49
Cement	22	29	37	36	36	36	n.a.
Textiles	68	69	73	72	73	72	74
Garments	80	83	86	85	84	84	86
Leather and fur	41	61	62	64	64 }	68	69
Footwear	51	56	63	66	67 }		
Food *of which*:	33	49	51	54	55	57	58
baking	28	58	61	69	70	74	74
confectionery	54	67	67	70	72	74	74
Total	35	43	46	44	46	48	48

Sources: Trud v SSSR, 1968: 120; Vestnik statistiki, 1969/1: 87; 1970/1: 90; 1971/1: 86; Zhenshchiny v SSSR, 1975: 38

Large numbers of women are also to be found in other occupations
previously reserved for men (see Table 10.3). While printing is a 'male
preserve' in the West, 72 per cent of Soviet printing workers are women.
Western women have been allowed to become bus drivers only in recent
years, but more than half of tram, trolleybus and bus drivers in the Soviet
Union are women.

As far as the more qualified work is concerned, here too women have
achieved much more than in the West. Indeed, they make up 59 per cent of
all specialists, although women only constitute 55 per cent of the
population between 25 and 59 years. In 1976, there were 16 times as many
women specialists employed in the economy as in 1940 and 93 times as
many as in 1928. More than $8\frac{1}{4}$ million of them had received technical
secondary education and almost another $5\frac{1}{2}$ million some form of higher
education. The following occupations, in particular, have higher proportions of female workers than in Western countries: engineers (40 per
cent), designers and draughtsmen (57 per · cent), scientific research
personnel (40 per cent), librarians (95 per cent), teachers in higher
education (43 per cent), doctors and dentists (77 per cent) and medical
administrators (53 per cent).

Table 10.3 '*Masculine*' *occupations with high numbers of women in 1970*

Occupations	Numbers of Women	% of Women
Chemical workers	392,000	68
Machine-building: machine-tool operators (except forge and press operators)	342,000	39
Workers in construction materials, glass and chinaware	312,000	56
Printing workers	149,000	72
Woodworking: planers, lathe and other machine-tool operators	133,000	53
Machine building: forge and press operators	120,000	66
Leather workers	80,000	68
Paper and boxboard workers	57,000	65
Tram, trolleybus and bus drivers	58,000	54

Source: Dodge (1975).

In contrast, 50 years and more after the British Parliament passed the Sex Disqualification (Removal) Act of 1919, making it illegal to discriminate against women entering the professions, only 4 per cent of architects, 8 per cent of barristers, 1 per cent of chartered accountants, 0.07 per cent of managers in manufacturing industry, 15 per cent of teachers in higher education, 14 per cent of hospital staff-doctors, 12 per cent of general practitioners and 8.5 per cent of dentists were women (*Crisis*, CIS Anti-Report, 1976: 4; Davies, 1975: 129–30). Women account for 15 per cent of all doctors in Sweden, 16 per cent in Denmark and 24 per cent in Finland, but only 7 per cent in the United States. Similarly, whereas women represent only 2 per cent of US dentists, the figure for Sweden is 24 per cent, and for Denmark 70 per cent (Deckard, 1975: 215). Canadian women accounted in 1971 for 5 per cent of all dentists, 3 per cent of engineers, 5 per cent of lawyers and notaries, 10 per cent of physicians and surgeons, 17 per cent of university teachers, 53 per cent of social workers, 76 per cent of librarians and archivists and 77 per cent of dental hygienists, assistants and technicians. These professional and technical occupations (excluding schoolteachers and nurses) accounted for only 1.5 per cent of all female workers (H. and P. Armstrong, 1975: 376–7). Among Bulgarian specialists (and Bulgaria used to be one of the most backward European countries before its state-socialist transformation) in 1971, women comprised 25 per cent of all engineers, 41 per cent of all doctors, 30 per cent of all economists, 37 per cent of zootechnicians and 30 per cent of agronomists. Thirty per cent of all Bulgarian scientists are women, but the growth in their proportion has stagnated during the last decade: during 1962–72,

Bulgarian women increased their share among scientists by only 3 per cent (Bártová, 1976a: 111).

It is worth noting, as well, that the proportion of women in the Soviet Union in established professional occupations did not decline significantly between 1959 and 1970, with the possible exception of doctors (as deliberate efforts are being made to increase the proportion of men). In fact, in spite of the gradual normalisation of the demographic composition of Soviet society, the proportion of women has increased in many of the more attractive, often previously masculine occupations. Between 1959 and 1970, the proportion of Soviet women engineers increased from 32 to 40 per cent, of technicians from 45 to 59 per cent, of technical workers in railway transport from 23 to 36 per cent and of writers, journalists and editors from 35 to 45 per cent (Dodge, 1975: 23–4).

Thus, many occupations that are considered 'naturally' suitable to men in the West have been opened up to women in the state-socialist countries. The percentages of women in such occupations are sufficiently high (although still falling short of complete equality) for them not to be dismissed as tokenism or as the outcome of the numerical preponderance of women in the population (which is now changing, anyway). This, however, does not mean that there is no sexual division of jobs in the Soviet Union. As in the West, large numbers of women work in low-grade sectors of the economy that are characterised by wages lower than the overall average.

INCOME DISTRIBUTION

Unfortunately, data on earnings by sex are not published in official Soviet sources. One can reasonably assume that if there were no discrepancies, that if male and female earnings were similar, the fact would be made public (although perhaps one should not make too much of this omission as Czechoslovakia does publish such data). However, an approach can be made to the problem, by comparing money-wage levels on the one hand, and sectors of the economy and branches of industry known to have high percentages of women in the labour force with, on the other, overall average earnings and average earnings in sectors known to have a large numerical preponderance of men.

When one looks at the data, the existence of an inverse relationship is self-evident – the higher the proportion of women, the lower the average wages. As in the West, feminisation of a profession or industry tends to hold down its status and financial rewards. This explains the effort to bring in more men. Recent enrolment figures for medical students show a shift in favour of men, but this will take some time to make itself felt in the composition of the profession as a whole. Judging from the enrolment figures in teachers' training, the attempts to masculinise teaching have so far not been very successful, despite the fact that the salaries of doctors and teachers have appreciably increased in recent years.[1]

Since 1917 women have received equal wages for equal work, but in the absence of equal work their wages have been much lower. However, as educational levels have risen and as women have penetrated the traditionally male professions to a considerable degree, wage levels as a percentage of male wages have risen. In 1966 the average figure was 69 per cent; at present it stands somewhere between 75 and 80 per cent (Holt, 1976*a*). Given that women in the West earn, on average, 40 to 60 per cent less than their male counterparts, the Soviet percentage is quite high, although it is far from parity.

POSITIONS OF AUTHORITY

To gain further insight into the extent of the sexual division of labour in the Soviet Union, we must examine more closely the vertical structure of occupations. In doing so, we find that the proportion of women in high-ranking jobs and political positions is significantly lower and declines sharply the nearer one gets to the top. Although women make up half the industrial labour force, they are employed as supervisors, shop chiefs, and in comparable leadership positions only one-sixth to one-seventh as frequently as men (Lennon, 1971: 51). To cite a typical example, there are 236 state-farm directors in the republic of Latvia only three of whom are women (Holt, 1976*a*). In 1969, men comprised only 15 per cent of all medical personnel, but constituted 50 per cent of all chief physicians and executives of medical institutions (Lennon, 1971: 50). This is officially attributed not to prejudice on the part of the appointing authorities, but to the fact that women lose more time (through child-bearing) at the beginning of their careers. Moreover, male doctors tend to have fewer domestic responsibilities than their female colleagues and can therefore take more advantage of further courses, consequently raising their qualifications and earning-power.

A similar pattern can be observed in the teaching profession, with perhaps more significant overall consequences, because the school is a major socialising agency (see Table 10.4). Women make up 70 per cent of the entire teaching force, with a big majority in every category of classroom teacher except one. Eighty-seven per cent of primary-school teachers and 75 per cent of the subject teachers in secondary schools' are women; only among teachers of aesthetic and technical subjects are they outnumbered by men. However, when it comes to promotion to school headships, they do much less well than their numbers might lead one to expect. It is true that women make up a majority of primary-school heads, but separate primary schools are very few in number. The normal organisational unit is the 8-year or 10-year school, which includes the primary department. In these schools, women have on average only about a one-in-four chance of becoming heads. Their proportion among deputy-heads is much larger, but even that does not correspond to their numbers in the profession. '

Table 10.4 Women teachers in day schools

All women teachers	Numbers	%
1950/51	999,000	70
1960/61	1,312,000	70
1970/71	1,669,000	71
1975/76	1,692,000	71
1976/77	1,673,000	70
Women teachers holding positions of responsibility (1976/77):		
Directors of primary schools	3,000	83
Directors of 8-year schools	15,000	33
Directors of 10-year schools	16,000	30
Deputy-directors of 8-year schools	16,000	60
Deputy-directors of 10-year schools	77,000	66
Class teachers (excluding teacher-directors)	1,443,000	79

Source: Vestnik statistiki, 1978/1: 89; Narodnoe Khoziastvo SSSR za 60 let, 1977: 581.

What this means is that most children grow up in a school where they are taught mainly by women under the direction of men. This situation may well reinforce traditional attitudes towards sex-roles: being used to seeing man in the dominant position, particularly in a largely feminised profession, children experience a graphic demonstration of the idea (often current in the home as well) of the man as the final figure of authority. There is some evidence to suggest that this does happen (Grant, 1972: 7).

The tendency for men to occupy the most important and responsible positions cuts across all professions. It is also evident in political institutions.

WOMEN AND POLITICS

The data reveal the relatively high proportion of women in the local Soviets[2] as well as the very small percentage of women in positions of greater influence in the governments of the republics. The significance of women in the upper reaches of the central government is even less. Women now constitute 47 per cent of deputies to local soviets, 38 per cent of deputies to Autonomous Republic Supreme Soviets, 31 per cent of the USSR Supreme Soviet, 33 per cent of people's judges and 52 per cent of people's assessors. However, the proportion of women in the Councils of Ministers of the Union Republics is only 5 per cent and in the USSR Council of Ministers 1 per cent (*Vestnik statistiki*, 1978/1: 85–6).

If we are concerned not only with the extent and forms of political participation by women, but with the accession of women to positions of political leadership, then we must focus on the role of women within the Soviet Communist Party. The ruling party is a highly selective elite which insists on a monopoly of power and doctrine. Party membership is the indispensable condition for a professional political career as well as for high-level managerial positions in both the economic and the state bureaucracies. There were relatively few women communists at the time of the revolution and civil war – under 8 per cent in 1922. From 1932 to 1941, when the role of women in the labour force and in professional and managerial positions increased dramatically, their proportion in general party membership actually declined. The increased recruitment of women to meet the wartime emergency was not sustained in the post-war period, when many women who had moved into important positions were replaced by men returning from the front (a familiar pattern all over the world!). The present percentage of women in the party is less than 25 per cent (See Table 10.5; Warshovsky Lapidus, 1974; Rigby, 1976).

Table 10.5 Party Membership by Sex, 1929–70

Indicator	1929	1941	1945	1950	1959	1965	1968	1970
All Party members (mln.)	1·535	3·872	5·760	6·340	8·239	11·758	13·180	14·5[*]
Men								
(mln.)	1·325	3·295	4·781	5·028	6·632	9·383	10·386	11·5[*]
(% of total)	86·3	85·1	83·0	79·3	80·5	79·8	78·8	79[*]
Women								
(mln.)	0·210	0·577	0·979	1·312	1·607	2·375	2·794	3·0[*]
(% of total)	13·7	14·9	17·0	20·7	19·5	20·2	21·2	21[*]

[*] Approximately
Source Rigby, 1968: 361; *Kommunist*, no. 3, Feb. 1972: 35.

The relatively stationary percentage of women party members conceals a slight improvement in the chances of women being selected for party membership, since in recent years the ratio of young adult males to females has become more even. In fact, the proportion of women among the heads of organisations of governmental administration, *Komsomol* (the official youth organisation), party, trade-union and other social organisations (Soviet data are extremely vague!) has increased from 26 per cent in 1959 to 32 per cent in 1970 (Dodge, 1975). Nevertheless, the greatly increased participation of women in the economy in roles requiring expertise and executive authority would lead one to expect a much higher proportion of women in the general party membership as well as in leadership.

A number of factors account for the inability or unwillingness of women actively to seek political careers. Party membership of itself entails consistent and extended time commitment not only in attending to varied party responsibilities, but also in serving as a model employee at one's place of work. As one member of a local party committee complained in a letter to *Pravda*:

> . . . Each of us is obliged to attend in the course of one month: two sessions of the party bureau, one meeting for all party members in the garage, two sessions of the People's Control Group, and one general meeting each of the shop party organisation's communists, the column trade union, and the brigade . . .
>
> To this we still add the quarterly meetings of the People's Control Groups and of the party organisation *aktiv*, conferences, etc. Add participation in *ad hoc* commissions and People's Control inspections – sometimes lasting several days – and there goes your week! All our month's free days turn out to be taken by volunteer work . . .
>
> Of course, each of us has a family, too, for which time must be allotted (Quoted in Warshovsky Lapidus, 1974).

The accession to positions of political leadership requires such an enormous commitment of time and energy that many women who are already working at full-time jobs, and who carry the added burden of caring for the family, may not wish to take on party responsibilities as well. A woman's reluctance to accept distant job assignments, if these should entail separation from her family, also limits her chances of seeking or accepting appointments to influential political posts, as advance within the party hierarchy requires a high degree of mobility. Thus, women who do undertake an active party role tend to do so at the local level. About one-third of secretaries of primary party organisations are women. At the level of real significance and power – the Central Committee – the role of women has been miniscule. The proportion of women in the party Central Committee and central auditing commission is only 4 per cent and in the Politburo, its executive, nil.

Another key factor in the political role of Soviet women lies in the recruitment policies of the party. These have tended to alternate between an emphasis on selectivity (limiting membership and selecting it primarily from members of the technical and managerial elite) and an emphasis on widening the basis of the party to bring in broader strata of the working class. The proportion of women party members rose noticeably during periods when deliberate efforts were made to recruit women, that is, in the

1920s (particularly through the efforts of *Zhenotdel*) and during the Second World War. On the whole, there has been considerable hesitation in the party to promote women to positions of real authority within the party, or anywhere else.

In fact, access to *top* jobs and positions of political influence is perhaps more difficult for Soviet women than it is for women in the West. If most members of the highly selective and powerful Soviet ruling elite are 'male chauvinist' (and one's general impression is that they are), their prejudices are more effective in keeping women out of top jobs than the prejudices of any similar group would be in a less-controlled society. Hence, we note the absence of Thatchers, Castles and Williams's in Soviet politics, of Mary Quants in Soviet industry or of Dorothy Hodgkinses and Barbara Wards in intellectual life. Although sex-role stereotyping and domestic responsibilities restrict women's entry to top jobs both in the East and in the West, for women who do pursue careers, access to top positions of authority is probably easier in the West. Nevertheless, general opportunities for employment and child-care arrangements are superior in Eastern Europe.

11 Maternity and Child Care

Compared with the Western capitalist countries, the social provisions for maternity and child care are key areas of privilege for women in the state-socialist countries. In socialist theory and practice, maternity and child care have been considered as social rather than individual matters. As Kollontai (1972a: 25) put it:

> The second demand is the acceptance in practice and not only in words that maternity is 'sacred'. Society must arrange all forms of 'aid stations' for women that will give them moral and material support during this very important period of their lives.

Krupskaya (1938: 192–3) saw matters in a similar light:

> How can one help the mother, suffering under the weight of childbirth, child-rearing and education? The answer is clear – the government needs to undertake not only to look after the woman during her pregnancy and during and after childbirth; but it must also establish tens of thousands of crèches, kindergartens, children's colonies, children's communities, where children would receive care and food, where they would live, develop and learn under conditions ten times better than those which could be created by a caring mother singlehanded.

This was also the policy of the Department for the Protection of Motherhood and Childhood, the founding of which Kollontai, in her autobiography, regarded as her most important achievement. The department was set up in 1918 and its guiding principles were as follows:

1. Child-bearing is the social function of the woman and the duty of the government is to enable her to fulfil this function.
2. It is the duty of the government to educate the mother-citizen.
3. The child must be physically protected; breast-feeding is therefore a social duty of women.
4. Bringing up of the child is to take place in the atmosphere of a socialist family.

On 25 May 1918, at a congress of the commissars of social welfare, a resolution was passed to set up sub-departments of protection of motherhood and childhood within each *guberniya* (district). The number of these sub-departments rose from 28 in 1919 to 524 in 1923, but the actual number of institutions directly caring for young mothers and babies was negligible. In 1923, the critical condition of the country forced the central government to withdraw support for this work, and it was transferred to local enterprises, factories, consumer and housing co-operatives, *Zhenotdel* (the women's section of the party) and village soviets. This reorganisation naturally slowed down expansion (local organisations were also short of funds) and the total number of institutions directly caring for mothers and children did not reach the (low) 1922 level again until 1927 (Smith, 1928: 175). A real expansion of health facilities for women and children has taken place only in the last three decades (see Table 11.1).

Table 11.1 Women's Clinics, Children's Clinics and Health Centres (in '000s)

Year	1940	1950	1960	1965	1970	1975	1976
Number	8·6	11·3	16·4	19·3	20·9	22·1	22·3

Source: *Vestnik statistiki,* 1978/1:92; *Narodnoe Khoziastvo SSSR za 60 let* 1977:632.

MATERNITY BENEFITS

The length of paid and unpaid maternity leave and other maternity benefits (the safeguarding of jobs and seniority), together with the widespread provision of child-care facilities, are the most visible privileges women in the socialist countries enjoy over those in the capitalist ones. Every employed Soviet woman receives 16 weeks maternity leave on full pay (26 weeks in Czechoslovakia), half of it before the child is born. She may stay away from her job (without pay) for the rest of the baby's first year (3 years in Hungary, Bulgaria and Czechoslovakia) without losing seniority or position. This is especially important for safeguarding length-of-service bonuses, pension qualifications, and the like. A new Soviet mother must also be given her regular annual paid vacation immediately after maternity leave if she so chooses, regardless of normal vacation schedules (Mandel, 1975: 6, 114).

Only the Scandinavian countries provide better guarantees and benefits. For instance, Sweden, with one of the best social welfare systems in the world, has transformed maternity benefits into parenthood benefits. Paid maternity leave, which covered mothers staying at home with children for 6 months, has now been extended to fathers who wish to do this instead. Sweden has also experimented with part-time jobs for both parents of young children. Elsewhere in the West, maternity provisions are inferior, although they vary from one country to another. For instance, in France an employer is not allowed to dismiss a woman during pregnancy and maternity and she has the right to be reinstated for up to a year. In Italy, there is a statutory 20-weeks period of paid maternity leave, plus 6 months' optional leave, and entitlement to paid leave during a child's illness.

In the United States, however, the cost of such benefits falls more on the employer than on the state, with the result that women become less attractive as employees. At best there are some agreements providing pregnancy benefits for employees of government and local authorities, and many private employers have reasonably generous informal policies for non-manual women workers. Most company schemes in Britain count pregnancy against sick-pay entitlement, a policy that favours white-collar as opposed to manual workers. The latter often have less than 13 weeks' entitlement to sick leave at full pay, while the former may have several months' full entitlement soon after joining the firm.

Also in Britain, although the policy cannot be regarded as more than a modest concession, a lump sum of £25 is payable to the new mother, provided that she or the father have paid 26 weekly National Insurance stamps in the appropriate year. A working woman may, if she is in benefit, receive an allowance of up to £6.75 a week (with the high rate of inflation, this amounts to very little indeed) for 18 weeks, starting on the eleventh week before the expected birth. Thereafter, it is a straight fight between her and her previous or prospective employer (Davies, 1975: 140–1).

In Canada before 1971, paid maternity leave was mandatory only in the provinces of British Columbia and New Brunswick and in the federal civil service. This legislation prohibited employers from dismissing a woman for reasons arising out of pregnancy and childbirth unless she had been absent for at least 16 weeks. The 1958 regulation for federal civil servants provided for maternity leave without pay, commencing 2 months prior to the expected date of birth. The employee was to return within 6 months after the birth. By 1962, maternity leave became an entitlement for both married and unmarried women, although still without pay. It should be noted that, on returning to her employment, the woman is required, if she wishes to be reinstated without a break in benefits, to pay both her own share and that of the government toward superannuation and medical insurance plans. There is no provision for extending the post-natal leave. The Royal Commission on the Status of Women in Canada found that women rarely received their salaries or wages for all or even part of the time of their maternity absences. In the few reported cases in which this was the practice, the leave with full pay ranged from 1 to 6 weeks. Sometimes employees received benefits from unemployment insurance to which they had contributed. Some Canadian employers gave no protection whatever; they simply required women to terminate their services when they were no longer able to work.

Following recommendations made by the Royal Commission on the Status of Women in 1970, the Unemployment Insurance Act was changed to include provisions for 15 weeks of maternity benefits. The reason for grouping together two entirely separate conditions – unemployment and maternity – was that unemployment insurance comes within the jurisdiction of the federal government and, as such, was the only way to extend coverage to most working women throughout Canada. At about the same time, the Canada Labour Code was amended so that, in organisations under federal jurisdiction, 17 weeks' leave was guaranteed for all women with one year of service, and dismissal on the grounds of pregnancy was prohibited. To date, six provinces (British Columbia, Saskatchewan, Manitoba, Ontario, New Brunswick and Nova Scotia) have enacted similar laws. Further, in several provinces, the law guarantees the woman the same or comparable work on return.

Despite these improvements, many Canadian women still face financial and psychological difficulties during maternity. Unemployment insurance provides two-thirds of insurable earnings but requires 2 weeks before any money can be collected. The income women receive from unemployment insurance during maternity leave is therefore substantially lower than the amount they normally earn. Furthermore, the mechanics of unemployment insurance are very burdensome. The expectant mother is required to obtain a separation paper from her employer saying she is no longer on the payroll. She also has to obtain a certificate of pregnancy from her doctor, wait for 2 weeks, and then queue at the Unemployment Insurance office to apply for payments. In addition, women on maternity leave in most companies have to pay both their own and their employer's share of contributions to all plans except pension, which goes into temporary suspension.

The inflexibility of unemployment insurance and leave regulations causes further difficulties. Under federal law and the laws of most provinces, the woman must divide her leave in a prescribed fashion before and after the birth – for example, in Saskatchewan, 12 weeks before and 6 weeks after. But many women would rather work until the birth, and spend more time with their newborn baby before returning to work (Bennett and Loewe, 1975).

CHILD-CARE ARRANGEMENTS

When we now look at the provisions made for children, East-West differences are equally great. In fact, some authors have suggested that children in the Soviet Union are rather privileged. It is a privilege not of material goods – although the chances are that they eat better and have better medical care than the rest of the population – but a privilege born of the care and concern of the adults in society (Bronfenbrenner, 1970; Sidel, 1972). However, we need to assess the extent to which 'adults' refers only to women and the extent to which child care is shared between individual families and public facilities.

Child care in the Soviet Union has remained women's responsibility – children are looked after by their mothers and grandmothers as well as by women teachers in nurseries and kindergartens. There seems to have been no effort to recruit men into fields in which they would be dealing with small children. As thousands of letters published in the mass media and many sociological studies point out, the following is what the overwhelming majority of Soviet women want:

> The right to enter any profession, yes. The right to have the number of children you personally wish, yes. The right to make decisions jointly with your husband, or not to have a husband, or to get rid of him, yes. Most divorces are now initiated by women in the USSR. But if you have a child, or more than one, rearing is yours, the woman's task. So the relationship is 'equal' in your eyes if the husband does everything but participate in child-rearing and say, major cooking (Mandel, 1975: 227–8).

Surveys have shown that a majority of mothers would rather have their children cared for at home, if not by themselves then by a grandmother, a relative, a friend, even a paid child-minder (Mandel, 1975: 229; Jacoby, 1974). Many grandmothers are, however, thought to be rather backward in their knowledge of and attitudes to socialisation. Although some cities (Minsk, for instance) have instituted child-care classes for *babushki*, this has met with some resistance, and there is a general feeling that this is not a satisfactory solution (Grant, 1972: 7; Mandel, 1975: 222–3).

It should be noted that there are some signs of increasing male interest in nurturing children. Mandel (1975: 236, 237) photographed a young couple – not only was the father pushing the pram, but it was he who would stop and bend over and tuck the cover in around the baby's chin or put the pacifier in its mouth. Mandel also came across two young men in their twenties, clearly working-class, pushing baby carriages side by side. As they strolled along, they fussed over the babies exactly as mothers would. They quietened them, arranged their clothing, covers, and so forth, and exchanged advice with each other. When one baby cried a lot, the father picked it up and carried it in his arms.[1]

NURSERIES AND DAY-CARE CENTRES

The main relief for mothers comes from public nurseries, kindergartens and schools. The network of these institutions is more developed than in the Western countries, where there has been considerable opposition to the idea that the state should play a crucial part in bringing up small children.

Many nurseries were set up during the last war in Britain, the United States and Canada, when the demands of the economy required that many women be relieved of child care. However, with the return of men from the armed forces to civilian life, many women workers were made redundant and the substantial state support for day care during the war quickly terminated. A different view then became current on the question of public facilitation of the employment of mothers with small children. John Bowlby's writings on child development emphasised the central importance of the mother-child relationship, especially in the first 2 years of the child's life, and the drastic effect of separation.

At their peak in 1944, state day nurseries in the United Kingdom were providing places for nearly 72,000 children. By 1969 the number had fallen by over two-thirds to 21,000. In 1975, of the 4 million children under five only 215,000 were receiving any sort of nursery education (state, private or voluntary) and only 29,000 were in local-authority nurseries. British postwar child-care policy discouraged provision of day-nursery places except for children with special needs. The priority groups for whom local authorities were encouraged to continue to provide places fell into three main categories:

1. Children whose mothers were constrained by individual circumstances to go out to work.
2. Children whose home conditions were in themselves unsatisfactory from the health point of view.
3. Children whose mothers were incapable, for some good reason, of undertaking the full care of their children.

However, demand for day-nursery places, far from declining as expected after the Second World War, has steadily increased as more married women have entered paid employment. The expansion of nursery education put forward in the White Paper of December 1972 was brought to a halt in August 1975 by drastic cutbacks in funds allocated to nursery education. The new nursery-building programme began in 1974/75 with an annual budget of £15 million, scheduled to increase to £30 million by 1977/78. By 1976/7 it had already been cut back to £8.5 million. Several local authorities decided not even to spend the small sums available, because of their inability or unwillingness to meet running costs.[2]

In 1961, no more than 15 per cent of Canadian women with children under 6 were in the labour force, apart from women graduates or those whose husband's annual income was below $3,000. In both these latter categories, the rate was 36 per cent (Judek, 1968). Having pre-school children inhibits Western female labour participation more powerfully than any other variable. Shortage of nursery accommodation means that many mothers must wait until their first or youngest child is five or six, old enough to go to primary school, before they are able to work outside the home. Adequate social provision for children has thus become one of the major issues in the current Women's Liberation movement; and, unlike East European practice, the women's movement has argued that men should participate in the running of day nurseries on the same basis and in the same numbers as women. In Eastern Europe, nurseries are staffed exclusively by females.

Table 11.2   Pre-school institutions in the USSR, 1928–76 (in '000s)

	1928	1940	1945	1950	1955	1960	1965	1970	1975	1976
Total	4·3	46·0	48·4	45·2	54·2	70·6	91·9	102·7	115·2	117·6
Nurseries:										
Urban	1·5	9·2	8·2	9·3	11·2	14·7	14·5	12·5	–	–
Rural	0·3	12·8	11·8	10·3	11·3	12·3	9·8	7·0	–	–
Total	1·8	22·0	20·0	19·6	22·6	27·0	24·3	19·6	15·8	15·0
Kindergartens:										
Urban	2·2	14·4	18·0	17·0	21·0	28·6	42·3	49·0	–	–
Rural	0·3	9·6	10·5	8·6	10·6	15·0	25·2	34·1	–	–
Total	2·5	24·0	28·4	25·6	31·6	37·4	39·0	35·4	34·1	33·9
Joint nurseries and kinder- gartens*	–	–	–	–	–	6·2	28·5	47·4	65·3	68·7

* Institutions accepting children aged 0–7; the proportion of these is growing.
Sources: *Narodnoe khoziastvo SSSR*, 1972: 634–5; 1973: 708–9; 1975: 602; *Vestnik statistiki*, 1978/ 1: 93.

In the Soviet Union, following the early years of industrialisation and mass female introduction into the urban industrial paid labour force, day-care facilities expanded rapidly (from, as one can see in Table 11.2, 4,300 in 1928 to 46,000 in 1940). However, glorification of motherhood (to the extent of awarding medals to 'productive' mothers), the restrictive policies of 'strengthening the family' and the Stalinist model of industrialisation led in the 1930s, 1940s and 1950s to a stagnation in the growth of pre-school institutions. A marked change has occurred only during the last two decades, during which the network of day-care facilities and the proportion of children enrolled in them has been expanding considerably (see Table 11.3).

The USSR now provides day- or 24-hour care for virtually every urban child whose parents desire it, and for every farm child during the planting and harvesting season. Fees are charged, but may cover only one-tenth to two-thirds of the total cost for the children (Osborn, 1970: 59). They are

Table 11.3 *Children in permanent pre-school institutions (in 'ooos)*

	1928	1940	1945	1950	1960	1965	1970	1975
Total	186	1953	2066	1788	4428	7673	9281	11523
In urban areas	166	1422	1453	1380	3565	6193	7380	8980
In rural areas	020	531	613	408	863	1480	1901	2543
Of nursery age:								
In nurseries	56	781	595	619	1313	1466	1182	1053
In nursery-kindergartens	–	–	–	–	142	954	1398	2067
Total	56	781	595	619	1455	2420	2580	3120
Of kindergarten age:								
In nursery-schools	–	–	–	–	217	1973	3911	5812
In kindergartens	130	1172	1471	1169	2756	3281	2791	2591
Total	130	1172	1471	1169	2973	5254	6702	8403

Sources: Narodnoe Khoziastvo SSSR, 1972: 634–5; 1973: 708–9; 1975: 602–3; *Vestnik statistiki*, 1971/9: 90; 1975/1: 93–4; 1978/1: 93–4.

remittable in whole or in part in the case of badly-off parents. Children are accepted from the age of 3 months, although relatively few mothers place them before they are a year old. The ratio between staff and children is higher than in most private day-care centres in the West; urban nurseries in the Soviet Union average 108 children and 14 staff – 1 nurse to 7–8 children (Osborn, 1970: 58). A 20 per cent pay rise for pre-school teachers in 1972 was designed to attract and keep better-trained personnel in the field. The director of a day-care centre must now have higher school special education; kindergarten teachers undergo 2- or 3- year courses at a teacher-training college (Weaver, 1971: 43–55).

Many visitors to the Soviet Union have been impressed with the quality of nurseries. Considerable attention is paid to developing children's sensory-motor functions and their language abilities during their first year at a Soviet nursery. Through play, children are further stimulated to advance through each stage of development from crawling to standing to walking. They are methodically encouraged by teachers who follow a plan laid down by the pre-school institute. The teachers know at what age children should be able to roll a ball, climb, take short walks and play with special toys geared to aid their development (and reinforce sex-role stereotypes!).

The kindergarten and the nursery are thought of as collectives, and the children are taught to consider themselves as part of the collective. There is, neverthless, a good deal of individual instruction, in addition to group instruction. Much attention is paid to holding the child's interest.

Following the guide-lines of Makarenko, a prominent Soviet education-alist in the 1930s, the young child is taught a few basic rules of 'socialist morality': politeness, unselfishness, tidiness, working for others and self-discipline (Weaver, 1971: 104).

The main problem in day-care centres seems to be the higher incidence of colds and children's diseases. It has been observed that the children of housewives are less liable to fall ill than those of any other group, and that children brought up in institutions are ill much more often than those kept at home, in spite of the provision of medical inspection and care in the institutions (*Zdravookhranenie Rossiskoi Federatssii*, no. 11, 1970: 29–33). However, it is instructive to make a contrast between infections and nutritional diseases. A survey carried out in the city of Gorki showed that 2·8 per cent of children in nurseries were suffering from rickets, but 3·9 per cent of those not in nurseries had the disease (Slesarev, 1965: 160).

EXTENDED-DAY SCHOOLS AND HOLIDAY CAMPS

Some older children are now given care at school after normal hours until their parents are able to take them home. The extended-day school lengthens the school day to a total of 9–12 hours. It also provides all meals. As an institution, it began as a voluntary parents' movement about a decade ago, when the built-in after-school child-supervisor, the living-in mother-in-law, widowed by the Second World War, ceased to be a universal phenomenon. Experiments began in 1955, and the schools were recommended for the entire Russian Republic in the following academic year. However, as one can see from Table 11.4, the number of such institutions only began to grow rapidly in the 1960s after it had been decided that boarding-schools were not as effective as had previously been thought.[3]

Table 11.4 Extended-day schools and groups, 1960–70

	1960	1965	1970
Extended-day schools:*			
Urban	8,427	18,302	24,726
Rural	3,266	17,158	39,525
Total	11,693	35,460	64,251
Children in extended-day groups (in millions):			
In urban schools	0·458	1·484	2·668
In rural schools	0·153	0·961	2·520
Total	0·611	2·445	5·188

* Including schools with extended-day groups.
Source: Narodnoe obrazovanie, nauka i kultura v SSSR, 1971: 92.

Similar provisions exist in the United Kingdom, where the school day usually finishes in mid-afternoon and the children may be away from home until 4 p.m. or later. A hot lunch is usually available, although some local authorities (Leicestershire) have cut back or eliminated meals in order to save money. In West Germany, by contrast, where the school day ends as early as 2 p.m., married women have a correspondingly shorter time in which they are available for work outside the home. Similarly, the Canadian kindergarten typically operates on a half-day basis, and later grades not only have noon break when in some instances children are not allowed to remain at school, but begin later and end earlier than the standard working day. There are few supplementary programmes to serve the needs of 'latch-key' children whose school hours fill only part of the standard working day, and there are also several school holidays on normal working days.

The Soviet extended-day schools and groups are not, however, without their faults. For instance, 13 years of experience with the extended-day programme in Tula province illustrates a pattern of deterioration. The Tula authorities initiated extended-day groups as well as entire schools in 1960, but 13 years later only extended groups were in operation, the experimental extended-day school being abolished after 7 years. The main faults with the programme lie in the fact that children undertake most of their activities in one room – classes in the morning, homework and play in the afternoon (Kozhevnikova, 1973). In Czechoslovakia, after-school centres are unpopular among the children for the same reason – they are too much like school.

Soviet children are also cared for during the summer holidays. Although many parents prefer to take their children with them on vacation or send them to the close relatives' farms that nearly every family has, many couples are not able to take their annual holiday at the same time. In 1970, 19 million children went on organised holidays, compared with less than 6 million in 1950, and there were twice as many children's holiday camps in 1974 as in 1960. Residential summer camps in the West are fewer in numbers and tend to be class-biased.

Therefore, as was envisaged by the Bolsheviks in the early years of the revolution, pre-school institutions, children's organised holidays and after-school-hours guidance and supervision for school-aged children have become permanent features of Soviet life. The Soviet Communist Party today sees pre-school institutions as supplementing and guiding parental upbringing. The child progresses from a small group (the family) to a larger one (the day nursery) finally to take up his or her place in society. Demand for nurseries exceeds supply, but the gap has been considerably narrowed.

FAMILY ALLOWANCES AND RELATED STATE POLICIES

In contrast, family-allowance schemes – another aspect of state acceptance of responsibility for child-raising – are underdeveloped in the Soviet Union compared with the rest of Eastern Europe and some Western countries. The first family-allowance programme was introduced only in 1936 (the year when the policy of strengthening the family was initiated and when abortion was prohibited), but payments began only with the seventh child. Later, when the outcome of the war was no longer in doubt, motherhood was declared a patriotic duty. Mothers with large families were given not only financial help, but medals and honorary titles of various degrees and classes. All single mothers were given special privileges in comparison with married women. The state took upon itself, whenever necessary, partial or even full support of their fatherless children if the mothers applied for such help. In 1945, shortly after the promulgation of this new law, 280,000 single mothers applied for state aid. By 1950, this number had increased to over 1,700,000, and by 1957 it had reached a total of 3,200,000. After 1957, the number of single mothers claiming state support started to decline (St. George, 1973: 70).

The 1944 law was an emergency wartime measure; in response to the impending demographic catastrophe. Twenty million people, mainly men, were slaughtered during the Second World War. The exact disparity between the sexes was never officially published, but an estimated 10 to 15 per cent of women in the fertile age category could not be fitted into the framework of the monogamous pairing family after the war. Twenty-seven years after the end of the war, there were still 19 million more women than men in the Soviet Union. The relatively peaceful last quarter-century has produced a certain normalisation and the sex disparity among the younger generation has virtually disappeared.[4]

To digress briefly, the Soviet birth rate remained high in international terms until 1960, after which it fell sharply (see Table 11.5). The small numbers of girls born in the difficult war and immediate post-war years were coming to child-bearing age at this time, and women in the older age-groups, 25 and over, were restricting births more than formerly by abortion and contraception, mainly for reasons common to other industrial societies. The present birthrate (which is still relatively high) is

Table 11.5 Crude birthrate in the USSR (per '000)

1940	1950	1955	1960	1965	1970	1971	1972	1973	1974
31·2	26·7	25·7	24·9	18·4	17·4	17·8	17·8	17·6	18·0

Source: *Zhenshchiny v SSSR*, 1975: 101.

maintained largely by the less urbanised ethnic minorities in the Asian parts of the USSR and by peasant women generally.

The results of family-planning studies reviewed in Macura (1974) suggest that most married couples in Eastern Europe tend to avoid having large families. This trend is especially striking among better-educated and gainfully employed women living in towns, but it is developing rapidly, especially among the younger generation, throughout the urban population and increasingly in rural areas. The average expected family size is generally close to, and for a sizeable group of women below, replacement level. However, many women have fewer children than they would like. The reasons are mainly economic and professional. Career orientations, the need for additional family income, inadequate housing and child-care facilities force women to think twice before deciding to have an additional child. The ideal of childlessness still remains rare. A sizeable proportion of women consider two children as the right number and an appreciable proportion would like to have a third. Even in Hungary, where the 'depreciation' of children as an economic and spiritual asset seems to have been most advanced, more than 80 per cent of women consider a family of two to three children as ideal, both in general terms and for themselves. Various circumstances prevent them from having as many children as they really want.

Eighty to eighty-five per cent of Soviet families have only one or two children. In 1960, 65 per cent of all births were first- or second-order births and were, thus, not eligible for family allowances, unless the children were illegitimate. Third-order births constituted 14 per cent of all births and attracted a lump-sum payment of 20 roubles, which was less than 2 per cent of a skilled worker's annual wage. Fourth-order births comprised 8 per cent of all births and brought in 65 roubles a year from the child's first birthday until its fifth, which was still only 6 per cent of the average worker's annual wage. Only a very large family derives considerable benefits from the family-allowance programme. With the tenth child, payments total 445 roubles annually, which is 41 per cent of the average worker's annual wage, but very few families have this many children.

Since 1958, family-allowance payments have formed a decreasing proportion of national income: whereas in 1958, they amounted to 0.4 per cent, in 1963 they had dropped to 0.28 per cent. In 1961, only 0.32 per cent of the national income consisted of family-allowance payments, while in France the percentage was 4.8 (Heer and Bryden, 1966).[5] Informed opinion, however, is now beginning to favour larger family allowances paid over a longer period (see, for example, Yurkevich, 1970: 40–1) and is having some impact. In 1974, benefits for low-income families were introduced. Now, families in which the *per capita* monthly income is under 50 roubles receive 12 roubles a month for every child under 8 years of age (Kotlyar and Turchaninova, 1975: 114). As the average monthly wage in the Soviet Union in 1976 was 158 roubles, this measure will mainly assist families in which the woman takes up the 10 months unpaid post-natal leave after the birth of her child. The benefits are therefore, to some degree, an alternative to using nursery facilities.

In 1973 the regulations on sick leave were altered so that parents could take 10 instead of 3 days with full pay. This regulation applies equally to men and women, but in practice it is always the women who stay at home. On the whole, the new measures presuppose that the family is the unit responsible for the main burden of upbringing, and that child-rearing is women's work. There is no provision in Soviet law for paternity leave – although one should point out that breast-feeding is widely supported, as a cultural datum.

More recent planned measures tend to reinforce these assumptions. The new Five-Year Plan adopted at the beginning of 1976 advocates that women be paid for part of the one year of post-natal leave, which the law at present allows to be taken unpaid, although it is not specified for what part of the year and at what rate. Further, it is promised that women will be given the opportunity to take work home or to work for a part of the day or week in order better to combine their work and child-rearing duties.

There are, however, reasons to believe that these government plans will not be realised. One reason is economic. Soviet law has for several years allowed enterprises to take on women part-time, but as such labour is comparatively more expensive (holiday and pension rights are retained in full), managers of larger enterprises have been reluctant to introduce part-time work for women (Kotlyar and Turchaninova, 1975: 103–4). The interests of managers and central planners do not always coincide. Moreover, industry could not cope with the mass exodus of female labour, even if it were to ensure greater labour resources in 20 years time. But the most important factor in the situation is women's unwillingness to accept the trimming of family income or their productive roles.

It might have been expected that, in view of their domestic burden, women would have leaped at the chance to be rid of some of the pressure, but surveys seem to indicate that women see their economic role as too important to surrender. Research carried out in Leningrad over a decade ago established that while 80 per cent of women thought it was right for women to stay at home for the first 3 years or so after the birth of a child, they personally did not want to sacrifice those years. The women suggested that part-time work be introduced (Yankova, 1970a; Holt, 1976a).

More recent surveys suggest that even this alternative (of part-time work) is no longer generally acceptable. Research conducted in a Moscow watch factory and in enterprises in Moldavia employing a high proportion of women revealed that only 6–12 per cent of the women wanted part-time work. The majority of the respondents were mothers with pre-school children (Kotlyar and Turchaninova, 1975:99). Less than 1 per cent of a sample of Ukrainian women declared that they wanted to devote all their time to bringing up their children; only 15 per cent expressed approval for the idea of part-time work. The most popular suggestion was that mothers with small children should work slightly shorter days – but even this was favoured by only 23 per cent of the sample (Holt, 1976a).

In other words, the vast majority of women when asked directly whether and under what conditions they would stay at home replied that under no conditions would they be willing to do so. The Ukrainian survey also showed that women's attitudes depend upon the jobs they hold and the qualifications they possess: there was a higher instance of negative responses to the suggested benefits among women with higher qualifications and hence more satisfying jobs. It is therefore quite probable that, without more concessions from the government, women will prove very reluctant to co-operate with the plan to bear and raise more children in the home.

12 Birth Control: A Woman's Right to Choose?

Having examined the extent of the state's assistance to women who have children, we now turn to the situation of women who do not want to have children. In what ways has the Soviet state interfered with a woman's right to choose not to bear a child? How do we account for the early Soviet abortion policy (in 1920, the Soviet Union became the first country in the world to legalise abortion) and how do we explain the change of direction in 1936 (when abortion was prohibited) and in 1955 (when abortion was re-legalised)? Furthermore, why has abortion remained the *major* method of birth control in the Soviet Union rather than a safety net for the failure of contraception, as it is in Western countries? How do we account for the apparent contradiction between the persistent Soviet playing-down of contraception and its simultaneous attempt to cut down the abortion rate?

Before one can begin to answer these complex questions, the problem of sources has to be faced. Because of our lack of knowledge of the social history of the early Soviet period, we have no clear idea of the moves that led to the 1920 law or of whether there was any inner party discussion on the subject. We do know that it was the Ministries of Health and Justice that were immediately responsible for drafting the abortion bill and we also know that the Ministry of Health spent a year before the legislation was enacted soliciting the views of medical and legal circles and the opinions of women's organisations (Higgins, 1976). But, with gaps in our knowledge, it is difficult to assess whether the whole initiative for the legislation rested with these two ministries. Did they do the work and then receive support from above, or were they initially encouraged from above? Were there any pressures for legislation from other sources? What part, if any, had the women's organisations in acting as a spur or pressure group? According to Kollontai, the women's sections took the initiative in pressing for some changes in the law, but we do not know if there was any grass-roots demand from women themselves.

In contrast to this, we do know that legal and medical circles were professionally interested in the abortion question both before and after the revolution. The Pirogov Society of Russian Physicians argued at their congress in 1913 that repealing the repressive abortion law would cut the mortality rate amongst women considerably, would ease the hospital situation (hospitals in the big cities were overwhelmed with women who had undergone some form of illegal abortion and, as a consequence, required serious medical attention), and would allow abortions to be combated more effectively. In 1914, the issue was raised at the Congress of the Russian group of the International Union of Criminologists; a motion was passed accepting abortion as a non-criminal act and recommending that the law be repealed. The matter was the source of lively debate for several months until the outbreak of the war closed the discussion for the time being (Knight, 1976).

Lenin's article, 'The Working Class and Neo-Malthusianism', written in 1913, should be seen in the context of this debate, as it is essentially a polemic directed against the 1913 congress of the Pirogov Society. In this authoritative article, Lenin refers to two strands in the Bolshevik attitude towards abortion. Firstly, he rejects 'social neo-malthusianism' which he sees as a protective measure of the rich against the proliferation of the poor. The advocacy of birth control as a means of relieving the suffering of the working class is viewed as a 'petty-bourgeois attitude'. The crucial issue is the fight for socialism, not for birth control. Secondly, he says:

> Of course this does not prevent us from demanding the complete abolition of all the laws condemning abortions or dissemination of medical birth-control information. All such laws are nothing but the hypocrisy of the ruling classes . . . it is one thing to demand the basic freedom of medical information, safeguarding the most basic democratic rights of all citizens, and another to apply neo-malthusianism as a social measure (1965: 30).

The Bolsheviks' attitude to abortion is therefore analogous to their attitude to bourgeois legislation in general. They were concerned with removing the social and economic *causes* of abortion rather than trying to prevent abortion by repression, and they also recognised illegal abortions as an inevitable outcome of repressive legislation.

However, the Bolsheviks did not legalise abortion until 1920 and this timing separates it from the 1917 decree on marriage and divorce, the 1918 laws on civil registration of deaths, births and marriages, and the codification of these measures in 1922. (It was not until 1936 that legislation grouped abortion with other aspects of family policy.) The 1920 decree was passed ostensibly on the grounds of the country's poverty, lack of child-care facilities and the recognition of the futility of prohibiting abortion under the circumstances.[1] The law made quite explicit the regime's disapproval of abortion, which it regarded as a serious 'evil' to the community, to be fought by propaganda.

Apart from the moral undertones, abortion was seen as an evil in the sense that it was detrimental to the health of a woman, even in the best of conditions. An illegal abortion was seen as worse, insofar as it involved unqualified practioners working in insanitary conditions. Thus, the decree was primarily a health measure; the official argument behind the legislation was made essentially in medical terms, with medical justifications. It was presented as a temporary solution to current shortcomings, although there was no indication of the time-span envisaged for the 'gradual disappearance of this evil'. It was assumed that the construction of socialism would remove the material conditions that forced women to resort to abortions. Improved maternity and child-care facilities were seen as eventually leading to the disappearance of abortion as a mass phenomenon.

The official justification of the 1920 legislation therefore concentrated on the health aspect of the operation and gave material inadequacies as the causal factor. What it did not do was to place abortion within the wider context of birth control. In not doing so, it avoided the vast number of tricky problems surrounding the birth-control issue, especially its neo-malthusian connotations. The latter was an important consideration, particularly as the opponents of legalised abortion constantly prophesied a declining birth rate. Another set of problems concerned the 'private' sphere – relationships between men and women, sexual liaisons, 'morality' – issues with which the party ideologists were reluctant to deal in any categorical form from above.

This reluctance was reflected in the vague and ambiguous attitude towards birth control in general and contraception in particular. Research and development in the sphere of contraception appears to have been slow. There were a number of commissions and studies set up to investigate what methods were in use and develop new devices, but the application of this research was very limited. Contraceptive devices such as condoms, rubber caps and chemical pessaries were produced and sold on the streets and in shops, but they were never produced in sufficient quantity and the quality was poor. Moreover, they were not publicised as a major alternative to abortion as a birth-control method, despite constant calls from some medical cricles that this should be done (Higgins, 1976).

The medical practioners who were concerned with the harmful effects of repeated abortions had no problems in demanding that contraception should replace abortion as a method of birth control, since the medical advantages of the former so greatly outweighed the latter. Abortion *was* a dangerous operation. Surveys in the early 1920s showed that even when abortions were performed by qualified doctors (i.e. legally), the death rate was 4 per cent and over half the women suffered from after-effects (Holt, 1976b). By contrast, the Bolsheviks were more interested in the social rather than the medical implications of the abortion issue.

From their point of view, the 'private' sphere of sexual morality in the 1920s was chaotic enough as it was, and free access to contraceptive devices would merely 'loosen morals' further. While legalisation of abortion could be justified on medical and economic grounds as a temporary measure, there could be no simple medical argument for contraception. A decision to endorse a birth-control policy that would leave choice in the hands of the individual, and that might have unforeseen demographic and moral consequences, would be a much more complex decision – indeed, one which the Soviet authorities have been unable to make to this day.

In fact, of course, Soviet women have used whatever methods were available, although supply could never fully satisfy demand. The economic constraints of the 1920s made it impossible to provide access to free abortion for all women seeking it. Many hospitals had been devastated during the civil war; what few remained were dealing with infectious diseases – the cholera and typhus epidemics of 1920–3. Moreover, there was a severe shortage of medical personnel. The rural health service was especially inadequate. The Ministries of Health and Justice responded to the excess demand for abortion over supply of facilities by setting up abortion commissions in November 1924. These handled applications for permits for free abortions, which were classified and then ranked. At the head of the queue would be unemployed single women, followed by single workers with one child, women workers with several children, wives of workers with several children, all remaining insured persons, and finally all other women. The ranking was based on the argument that those in most need were first in line. Those who failed to get a permit could resort to illegal abortions in the private hospitals which had sprung up, chiefly in Moscow and Leningrad, or could pay for an operation under a pay-bed scheme operated by the local departments of health. Fee-paying beds provided some mechanism for regulating demand and financing more beds for abortions. Rural dwellers were in a disadvantaged position, as many women were unable to travel to large centres to visit the abortion commissions (Higgins, 1976; Knight, 1976).

Another obstacle to implementing the 1920 legislation sprang from the hostile attitudes of some doctors to abortion. The questionnaires sent out to provincial doctors by the Ministry of Health in 1919 revealed that many of them were opposed to the legalisation of abortion. Yet these were the doctors on whom the implementation of the new legislation depended. Moreover, many not only displayed hostile attitudes but effectively barred the way to those women seeking abortion, by delaying operating on the grounds of the lack of vacant beds. The women were told to return in 2–3 months, which was equivalent to refusing abortion outright (Higgins, 1976). (It will be interesting to see how the proposed abortion legislation is implemented in Italy, where many doctors are Catholics and thus opposed to abortion on ethical grounds. The situation might turn out to be quite similar to that existing in the USSR in the 1920s.)

Despite these obstacles, the number of legal abortions increased significantly during the 1920s. The figures for Moscow, Leningrad and other large cities were pronounced as 'massive' and 'horrifying' by many of the more respected party members, men and women alike (Geiger, 1968: 77). Thus, by the early 1930s, a campaign against abortion had been launched; it involved widespread propaganda and trials – resulting in severe sentences – of doctors operating clandestine abortion clinics. In 1935, new regulations were introduced forbidding abortions in the case of first pregnancies or in those where more than 3 months had elapsed since conception, and stipulating a minimum of 6 months between operations.

Then, on 26 May 1936, a draft law amending important aspects of Soviet matrimonial law and making abortion illegal was published, and public discussion of its contents was invited. Debate took the form of letters to the press and factory meetings. Schlesinger (1949: 251–69) reprints some of the letters. Although only one of the eight sections of the law dealt with abortion, it was certainly the abortion issue that the public considered the crucial one.

The law passed a month later (on 27 June 1936) differed from the original draft only in minor ways unrelated to the abortion provisions. The law did not compromise on the abortion issue and abortion was prohibited for all but the strictest medical reasons. It is generally accepted that public opinion was ignored and that the legislation was stricter than desired by the majority of the participants in the discussion (Knight, 1976). Other aspects of the new law worth mentioning were the extraordinary emphasis on the 'duties' of motherhood and the grouping of abortion with other aspects of family policy. What is also interesting is the attempt to legitimise, in Leninist terms, the 1920 decree by the assertion that socialism had been attained, so that resort to abortion was no longer necessary. In this sense, the 1936 law is not as inconsistent with the 1920 decree as is commonly assumed, since the medical justification is essentially the same in both cases. The prohibition of abortion in 1936 was justified on the same grounds on which abortion had originally been legalised – the danger to a woman's health. The operation itself was now considered so dangerous that the state had to protect women from its possible consequences.

Of course, this was not the reason for the enactment of the 1936 law, which has been subjected to a variety of greatly oversimplified interpretations. For example, Heer (1968) argues that it was a measure intended to check the fall in the birth rate due to the rise in the abortion rate. This approach, seeing the birth rate as being inversely related to the abortion rate, fails to take into account other factors which are responsible for the irregularities in the birthrate, such as the age and sex-structure of the population. It also ignores socio-economic determinants of the birth rate, such as the housing shortage. Geiger (1968) sees the 1936 legislation essentially as an attempt to 'strengthen' the family as a social unit (in contrast to earlier policy, which had aimed at 'weakening' it) as a means of ensuring social stability, although factors such as the party's concern over the birth rate, problems of labour shortage and the rise of Hitlerism are also suggested as relevant.

Knight's conclusion on the various arguments is that it is neither sufficient to see the 1936 law as a purely pro-natalist measure, nor simply as an attempt to 'strengthen' the family. If the birthrate alone had been at issue, other policies such as raising real wages, improving housing and providing much more extensive child-care facilities would probably also have been adopted and the risk of simply raising the rate of illegal abortions avoided. In Knight's view, both the content and the timing of the law must be considered in the context of wider policy aims and a trade-off between these when they conflicted. These wider aims were the maximisation of economic growth, social stability and nationalism. In conditions of scarce resources for non-productive sectors (such as housing and child-care facilities), the government found a cheap policy solution which attempted to raise the birthrate and retain women in the labour force through a combination of repression and ideological pressure promoting the role of worker and mother, as well as that of Soviet patriot.

Abortion was re-legalised in 1955, ostensibly on the grounds of the prevalence of criminal abortions taking place outside hospitals. Heer (1968) sees the legislation essentially as a popular gesture of the post-Stalin leadership to the population, which was still living in crowded housing conditions, with no desire to have large families. Thus, the futility of prohibiting abortion under the circumstances was again officially re-cognised. Since the birthrate was not falling in the mid-1950s, the rapid increase in the number of legal abortions in the first 2 years of the new legislation was caused by the decrease in the number of illegal abortions (see Table 12.1).

Table 12.1 Abortions in the USSR, 1954–66

Year	All abortions (% of previous year)	Abortions out-side hospitals* (% of all abortions)	Abortions in-side hospitals (% of all abortions)
1954	–	80	20
1955	131	77	23
1956	182	30	70
1960	110	20	80
1965	102	16	84
1966	98	16	84

* i.e., basically illegal abortions.
Source: Ye. A. Sadvokasova, 1969: 117–18.

There are no official statistics on the number of abortions performed in the Soviet Union each year, but the rate is undoubtedly high. Sixty-seven per cent of women who, in the course of their fertile lives, have been pregnant, are estimated to have had an abortion. Of these, 49 per cent have had three or more, 23 per cent have had two and 29 per cent have had one abortion (Sadvokasova, 1969). The annual number of abortions substantially exceeds that of live births and the abortion rate for employed women is $2\frac{1}{2}$ times higher than that of full-time housewives (Sadvokasova, 1963: 45–50).

Abortion on demand is legal up to and including the 12th week of pregnancy; later, only if medically indicated. Any woman wishing to terminate pregnancy must apply to her regional women's clinic, whereupon she is examined by a physician, always a woman, who determines whether abortion is medically safe. Until 1961, the opinion of two or more physicians was necessary, but now a single physician's opinion is sufficient. Permission is not required either of the father of the unborn child or of parents in the case of under-age girls. Unmarried women have the same right to abortions as married women. Abortions must be performed in hospitals; never at home and never by anyone other than a qualified physician. Mandel (1975) claims that the vacuum method is used, but Holt's experience (personal communication) is that the old-fashioned methods with local anaesthetics are used in hospitals and the vacuum method only in illegal abortions, or perhaps in party clinics. For abortion by choice there is a fee of 5 roubles, about a day's average pay. (The procedure is free if it arises from medical factors at any stage of pregnancy.) The Soviet labour code specifies that a voluntary abortion qualifies a woman to take unpaid sick leave (usually 5 days), thus protecting her against dismissal or disciplinary action for an unauthorised absence (Mandel, 1975: 116; St. George, 1973: 105–6).

Despite the extent and easy access to abortion, it is still officially disapproved of. For example, I was told of one clinic that had two posters: one of the happy mother, and one of a sad woman about to have an abortion. As in the 1920s, abortion is seen as a necessary 'evil' and the Soviet regime's aim is to reduce the number performed. It is hoped that this will be achieved by the greater use and availability of modern forms of contraception. Dr Kazhanova, the head of a large Moscow clinic, told Mandel that the ratio of abortions per live birth had gone down from 3-to-1 to 1-to-1 since the introduction of the Pill and the IUD. But the 8,000 women equipped with modern preventive measures by her clinic constitute only 3–4 per cent of those in the fertile ages in her area. And this is Moscow – the proportion, low as it is, is undoubtedly much smaller in other parts of the USSR. As far as I know, the Soviet Union still does not produce its own Pill but imports the Hungarian one. It is easily available only for those with connections, and it is certainly misleading to say, as Mandel does, that it can be obtained on prescription. Moreover, it is not just peasant prejudice (as Mandel argues) but unavailability that prevents women from using it.

Given the unavailibility of the Pill, no significant reduction in the number of abortions can be looked for in the short run. An experiment in intensive contraceptive propaganda in seven towns succeeded in only cutting the rising abortion rate, not in reducing it. Contraceptive use prevented 35–50 per cent of abortions which might otherwise have occured, compared with 20–25 per cent in the country at large. However, this level would be inadequate to bring about an absolute reduction in the number of abortions, given a rising rate in the 1960s (abortions in 1966 were four times greater than in 1954, before re-legalisation).[2] In other words, intensification of contraceptive propaganda and use would be needed to stop 40–45 per cent of abortions within one or two years (Verbenko *et al*, 1968: 39; Sadvokasova, 1969: 117–18, 191). This could only be done by better contraceptive techniques than those currently in use – a development that the Soviet government is still reluctant to foster.

Thus, a 'woman's right to choose' has not been accepted as policy in the Soviet Union, although abortion has been relatively freely available during the last two decades. The birthrate in European Russia is one of the lowest in the world and all surveys fail to indicate any significant level of unwanted children. In fact, some recent surveys suggest that many women would want more children if income and housing were improved.

In the official view, a woman bearing and rearing children is fulfilling not only her 'natural' desire, but also her obligation to society. Voluntary childlessness is usually frowned upon because it is 'selfish'. More importantantly, the state has assumed the right not only to regulate abortions, but also to provide or withhold modern methods of con-traception. The current pro-natalist policy has so far preserved the right of Soviet women to decide on the number and spacing of their children, but this may well change. Some of the other East European countries (namely Rumania, Bulgaria, Czechslovakia and, most recently, Hungary and the GDR) have adopted more restrictive attitudes towards abortion. It could well happen that the Soviet Union will also begin to rely on more restrictive measures, as it has done in the past.

Concluding Note to Part III

What general observations can we now make about sex-equality and the integration of women's productive and reproductive roles in the USSR? Compared with the West, indeed with any other country, women's progress in the social sphere of production has been quite remarkable in the Soviet Union. While in 1920, 67 per cent of the population was illiterate, and 76 per cent of those were women, the latter now dominate the scientific profession. The USSR leads all other countries in the percentage of women employed and in the female share of the labour force (the latter is also due to the numerical majority of women in the population). Women now comprise 51 per cent of wage- and salary-earners and 52 per cent of collective-farm workers. The near-universal expectation that women should work and see work as a central and continuing feature of their lives has had profound psychological consequences in terms of women's 'seriousness', confidence and their concern with intellectual and social problems. Soviet women are assured free access to higher education, and as many women as men attend universities. The proportion of women studying and actually practising 'male' professions (engineering, technology, medicine, higher education) is beyond comparison with any other country in the world. Soviet women are not dependent on their husbands for money and are completely free to choose whether to live with a man or not. Most divorces are initiated by women. However, the proportion of women in higher-ranking jobs and political positions is significantly lower and declines sharply the nearer one gets to the top.

Women's achievements at work have been accompanied by only minimal restructuring of other institutions. The family 'collective' (essentially the father, mother, children and possibly a grandmother) and compensatory boarding-schools are the only forms of intergenerational living arrangement considered acceptable and supported. The family is seen as a central social institution and as an indispensable means for proper child socialisation. Parental upbringing is regarded as a responsible task in which the state actively co-operates and provides help in the form of public child-care facilities, the school, after-school care, youth organisations and clubs, holiday camps, etc. Almost every urban child can now be placed in these institutions if it is the parents' wish. In Soviet legal philosophy, the family is seen as subordinate to society, as an instrument of the socialist state, and the strengthening of the family and its support is a major concern of the Soviet government. The divorce rate is quite high, although it is currently falling somewhat. In the last decade the proportion of 'young' marriages (of up to 4 years duration) dissolved has fallen from 40 per cent of all divorces to 33 per cent.

Child socialisation has remained primarily women's responsibility, as has housework, although there is some indication that men are now taking greater interest in these activities. The Soviet Union regards motherhood as a social function, as distinct from the previous notion (still current in many Western societies) that it is a free natural 'accident' for which only the mother is responsible. Soviet motherhood is as much a social function as working, and therefore disability due to pregnancy brings public maintenance, preservation of job rights and other benefits. However, there does not seem to be a distinction made between child-bearing and child-rearing – both are considered to be women's tasks. All nursery teachers are women. The views held on sex-roles in marriage are still very traditional, although these attitudes are being eroded by urbanisation and by education – even if only partially and rather slowly.

Despite the effects of almost universal employment, the overwhelming majority of women do, in fact, accept a role involving less autonomy and initiative than men. This is marked not only in relation to their sexuality but also in the many areas of behaviour bearing on family and work relations between men and women. Women occupy a disproportionately small number of positions of authority, both in the economy and in political institutions. The regime, led almost exclusively by men, has had few advocates within the innermost circles who would fight the broader battle to liberate women from the 'tyranny' of husbands and the home. The resources allocated to the consumer sphere, and to the socialisation of housework have been wholly insufficient. Because the regime has been primarily concerned with the goal of extensive growth of capital stocks, easing women's burden in the home has been assigned a very low priority. With society's greater affluence, more is being invested in the consumer sector, but the assumption that technological improvement solves all problems is mistaken. 'Technological determinism' cannot resolve such issues as the element of co-ordination involved in housework and the social effects of sex-role socialisation.

There has been no specific campaigning against sex-role stereotyping. Indeed, one can detect it in the literature produced for children, as well as in the socialisation process in the home and in pre-school institutions. School curricula also lend support to popular convictions (of both sexes) that cooking, mending and baby-care are women's work. Over half of the male population do little or nothing in the house. Women prepare most meals and give most parental help in their children's school work. The care of children is the household activity that consumes most of the time saved in other ways.

Thus, a reduction in the amount of domestic work, achieved through the improvement of public household services, greater individual use of modern household technology and greater involvement of men, all of which are certainly taking place, does not necessarily mean that women enter the social sphere of production on an equal footing with men. Rather than seeking the same degree of recreation, sleep and further self-education as men are currently enjoying, Soviet women are quite likely to devote their newly gained leisure to bringing up their children. As there is also an emphasis on a higher birthrate, women's responsibility for child care is likely to be the main factor holding them back. As domestic work involves an element of co-operation and organisation that can be delegated neither to socialised household facilities nor to other members of the family, and as there is no indication that reproduction of labour power will become a male responsibility, Soviet women are unlikely to achieve equality in *all* areas of life for some time to come. As we shall see in the following chapters, Czechoslovak women are in a very similar situation.

Part IV
Women in Czechoslovakia

13 Historical Background and Legal Changes

As less is generally known in the West about Czechoslovakia than about the USSR, I think it important to provide a somewhat lengthier introduction to this section. Czechoslovakia as an independent state arose in 1918 after the break-up of the Austro-Hungarian Empire. Of all the states newly created after the First World War, Czechoslovakia was the richest and economically the most highly developed, as the Czech lands inherited two-thirds of the industrial base of the Austro-Hungarian Empire. Czechoslovakia was a democratic republic, the only Western-type liberal state in the whole of Eastern and Central Europe. The first president was Professor T. G. Masaryk, a humanistic philosopher and a supporter of women's equality.

The new constitution gave women full voting rights and guaranteed them equal rights in other spheres of civil life. The existing discrimination against women in higher education was abolished. (In the Austro-Hungarian Empire, women were excluded from the study of law, technical sciences, art and agriculture.) The marriage bar for women teachers and civil servants was abolished in 1919. (Prohibition against married women in the Canadian federal civil service was lifted only in 1955.) And maternity leave was guaranteed for 6 weeks.

Despite this progressive legislation, sex discrimination remained widespread. As soon as the First World War was over, women were dismissed from most of war industry, mainly (as in other parts of the world) as a result of male demands. A decade later, the economic depression of the 1930s hit Czechoslovakia particularly hard – there were more than a million unemployed out of a population of 14 million and women were the first to lose their jobs. Throughout the inter-war period, female wages in industry were only a half or even a third of those earned by men, and the principle of unequal pay for the same work remained legally sanctioned.

Sex inequality was also explicitly embodied in the family code. The matrimonial law, passed on 22 May 1919, introduced only minor changes in the traditional 1811 family code of the Austro-Hungarian Empire, and these changes did not fundamentally affect the status of the woman within the family. The indissolubility of marriage was ended with the introduction of a procedure for divorce; both forms of marriage, civil and religious, were given the same legal status, and the prohibition of marriage between Christians and those of another religious faith or without a religion was deleted. However, the so-called paternal authority, that is, the status given by law to the father as the head of the family, remained intact. The code laid down that a wife had to adopt her husband's name, live with him, help him in farming or business, keep house, and see to the execution of her husband's orders. These requirements explicitly upheld female inequality within the family, and although various reforms of the family law were suggested in the inter-war period (such as the replacement of the concept of paternal authority with that of parental authority), no change actually occurred.

The inter-war period ended, of course, with the German occupation, following soon after the signing of the Munich agreement in 1938, and destroying any illusion that Czechoslovakia could find a secure place for itself in Europe without changing the direction of its foreign policy. Accordingly, the authority and prestige of the Soviet Union were strengthened, especially towards the end of the Second World War when a large part of Czechoslovakia was liberated by the Red Army.

After the war, the government from 1945 to 1948 was in the hands of a coalition cabinet of four Czech and three Slovak parties, associated in the National Front. The communists held several key positions, including that of prime minister, thanks to their victory in the elections of May 1946. They came to power in February 1948 through parliamentary manoeuvring and with a minimum of violence, although strong-arm tactics and the threat of violence were not entirely absent. The events of February 1948 aligned Czechoslovakia permanently with the 'people's democracies'. Once in power, the communists still demonstrated a certain awareness of the strong democratic tradition of the Czechs, leaving intact, in theory if not in practice, a number of former institutions. For instance, the importance of the presidency and many parliamentary forms were preserved. The Communist Party's programme at that time mentioned a 'specific Czechoslovak road to socialism,' although this idea never received any theoretical analysis.

The communists also fulfilled some of their promises to women. The May 1948 constitution enacted principles of equality between women and men in all aspects of social life. Motherhood, marriage and the family were given special protection by the state. The distinction between legitimate and illegitimate children was deleted from the law. These principles were declared to be socialist and served as a basis for the revision of the family code, which was approved in December 1949 and came into operation in January of the following year. This legislation was directed towards overcoming the inequality of relationships within the family that had existed in the earlier 'bourgeois' code. However, wider aspects of the family's relationship to society were neglected, on the assumption that the relationship between the family and the newly developing socialist society was still at an early stage.

The whole question was left open for another 11 years, until the enactment of the new socialist constitution of July 1960. It officially marked the end of the transitional period from 'people's democracy' to 'socialism'. In the field of family relations, the constitution noted the social dependence of family relationships on society as a whole. The upbringing of children was emphasised as the most important social function of the family and was to involve both parents equally. Going beyond mere acknowledgement of the ideological principle of social equality of men and women, the constitution specified the basic means necessary for the actual realisation of female equality. In other words, it formally granted equal rights to women (in the same way as the 'bourgeois' constitution of 1918 had done), but it also provided guarantees for their implementation. Article 27 stated:

> The equal status of women in the family, at work and in public life shall be secured by special adjustment of working conditions and special health care during pregnancy and maternity, as well as by the development of facilities and services which will enable women to participate fully in the life of society.

The last principle, the encouragement of the use of public facilities and services, is important as it recognises, in a modified form, the Marxist principle of the socialisation of housework. But it is important to note that co-operation between the nuclear family and public institutions is advocated, rather than the total socialisation of the family suggested by Engels and some Bolsheviks in revolutionary Russia. In relation to housework, official ideology and propaganda generally emphasised public facilities rather than the family, while, in relation to child care, there has been more emphasis on the family as the primary socialising agency.[1]

However, as we shall see in the following chapters, the ideology of women's equality expressed in the constitution, and in civil, family and labour laws,[2] has borne little relation to what has happened in practice. In the early 1950s, at the height of Stalinism, official propaganda and social science often confused legal and ideological principles of female equality with the daily reality of social relations. Legal aspects of women's equality were magnified and overemphasised; formal legal equality was used as a disguise and substitute for various inadequacies with which the party was unable or unwilling to deal.

In fact, of course, a 'specific Czechoslovak road to socialism' was never put to practice, largely because of the Cominform decision on Yugoslavia, which denounced efforts to develp patterns of socialism different from that existing in the Soviet Union. In the end, it was this model which Czechoslovakia adopted. During the years 1949–53 the government and party proceeded to change the industrial structure, giving marked priority to the expansion of capital-intensive sectors and above all to 'male' coal-mining, metallurgy and engineering. In COMECON Czechoslovakia was expected to play the role of supplier of capital goods for the other people's democracies, which were in turn starting to industrialise on the Soviet model. Simultaneously with this shift in its economic structure, Czechoslovakia introduced the Soviet system of centralised administrative control, without which the structural changes in the economy could not have effected at all, as they did not correspond to home demand (Selucky, 1970: 28).

Because of the extensive mode of economic growth and the expansion of heavy industry, the state neglected the development and technological improvement of the consumer industries, such as housing, convenience foods, artificial textile fibres, modern household gadgets and the whole tertiary sector of trade and services. The chequered experience of the Soviet model of socialism in Czechoslovakia, the outcome of various attempts to reform it from within, culminated in a long-drawn-out economic, political and moral crisis of the 1960s, leading to the 'Prague Spring' in 1968.[3]

14 Housework

The time taken up by private housework in Czechoslovakia is almost as high as in the Soviet Union. It has been estimated that housework in individual Czechoslovak families takes up to 5 million hours a year, which is roughly the same amount of time as is spent on paid labour by the whole population.[1] Why has housework remained organised on a private basis, despite an ideology advocating its socialisation? In accordance with the 'new socialist style of living', rationalisation of domestic work within the family was initially considered as anti-socialist (Háková and Svarovská, 1961), even counter-revolutionary (Landová-Štychová, 1961).[2] The Czechoslovak ideologues assumed that 'gradually all domestic activity would be shifted from the family to society, which would ensure the development of the appropriate type of service' (Brablcová, 1967). The opponents of individual housework particularly emphasised its negative consequences for a woman's personality.

> The woman, excluded from other activities and isolated in the home, makes out of her livelihood a complicated system of fetishes . . . The house becomes for her the centre of the world, the only proof of her individuality, which she cannot otherwise realise (Fukalová, 1967: 23).

Betty Friedan would not disagree with this view.

However, the initial Czechoslovak concept of socialised housework was in direct conflict with the Soviet model of socialist development, which assigned a low priority to the consumer sector of the economy. The realisation that the model had failed to work in Czechoslovak society came in 1962 and 1963, when the once-prosperous economy suffered a serious economic crisis. The ensuing economic reforms, among other things, abandoned the ideological concept of socialised housework and replaced it with a more pragmatic approach. Vlasta Brablcová, a Czech woman sociologist and economist who briefly held a government post, wrote that, in view of the difficulties of automating services, it was impossible to expand manpower in this sphere, and that in the face of changing consumer preferences it seemed likely that both socialist and capitalist countries would take the path of mechanising domestic work through home appliances. What this has meant is that the domestic burden has been placed on the family in general, and on women in particular. Table 14.1 shows just how great the female burden is.

Table 14.1 *Time spent on housework by employed women in Czechoslovakia (%)*

Activity	Working day	Saturday	Sunday	Average
Preparation of meals	32	32	45	37
Food purchases	22	10	–	9
Washing-up	12	12	14	13
Cleaning	18	25	15	19
Washing	9	17	17	15
Ironing	7	4	9	7
Total: %	100	100	100	100
minutes	224	400	400	342

Source: Bauerová, 1974: 146.

SHOPPING, PREPARATION OF MEALS AND HOUSEHOLD SERVICES

Shopping and the preparation of meals are the most time-consuming tasks that have to be undertaken almost every day. As in the Soviet Union, goods have to be searched for, both because they are in short supply and because of the lack of retail outlets. In 1971, there were 67,035 shops or stalls in Czechoslovakia for the population of 14 million, which is a better ratio than in the USSR, but very much below Western standards. There is one shop-assistant per 96 customers in Czechoslovakia, while the equivalent for Western Europe is only 27. Furthermore, shops are very unevenly distributed – the capital, Prague, for instance, is much better off than the rest of the country. Most of the existing shops are old-fashioned, although the number of supermarkets stocking a wide range of products is growing, especially in the new housing estates. It has been found that, on average, women workers devote 55 minutes to shopping every day (Votruba, 1973 and Tomášek, 1975).

Between 7 and 8½ hours are spent every week on the maintenance of clothing, 5 of which are devoted to washing and ironing. Public laundries now take care of only about 5 per cent of the family wash; the goal is something like 10 per cent by 1980. Laundries are used only occasionally (mainly for linen) and then only by 17 per cent of Czechoslovak families. In 1964, only 2.3 kg of clothes per citizen were washed commercially, and there has been a decline since that time. In 1974, Czechoslovak laundries washed only 2 kg of clothes per citizen, 2.3 kg in the Czech lands and 1.7 kg in Slovakia. The figure is higher in the big cities: 4 kg in Prague and almost 8 kg in Bratislava (*Statistická ročenka ČSSR*, 1975: 403). As we know that one person requires an estimated 80 kg of clean clothing a year, it can be seen that public facilities account for only a small proportion of all clothes laundered. One reason is that the waiting-time for the existing service is 2–3 weeks, with an extra charge for more rapid service. There are no home deliveries and it is often quicker to wash clothes at home than to queue in a public laundry. Village laundries are virtually non-existent and public launderettes were introduced only recently.

Research undertaken in Czechoslovakia in 1959 revealed that only 8 per cent of households used the services of laundries for washing large items. Forty-four per cent of households washed such items in their own washing-machines and more than 30 per cent washed them by hand (Fukalová, 1967: 53). More families have washing-machines today – an estimated 67 per cent of households in the 1970 census. In familites with two or more children, more than 80 per cent of households had a washing-machine, which is a higher proportion than in the Soviet Union and not much lower than in the West.

However, most of the existing washing-machines are rather old-fashioned, frequently without a wringing device. Fully automatic washing-machines were not generally available in Czechoslovakia until 1972. Their cost is very high and at the estimated rate of production it will be 1985 before they become available to even half of Czechoslovak households. In 1972, only 4 per cent of households owned an automatic machine, although 21 per cent were intending to buy one, especially those in higher-income brackets (*Vybavenost* . . . , 1973).

Dry-cleaning has a somewhat better record, with 73 per cent of women using dry-cleaners frequently or very frequently. But here again there are complaints about quality and waiting-time. The customer is asked to remove buttons, and not all establishments accept all fabrics. 'Express' service takes five days, but the charge is one-third higher. Self-service cleaners, common in the West, are all but non-existent in Czechoslovakia.

Housing standards, in general, are higher in Czechoslovakia than in the Soviet Union, and there has been a substantial improvement in recent years. While in 1960 only 10 per cent of Czechoslovak households had central heating, by 1970 this had increased to 30 per cent. However, only 17 per cent of all households had hot running water, while 23 per cent were without running water at all. Fifty-two per cent owned a vacuum-cleaner, 9 per cent a 'kitchen robot' and 60 per cent a refrigerator; 24 per cent had modern kitchens (*Statistická ročenka ČSSR*, 1972: 97).

Gainfully employed women spend 5, 6 or more hours on domestic cleaning every week. Maintenance and cleaning of the home takes up one-fifth of the time spent on housework. Since the introduction of the 5-day week in the late 1960s, women have spent proportionately more time on house-cleaning than they did before the shorter working week was introduced. It is the domestic equivalent of Parkinson's law again – the shorter working week made it possible for the employed woman to enjoy more leisure, but she has used the available time to raise her standards and do more cleaning and general home maintenance. It is also interesting to note that the proportion of time spent on domestic cleaning has also increased among full-time housewives (Bauerová, 1974: 150).

Only a few families take advantage of the existing house-cleaning services, ironically called 'Liberated Housework' (*Osvobozená Domácnost*). An investigation among 500 women occupying leading economic positions revealed that 80 per cent used them regularly and 17 per cent used them occasionally. Occasional use means that these services are used a few times a year, on special occasions (after moving or interior decorating, during the pre-Christmas or spring clean-up, etc.). These services are used almost entirely by bureaucratic organisations and not by individual families (Bauerová, 1970: 456).

Household services are few in number, their quality often poor and their cost prohibitive for daily use. If we look at the proportional expenditure on household services by individual Czechoslovak families, we see no increase at all over the last decade, rather the contrary (see Table 14.2).

Table 14.2 Proportional expenditure on household services (%)

Households	1961	1964	1965	1971	1976
Working-class	11	11	12	12	11
White-collar	13	13	14	14	13
Collectivised farmers	10	11	10	10	10

Source: Statistická ročenka ČSSR, 1972: 466; 1977: 508.

Collectivised farmers spent proportionately less on public household services in 1971 than they did in 1964, and working-class and white-collar families only a fraction more. Proportional household expenditures in 1976 were exactly the same as in 1961. In the mid-1960s, during the period of economic reform, public household services were put on a paying basis in order to enable them to modernise, mechanise and pay higher salaries to their employees. Between January 1964 and the end of 1970 services as a whole recorded a retail price rise of 40 per cent. However, while their receipts rose in absolute figures during this period, their share in total consumer spending dropped from 31 per cent in 1966 to 24 per cent in 1970 (Scott, 1974: 195).

The last Five-Year Plan (1970–75) called for a 20–30 per cent increase in the volume of household services. At the same time, it was admitted by government officials most closely connected with the problem that a real analysis of needs and a realistic conception on which the desired reconstruction and expansion could be based were still lacking (Kerner, 1973). The only woman member of the Presidium of the Communist Party of Slovakia pointed out that research in this area directed at a 'substantial rationalisation of housework is, at least as far as we know, minimal, not to speak of the fact that any existing proposals . . . find their way into practice very, very slowly. (Quoted in Scott, 1974: 197).

By far the greatest proportion of time and labour is taken up with the preparation of meals – on average 59 per cent of the time spent on housework. Public catering has done little to ease the burden. Canteen catering was expanding rapidly at a time when eating-places were heavily subsidised by plant managements. However, measures taken since 1963 to put them on a paying basis have resulted in closing some and raising prices in others; in all, 1,350 enterprise canteens were closed between 1964 and 1970 (Košnierik, 1972: 57). As a result, many people started bringing sandwiches for their lunch (which had to be prepared at home the night before) and now most have their main meal at home in the evening, which again has required more work. After 1971, the number of canteens began to rise again, from 8,463 in 1971, to 9,063 in 1974, and 10,073 in 1976 (*Statisticka ročenka ČSSR*, 1975: 424; 1977: 480) but the improvement is too small to have made a significant impact. At present, only 17 per cent of employed people take their meals at their place of work and 3 per cent use restaurants (Bauerová, 1974: 147). Even school canteens cater for only 40–50 per cent of pupils. Moreover, there are many complaints about the quality of canteen meals: portions of meat are said to be insufficient, and eating one's fill is attained by an excess of starchy food. However, judging from my personal experience, the meals offered are generally tastier than those obtainable in canteens in Britain or Canada.

Public household services and modern household gadgets have until recently not been of significant help to women in Czechoslovakia. Modern household appliances and gadgets are now more widely available, but there are many complaints about the quality of these aids. For example, 10,000 new refrigerators failed to function in 1971 and 1972 and the wait for servicing was at least 3 months, unless one had a moonlighting friend or bribed the repairer to come earlier. Many household products common in the West, such as dish-washers, clothes-dryers and home-freezers, are virtually unknown in Czechoslovakia. The country also lags behind the West in its range of new household chemical products. Carpet shampoos, dish-washing liquids, plastic bags and wrapping, treated fabrics, artificial fibres and disposable children's nappies made out of cellulose are either unavailable or of inferior quality.

The comparative under-development of the consumer sphere means that the housework undertaken in Czechoslovak families is heavy. Moreover, there has been little change over the past decade. Research on the time-budget of employed women, conducted by the State Population Commission in a big electronics factory in Prague in 1959–1960 revealed that employed women spent on average 5–5½ hours daily on housework,

$1\frac{1}{4}$–$1\frac{1}{2}$ hours on child-rearing and only 100 minutes on their own physical and mental recreation. The total rest period of these women, including sleep, averaged only 6 hours per day (Radvanová, 1963: 1483). Very little changed in the following decade – the time spent on housework in individual households was reduced by only half an hour a day during the period 1960–67 (Bauerová, 1974: 144).

In view of the small and selective contribution of their husbands, married women can expect to do housework for the rest of their lives. A nationwide sample survey on leisure activities, conducted in 1961, showed that employed women spent 22 per cent (5 hours, 20 minutes) of their non-work activities on housework, while men did not 'give up', more than 8 per cent (2 hours) of their day. Married men had almost one-third more leisure than employed married women (Svoreňová-Királyová, 1968: 96). This problem is not dissimilar from that in the USSR, Canada or the United Kingdom. Wilmott and Young carried out a survey in London in 1970 on the time-budgets of married men and women aged 30–49. They found that men spent 10 hours a week on household tasks, mainly at the week-end, while women in full-time employment spent 23 hours a week on housework. Leisure hours were found to be 32 hours a week for men and 26 hours a week for employed women (*Social Trends*, no. 5, 1974: 21).

One of the questions asked in a nationwide survey carried out by the State Population Commission between 1962 and 1964 read: 'Do you get any permanent help with housework?'. Individual answers were then classified according to the combination of socio-economic groups of both the husband and the wife. Considerable differences were found among various categories of people. Men working in agriculture helped least with housework, while the highest degree of egalitarianism existed in families where both spouses were engaged in manual work in the factory. However, in the latter case, this relatively frequent help from the husbands was offset by less help from the children. In rural families, the opposite was the case – children helped more than did the husbands (Musil, 1971).

A more recent nationwide sample survey produced similar findings (see Table 14.3). Unfortunately, it is not very clear from these data what exactly is meant by the term 'help'. Men and women tend to understand 'help with housework' differently, and the available Czech data on this issue are very limited. In a sample survey carried out in 1969, 28 per cent of female respondents claimed that their husbands helped them regularly with housework, but 48 per cent of the male respondents thought that they 'helped with housework regularly' – a discrepancy of 20 per cent! The most frequently cited activities in which the husband 'helped' were small repairs (92 per cent), stoking the boiler (58 per cent), washing dishes (46 per cent), washing clothes (37 per cent) and preparation of meals (32 per cent) (Večerník and Vítečková, 1976: 57). These findings are similar to those revealed in the Vilnius and the Vancouver studies discussed in Chapter 6, although the Czech data are not as precise. Housework involves more than

Table 14.3 Frequency of help from husbands with housework (%)

	Daily	On most days	Some-times	Not at all	No husband
Sample (1,225)	23	12	42	15	9
ČSR (893)	23	11	40	16	9
SSR (332)	23	15	44	11	7
Socio-economic group of woman:					
Unqualified worker (1,228)	22	14	39	16	10
Qualified worker (228)	26	10	38	10	16
White-collar without secondary education* (183)	24	11	39	14	13
White-collar with secondary education* (252)	29	14	41	10	7
Farmer (91)	19	12	47	18	4
Housewife (249)	15	12	49	21	2
Socio-economic group of husband:					
Worker (577)	24	12	42	18	4
White-collar (476)	26	15	46	11	3
Farmer (72)	15	10	54	19	1
Other (28)	39	11	32	18	0

* Equivalent to 'A' levels.
Source: Mínění žen o zaměstnání, domácnosti a rodině, part II, 1972: 13.

the number of hours devoted to it, but the available Czech data tell us little about the various aspects of housework, what proportions of wives, husbands and children contribute to them and how much. Housework is a complex set of activities and its study in terms of whether husbands 'help' their wives is not very helpful and illuminating. The very way the question is phrased implies that women are (or should be?) basically responsible.

Overall, the traditional pattern is strongest in farming families, despite the fact that agriculture has been completely collectivised and 'socialised'. In fact, however, the socialist transformation and the extensive employment of women have affected urban men to a greater extent than farmers. On average, Czechoslovak men were devoting twice as much time to housework in 1967 as in 1960. As we have seen in Table 14.3 only 15 per cent of husbands were reported never to help with housework at all; 33 per cent were reported to help daily or on most days. Children in the average Czechoslovak families help even less than do the husbands. Thirty-six per cent of children do not help at all, 25 per cent help sometimes and only 20 per cent help daily or on most days.

The traditional sexual division of labour persists in Czechoslovakia as it does everywhere else in the world. Although it is fixed culturally rather than economically (the material conditions of the traditional agricultural or capitalist production no longer exist), official policy generally and the educational system in particular have paid little attention to the eradication of sex-role stereotypes. In many instances, sex-roles have been upheld and reinforced, as we have seen in Chapter 7, in our discussion of the so-called girls' clubs. Another example is based on my own observation. While walking in one of the main streets of Prague, I came across a bookshop window labelled 'Books for Women', which was filled only with cookery books. This sort of thing reinforces the notion that cooking is 'women's work'. Both sexes seem to accept this view and women who are not good cooks feel guilty about it. The majority of the women with whom I have talked do not question or rebel against an existing sexual division of labour that locates them within the private sphere of reproduction of labour power. And naturally if women accept this responsibility, why should men question it?

Housework lies at the core of the public sexual division of labour. Because women are forced to spend so much time and energy on domestic work, they have little time left for relaxation, self-education, political participation, improving their professional qualifications, chances for promotion, etc. Furthermore, the work they perform in the home tends to influence the type of work they undertake when they enter paid employment, a conclusion we shall explore in the next chapter.

15 Employment, Earnings and Positions of Authority[1]

In this chapter, we shall examine the impact of the post-war increase in the proportion of women in the labour force of Czechoslovakia (from 38 per cent in 1948 to nearly 48 per cent in 1975) upon (1) the sexual division of labour, (2) the structure of remuneration and (3) the distribution of positions of authority. At present only the USSR (with 51 per cent) and the GDR (with 49 per cent) have more women in the labour force. By contrast, the proportion of women in the labour force in Western capitalist countries is much lower, ranging from 27 to 38 per cent, including many women employed on a part-time basis.

Part-time employment in the West is predominantly a female category, while in Eastern Europe it is restricted to students or older people after retirement. In 1971, 25 per cent of all employed Canadian women worked fewer than 35 hours a week, mainly in trade and services – an increase of 6 per cent from 1962, when 19 per cent of all employed women in Canada worked part-time. Part-time employment has many disadvantages: its income is substantially lower, while the amount of time and money spent on the journey to work is the same; the security of employment, sick leave, holidays with pay, social-insurance schemes and prospects for promotion are generally less favourable.[2] Many women in the West opt for part-time work because this is the only way in which they can earn some of the money they need and still have time for the other jobs forced on them by their inherited role in the family – taking care of small children in the absence of adequate nursery care, coping with housework, shopping, cooking and so on. The current Five-Year Plan in the Soviet Union also advocates part-time work for women as the solution to their 'double role', but, as I have argued in Chapter 11, there are reasons to believe that the plan will not be realised. A better solution, making shorter daily and weekly hours for all workers, male and female, has been considered neither in the West nor in the East, with the possible exception of Sweden.

Apart from the issue of part-time employment, the state-socialist and capitalist countries also differ in their labour-participation rates for mothers with small children. The rate is very low in the West, though rising, and very high in Eastern Europe. In the United States in 1950, only 12 per cent of women in the labour force had children under 6 years of age. By 1971, this proportion had increased to 30 per cent. By comparison, almost 80 per cent of all Czechoslovak women in the 20–30 age-category were employed in 1970 (63 per cent in 1961), yet this is the age-group to which most children are born and for which family responsibilities are heaviest. What this means is that most young mothers return to work immediately after the expiry of maternity leave which, however, can now be as long as 3 years.

Thus, Czechoslovakia is characterised by a nearly universal female participation in the labour force: the female participation rate has increased from 54 per cent in 1950 to 71 per cent in 1960 to 85 per cent in 1970, which is about as high as it could be. To what extent has this substantial growth in the proportion of women in the labour force widened occupational opportunities for women?

THE TYPES OF WORK WOMEN DO[3]

In 1948, only two sections of the economy employed more women than men: the health service and social welfare (60 per cent) and agriculture (54 per cent). By 1963, eight such feminised sectors existed: the health service and social welfare (76 per cent); the educational system (60 per cent); trade and public catering (71 per cent); housing administration (64 per cent); communications – non-production units (55 per cent); public services (53 per cent); and agriculture (53 per cent). By 1973, only 48 per cent of all workers in agriculture were women, but 75 per cent of those in trade and catering, 67 per cent of those in the educational system, 80 per cent of all workers in the health service and social welfare, 69 per cent among workers in finance and insurance and 64 per cent of those in communications. Women are also extensively employed in industry: the proportion of women among manual industrial workers had increased from 34 per cent in 1954 to almost 45 per cent in 1973. Traditionally, the greatest number of women are employed in the consumer sector: the food industry, textiles, ready-made clothes, and tanning and fur.

The increase in the proportion of women among workers in industry, trade and services over the last three decades corresponds to the overall expansion of the number of workers employed in these sectors. Naturally, the growth rate has been faster in those industries where women initially constituted an insignificant proportion of the work force. The fastest growth occurred in the building industry, where women increased their share of the labour force from 9 per cent in 1954 to almost 17 per cent in 1973. As far as professional occupations are concerned, the fastest growth has occurred in the judiciary and administration.[4] Women had increased their percentage from 36 in 1954 to 54 in 1976. The proportion of women among workers in science and research had also increased, from 22 per cent in 1954 to 35 per cent in 1976. Over 40 per cent of physicians in

Czechoslovakia are women (compared to 76 per cent in the USSR, but only 10 per cent in Canada).

One could list other examples and run the risk of overwhelming the reader with statistical data on the ever-growing numbers of working women and women with post-secondary education and professional jobs. This is fortunately not necessary, because the trend that has emerged is quite clear. Women have been absorbed primarily in occupations where a significant proportion had been employed before, although individual women are employed in virtually every listed occupation. On the whole, women in Czechoslovakia are more evenly distributed over the occupational structure than their counterparts in the West. Nevertheless, the differing proportions of women in different job categories are still quite noticeable. As in the West, sex continues to be an important criterion for the social division of labour. Sixty to eighty per cent of all Czechoslovak women are employed in traditionally 'feminine' sectors of the economy: teaching, the health service and social welfare, trade and public catering, posts and communications, and in the textile, clothing, food, tanning and fur industries.

Sex-typing also exists within the professions. Let us look at some research findings about the problems facing women doctors in Slovakia. Although the theoretical standards achieved by female medical students are higher than those of their male colleagues, when it comes to practice it is the male doctor who is considered more talented and skilful. Patients tend to prefer and trust male doctors more than female ones. The latter are not so much appreciated for their expertise as for their 'human' (presumably maternal) approach to patients. Women doctors are also further handicapped by their family duties, which prevent them from acquiring further qualifications and higher incomes (Bártová, 1973; Jančovičová, 1974). The so-called feminisation of medicine and education already worries many 'experts' because single and older women have to carry an unfair burden (mothers with small children tend to have a higher rate of abstenteeism), wages are generally lower and the younger generation is reared almost exclusively by women (Jančovičová, 1974; Bauerová, 1974: 78).

TRAINING AND EDUCATION

In contrast, women in the West face discrimination long *before* they start working – the whole of their pre-school and school education pushes them towards the role they are expected to play in society. Girls in the United Kingdom are steered towards home-oriented courses like domestic science and art, while boys are encouraged to take scientific and technical subjects. In 1974, only 26 per cent of all 'O'-level entries from girls were in science subjects, as opposed to 42 per cent of boys. At 'A' level, of school-leavers with two or more 'A'-level passes, 65 per cent of girls and 39 per cent of boys had no science subject (*Crisis*, 1976: 7).

Czechoslovakia has a better record, but considering that schools are not segregated, that girls are not discouraged from studying scientific and technical subjects and that boys and girls pursue some kind of further training in roughly equal numbers, the disparities and anomalies between the sexes in apprenticeship and the system of further education are quite striking. While in 1955 every third girl who left school directly joined the labour force, by 1961 only every tenth girl left school without pursuing some further education. At the end of 1965, women formed 32 per cent of all apprentices in training and 33 per cent of all trained apprentices. This is a relatively high proportion when compared with the United Kingdom, where in 1970 there were 110 women apprentices to skilled craft occupations and 112,000 men. In 1974, 43 per cent of English boys entering employment went into apprenticeship, but only 6 per cent of girls. Of these, three-quarters went into hairdressing, where the apprenticeship system has been attacked as a method of providing cheap rather than trained labour.

However, since 1965, the proportion of Czechoslovak girls among apprentices has *declined*. According to the results of a sample survey conducted in 1970, there were only 20 women apprentices for every 100 women with primary education, while of 100 men with primary education, 75 were apprenticed (Kadlecová, 1974). In fact, the proportion of women school-leavers who directly joined the labour force without pursuing some further training has increased in the last decade. In 1969, nearly 3,500 boys, but almost 16,000 girls, that is 82 per cent of the total, went straight into full-time employment on leaving school. In 1972, 3,207 fewer girls than had been expected applied for apprentice training. In fact, the recruitment quota for female apprentices has not been fulfilled since 1967 (Bauerová, 1974: 104).

Among girls applying for apprentice-servicing courses in 1971, there were ten applicants for every place available to learn jewellery-making, and ten for every apprenticeship in glass-painting. In order of popularity, there followed photography, dressmaking, window-arrangement, hair-dressing, pastry-making, and switchboard-operating, while boys wanted to be housepainters, electronic mechanics, automobile mechanics, but-chers, cooks and waiters (the latter two were also quite popular among girls). This division into girls' occupations and boys' occupations is intensified by the reluctance of most industries to take their quota of girls for fear of losing them later on. Of the 288 available types of apprenticeship training courses, most of them lasting 2 or 3 years, 99 are now exclusively reserved for boys (mainly in mining and metallurgy), 20 exclusively for girls, with 173 open to both, although not in equal numbers (Scott, 1974: 8, 12).

Roughly half of all apprenticed girls are in trades connected with textiles, the food industry, chemistry, building materials, porcelain-making and glass-making. There are very few girl apprentices in engineering, tool-making and electronics. Although girl apprentices predominate in the textile and clothing industries, in 1970 only one woman was training as a textile-machine mechanic, only ten as industrial dyers and not a single one as an industrial printer of textiles (Bauerová, 1974: 107). The more 'technical' the job is thought to be, the fewer girls apply.

When we now look at secondary education, we can see that women have more than doubled their enrolment. Between 1954 and 1965, the percentage of pupils enrolled in secondary schools increased by 67. Boys increased their proportion by 16 per cent, but girls by 114 per cent. Since 1958, more girls than boys have, in fact, been enrolling in further education.[5] Despite this significant increase, the segregation of girls' and boys' subjects has remained stable. Girls specialise in the humanities and boys in science. High-school training is essentially feminised in librarian-ship, nursing, kindergarten-teaching and clerical work – women comprise 87–99 per cent of enrolled students. Virtually no women are enrolled in forestry schools and only 22 per cent attend the various technico-industrial schools (Bauerová, 1974: 112).

More males than females are accepted for university places, although this is more a factor of girls' decisions than of the universities. Virtually every boy, but only every other girl, applies for a university place on leaving high school. The majority of girls apply for the humanities, yet this is where the competition is greatest, as there are many more applicants than available places. Women comprise 40 per cent of all enrolled university students (compared to more than 50 per cent of high-school students), 45 per cent of students of economics, less than 26 per cent of students of agriculture, 35 per cent of art stutudents, 58 per cent of students in humanities, law, social science and medicine and only 15 per cent of students in technical faculties (in 1934, however, only 4 per cent of students enrolled in Czech technical faculties were women). The proportion of women studying technical subjects is much higher in some of the other East European countries: 38 per cent in the USSR, 34 per cent in Bulgaria and 60 per cent in the GDR. Those Czechoslovak women who choose to study technical subjects tend to concentrate in the faculties of civil engineering, food and biochemical technology, textiles and chemical technology. Very few women study engineering, electronics and nuclear physics, although more study mathematics.

The subjects women study at high schools and universities determine to a great extent the sort of employment they eventually get. Data on women specialists were first collected in 1958, when women formed 38 per cent of all specialists with secondary and university education. By 1970, women had increased their overall share among specialists to 46 per cent (30 per cent in industry). The increase in the proportion of women specialists with secondary education is especially noticeable. In some branches of industry (the polygraphic industry and ready-made clothes) there were actually more women specialists than male specialists. A high proportion of women specialists also works in the textile, glass, porcelain and food industries (see Table 15.1).

Table 15.1 Women specialists in industry in 1970

Industry	Percentage of women in the total number of specialists	Percentage of women with higher education in the total number of specialists with higher education	Percentage of women with secondary education in the total number of specialists with secondary education
All industry	31	10	33
Fuel	17	5	20
Production and distribution of heat and electricity	23	6	25
Iron and steel	22	8	24
Non-ferrous metals	21	6	24
Rubber and chemicals	32	18	35
Engineering and metal-processing	27	8	29
Building materials	31	11	34
Wood-processing	35	11	37
Paper and cellulose	36	16	39
Glass, ceramics and porcelain	42	14	45
Textiles	49	20	50
Clothing	65	16	67
Leather, footwear and fur	40	10	42
Printing industry	51	20	53
Food	45	23	47
Other	38	15	42

Source: Bauerová, 1974: 120.

However, the data in Table 15.1 are slightly misleading because they fail to differentiate between women working directly in industry and women employed in technical administration. When we look at the ways in which technically educated women make use of their qualifications, it is difficult to find a woman in the position of foreman, technologist or director of an enterprise. The majority of women technicians and engineers work in the less-demanding administrative roles (Svoreňová-Királyová, 1968: 55; Čech and Jukl, 1976).

Thus, both men and women still hold traditional images of the type of occupation which is 'naturally' suitable for a woman. Women employed in administration, or women performing industrial tasks which require manual dexterity, are socially acceptable and generally approved of, while women technicians or women in leading positions are still considered something special. Typical was the comment of a woman economist published in the women's weekly *Vlasta* in 1966, accusing universities and secondary schools of applying stricter standards to women than men in entrance examinations. She added:

And so another campaign is born . . . The apparition of feminisation has emerged suddenly in monstrous guise stalking the colleges and secondary schools, the organs of government and institutions, and terrifying everyone. The name is woman; know thou that thou must relinquish any desire for medicine, teaching, philology, sociology and I know not what else. Some years ago we were astonished by the number of callings which had been invaded by women and in which they had proved their worth. Now we are carefully, pedantically weighing and choosing one occupation after another which women must not be allowed to enter.

. . . Imagine the enduring bitterness and disappointment that a fifteen-year-old girl with top marks will suffer when she is faced with the choice: either you study aircraft engines or you don't study at all. No one is interested in whether she has any particular feeling for engines. What is important is that this particular vocational school should fulfil its quota. Its unusual interest in girls is explained quite bluntly to their parents: female graduates will step up to the drawing board in the factory for 900 crowns monthly, something no man would do . . . (*Vlasta*, 20 July 1966; also quoted in Scott, 1974: 10–11).

The last comment points to the crux of the matter. Female concentration in specific sectors of the economy does not, in itself, constitute sexual inequality. What is more significant is the reward structure which is associated with this public division of labour between the sexes.

INCOME INEQUALITY

Table 15.2, which shows the structure of income distribution in the nationalised sector of the economy, highlights the existing discrepancies very clearly. Sex differences are, as a matter of fact, greater than the overall national income differential. The proportion of women earning 1,000–1,400 Kčs monthly is 39 per cent, compared with only 5 per cent of men or

17 per cent of the whole population. Half the men earn between 2,000 and 3,000 Kčs monthly, but only 13 per cent of women earn as much.

Table 15.2 Income structure in the socialist sector of the economy in May 1970

Income Category (in Kčs)	Number of employees (%)		
	Total	Men	Women
Up to 600	0·06	0·02	0·12
601–1000	3	0·9	6
1001–1400	17	5	39
1400–2000	36	28	46
2001–3000	35	51	13
3001–4000	7	12	1
4001–	2	3	0·22

Source: *Čísía pro každého*, 1973: 89

This unequal distribution of income between males and females has remained constant throughout the post-war state-socialist period, despite the overall rapid increase in female education and employment. In 1946 the ratio of average income of men and women was 100:65 and this sex-disparity has barely changed (see Table 15.3).

Table 15.3 Income distribution by sex

Average monthly Wage (Kčs)	1959	1964	1966	1968	1970	Accretion 1959–70	
						Kčs	%
Total	1,405	1,543	1,614	1,814	2,012	607	43
Men	1,598	1,781	1,871	2,105	2,336	738	46
Women	1,057	1,196	1,232	1,400	1,565	508	48
Ratio of Average wages: (%) Women/ All employees	75	76	76	77	78	3	3
Women/ Men	66	66	66	67	67	1	1

Source: Baštýř, 1971: 9

In 1946, females earned about 35 per cent less than men and, in 1970, women's earnings were still 32 per cent lower than those of their male counterparts.[6] In 1976, husbands' earnings accounted for 44 to 48 per cent of average family income, while wives' earnings amounted to only 12 to 22 per cent (see Table 15.4).

Table 15.4 Households' incomes derived from employment in 1976 (%) *

Households	Husband	Wife	Contributions of other family members
Working-class	48	21	4
White-collar	48	22	4
Collectivised farmers	44	12	1

* Income derived from pensions, family allowances and sickness benefits is excluded
Source: *Statistická ročenka ČSSR*, 1977: 508

This discrimination against women in terms of reward for their work operates in two ways, between, as well as within, industries. The overall average income of feminised sectors is below the average of 'male' sectors, but discrepancies among men and women occur within the same industry, even within the feminised sectors themselves. Female salaries in the educational system were 70 per cent of those of their male colleagues; the corresponding figure for health and social services was 62 per cent, in retail trade 74 per cent, in public household services 71 per cent and in public catering 75 per cent (Svoreňová-Királyová, 1968: 66). The situation within the feminised consumer industry, where women comprise 58 per cent of the total number of workers, is similar – women earn on average 30 per cent less than men (Háková and Svarovská, 1961: 313).

In 1968, women comprised 42 per cent of the total number of workers in industry, but 90 per cent of female jobs corresponded to the lowest three classes of the income tariff. Only 25 per cent of women were engaged in skilled work which corresponded to classes 4, 5 and 6, and only 2 per cent were in classes 7 and 8, the highest ones (Tomášek, 1968: 21). In 1965, at the Tesla-Pardubice electrical engineering plant, where women out-numbered men by more than three to two, only 0.3 per cent of women earned more than 1,200 Kčs monthly, compared to 70 per cent of the men (Kohout and Kolář, 1966: 547). No data are available to determine whether this wide discrepancy is at least partially due to job classification.[7]

When job classification is held constant, levels of educational attainment and family responsibilities account for some of the pay disparities. The findings of a survey on attitudes towards improving skills and qualifications showed that, while 50 per cent of the men expressed positive attitudes towards bettering their qualifications, only 29 per cent of the women in the sample responded in this way (Blucha, 1966). Table 15.5, which breaks down the negative replies, shows very clearly the adverse relationship between the housewife's role within the individual family and her equality in social life.

Table 15.5 *Negative attitudes towards the improvement of personal skills (%)*

	Men	Women
Higher qualification could not be utilised	43	18
Too old	37	23
Undue burden of housework	–	45
Other	20	14

Source: Blucha, 1966.

The majority of women could not increase their qualifications because of responsibilities within their families for housework and child care. No man faced such a problem. Even if various household tasks are shared (as is increasingly, although slowly, becoming the case), men are not ultimately *responsible* and, if a more urgent need arises (such as the possibility of increasing qualifications and income), they can always opt out of housework and concentrate on further training. Such a choice is still not open to the majority of women.

Sex-discrepancies persist even when the level of educational attainment is held constant. Many enterprises recruit women for work for which they are over-qualified and which is less well paid. In the spring of 1965, the Central Commission of People's Control and Statistics took a sample survey of 2,429 women – housewives and others – who in 1964 and 1965 re-entered employment after a gap of at least two years. Twenty-three per cent of the women in the sample accepted jobs for which they were over-qualified. Furthermore, their employers expected that only 9 per cent of the newly employed women would be promoted and transferred to a higher position (Srb, 1966). A higher level of educational attainment does not therefore automatically alter women's subordinate occupational roles!

When all the factors, i.e. level of skill, type of work performed and hours of work are held constant, the income differences between the sexes are still great. There is no explanation for it other than discrimination. In 1964, the Communist Party committee at one of the plants of the ready-made clothing industry in Prostějov, employing 70 per cent of women among its workers, found that, where women were employed in the better-paid, medium-grade jobs, as technical controllers, norm-setters, foremen, technologists, planners and designers, in almost every category a much higher percentage of women than men had the necessary training and experience. When it came to pay, however, women controllers earned less than men controllers, women foremen less than men foremen, and qualified men workers earned more than qualified women on the same job. Various reasons were advanced: women themselves were not eager for more demanding work; management tended to regard the man as a family head whose pay was vital; foremen favoured men in the distribution of work; men were stronger, tired less easily, had a higher output. None of these explanations, however, seemed adequate to the communist daily *Rudé právo* (Scott, 1974: 4–5).

In several light-industry plants, when it came to positions requiring training and responsibility, women had to fulfil all the necessary conditions to qualify, while a lack of education and experience was often overlooked in men (Kaliberková, 1968; Scott, 1974: 5). In an investigation of nearly 500 medium-level technical administrative personnel in two textile plants, men averaged higher pay and higher bonuses in every category, even though the women were equally and sometimes better qualified. Some women who had been promoted to these jobs pointed out that when the posts had been previously occupied by men they had had their own secretaries, and for the most part attended conferences and meetings while their work was done for them by this subordinate. When they were replaced by a woman, however, she had to do all the work, including that which had been done for the man by someone else (Bauerová, 1971: 123). A majority of these women acknowledged that men were objectively more desirable workers than women because they were not burdened by home worries. One-third added that many women themselves preferred less responsible jobs which left them more time and strength for their household duties (Scott, 1974: 6).

Despite the equal-pay legislation, income discrimination is practised against women who perform the same type of work as men within the same qualification and tariff categories. Most enterprises have income categories with a rising scale, and women are always appointed at the lowest possible level, while men (the 'breadwinners') are usually appointed at the top of the scale, particularly in areas where there is a shortage of labour. Baštýř has calculated that this latter type of income sex-discrimination accounts for 8 to 9 per cent of the overall 26 per cent of the discrepancy between males and females. Feminisation of certain lower-paid sectors of the economy accounts for two-thirds of the existing difference; the greater working experience and productivity of men, as well as the greater amount of overtime (women are too tied to their family duties to be able to work overtime), further account for the income discrepancy between the sexes (Baštýř, 1971: 813). These discrepancies are also reflected in the distribution of positions of authority.

POSITIONS OF AUTHORITY

With such a rapid development in women's education and employment, one might expect a corresponding improvement in the sexual distribution of positions of authority. Yet the latter has remained virtually unchanged. At present, less than 5 per cent of leading managerial and political positions are occupied by women, compared with almost 48 per cent of their overall employment (Bauerová, 1970: 450; Bártová, 1973: 203). Table 15.6 reveals that this discrepancy exists in all individual branches, but it is particularly startling in sectors with the highest concentration of women.

Table 15.6 Women in leading positions in Czechoslovakia in 1961 (%)

Directors of district and county bodies of state administration	4
Directors of productive, building and transport organisations	2
Leading technical specialists	2
Directors of working and production units	5
Constructors, designers, technical accountants	12
Leading economists	18
Inspectors and auditors	27
Academicians, professors, scientific researchers at universities	9
Medical directors of health institutions, main district and county leading doctors, heads of various hospital departments	12
Arbitrators, chairmen of courts and senates, judges and prosecutors	12
Leading employees in communication	28
Leading employees in internal retail trade	14
Leading employees in communal services and housing administration	30
Directors of organisations of administrative services, heads of administrative and economic units	15

Source: *Encyklopedie moderní ženy*, 1964; Čáp and Peltrámová, 1965.

Take, for example, the health service. Women comprise 44 per cent of all doctors and 80 per cent of all the medical personnel, but only 12 per cent hold positions of authority. In insurance and finance, women form 66 per cent of the labour force, but only 27 per cent of them are employed in leading positions. Yet they are doing very well compared with other economic spheres – less than 4 per cent of the executive and specialised positions in the co-operative movement in agriculture were held by women in 1966, compared with their overall labour participation of 51 per cent (Burešová, 1966). In 1972, women formed nearly 50 per cent of all workers in agriculture, but only 14 per cent of chairmen of co-operatives, leading economists and zootechnicians (Sagara and Mach, 1974).

Teaching – a predominantly feminine profession – offers another interesting example. As far as rural schools are concerned, women teachers predominate in primary schools, while men teach mainly in secondary schools. This trend is repeated in urban schools, although many more women teach at the secondary level. As far as the distribution of positions of authority is concerned, the highest proportion of headmistresses is found in one-class rural schools – 42 per cent. There are 17 per cent of women among the heads of basic educational rural schools (predominantly in smaller towns), but only 11 per cent of urban basic educational schools are directed by women (Bártová, 1973; Mrkosová, 1974).

One could go on and list other examples. In the food industry, in which half of the employees are women, only 5 of 579 plant directors in 1973 were women. A male executive in this industry explained that 'a woman in an executive post is an anomaly. Matriarchies exist only in primitive societies' ('Women and Leading Jobs in Industry', *Hospodářské noviny*, 21 December 1973). So general is the acceptance of the fact that management jobs belong to men that the trade-union paper saw nothing incongruous in publishing, as one of its human-interest stories for International Women's Day, an interview with the male head of Prague's central telephone exchange, whose main worry was how to congratulate all 760 members of his all-female work force in one day (Scott, 1974: 13–14)!

As in the rest of Eastern Europe, women in Czechoslovakia tend to concentrate in middle-range jobs. If they finally succeed in reaching positions of higher authority, these tend to be associated with lower-prestige institutions. This tendency applies to industry and education, as well as to political institutions. In Czechoslovakia, women form 51 per cent of the population, 48 per cent of economically active persons, 63 per cent of secondary vocational school students and 40 per cent of university students, but their share of political positions is only 20 per cent and it decreases sharply as one moves up the ladder of authority.

Initially, in the first stages of 'socialist reconstruction', the proportion of women representatives elected to the national committees at all levels showed an increase: from 17 per cent to 22 per cent of all representatives. In 1960, women comprised 22 per cent of all representatives in the National Assembly, 28 per cent of those elected to the district national committees, 37 per cent of those in county national committees and 21 per cent in local national committees (Kalmünzerová, 1972: 10). In the following decade, however, the number of women representatives in these institutions declined. In 1964, only 19 per cent and, in 1970, less than 18 per cent of all elected representatives were women. In response to directives calling for greater participation of women in public life, more women (an increase of 4 per cent) were elected in the 1971 election (Bártová, 1976b).

The highest proportion of women representatives is in the trades union bodies. In 1967, over 40 per cent of trades union members were women. Thirty-one per cent of all the officials of branch organisations were women, which is a relatively high proportion, but the number of women officials decreases rapidly in the higher trade-union bodies (Brejchová, 1967: 21). In 1974, almost 432,000 women were elected to all trade-union bodies and commissions, which represents 44 per cent of the total number of union officials. However, men tend to regard these as positions that carry little real power (as there is a parallel party organisation) but rather that require patient, plodding, day-to-day administrative work in which women are said to excel. The percentage of women holding leading jobs greatly increased only after the Eighth All-Union Congress in 1972. Whereas in 1948 women formed 10 per cent of all the members of the Central Council of Trades Unions (the supreme trade-union body), this figure increased to 23 per cent in 1955, to 26 per cent in 1963 and to 37 per cent at present (*Working Women in Czechoslovakia*, 1975: 68).

However, as in all state-socialist societies, effective political power in Czechoslovakia does not reside in the trades unions, the national committees or the National Assembly, but rather in the government and, above all, in the Communist Party. Since 1948, no more than two women have occupied ministerial posts at any one time, and these invariably have been the Ministry of Food and/or the Ministry of Consumer Affairs. At present, there are no women ministers or ambassadors. Within the Communist Party the situation for women is equally bleak. For instance, at the last party congress, only eight women were elected to the 115-strong Central Committee. As far as the specialist party bodies are concerned, the highest representation of women is in the revision commission – out of 45 members, six (17.6 per cent) are women, which is still a very small proportion (Köhler-Wagnerova, 1974: 54). There are no women in the Presidium of the Central Committee of the party.

A disproportionately small number of women in leading positions of authority is therefore evident in *all* areas of social life. As the new active forces – continuously increasing employment of women and the rapid increase in the level of their education – have not improved the political position of women, we have to look for negative factors which hold women back.

At the most general level, the cause of this contradiction lies again in the inter-relationship between social production and private reproduction, in the dual role of the woman. The woman as a mother and housekeeper becomes 'lost' as a worker, since, in most cases, she cannot devote herself to her occupation in the same way as a man can. Any position of authority requires almost total commitment – a high degree of concentration and time-flexibility, both of which present major obstacles to the employed mother. She finds it difficult to concentrate because she is constantly interrupted by the trivial activities inherent in housework and the bringing-up of children. Moreover, the fulfilment of domestic and family duties often means that she has to leave her work or an important meeting, or interrupt her experiment at a fixed hour. Her situation is obviously also connected with the still insufficient development of public services in the broadest sense of the word. The provision of basic family needs requires so much physical and mental effort in Czechoslovakia (and, as we saw, in the Soviet Union) that not much is left for other activities, such as recreation or further study. This, then, conditions the fact that although many women – especially up to 35 years of age – have acquired high qualifications, they stagnate when it comes to further self-realisation and the development of expertise. For example, Slovak women doctors spend only 2 hours daily on further study, while their male colleagues can afford to spend from 3 to 10 hours a day; the same applies to engineers (Bártová, 1973; Foret and Illner, 1976). Thirty-one per cent of Slovak men doctors but only 10 per cent of women doctors obtain a specialist qualification (the so-called second-degree *atestace*) at the usual age of 34. Twenty-five per cent of Slovak women doctors do not obtain the second qualification because of family responsibilities (Jančovičová, 1974).

Another cause of the low number of women in positions of authority, especially in the higher ones, is to be found in the anachronistic attitudes that survive among both men and women. Comparative research (in which Czechoslovakia took part) conducted on *Images of the World in the Year 2000*, organised in 1967 by the European Centre for Research and Documentation in Social Sciences, showed some interesting differences in attitudes between men and women concerning hopes and expectations of 'more or fewer women in leading positions'. The *expectations* of males and females were quite similar, but their hopes differed quite radically. Women's hopes were much higher than those of men and they were similar to or exceeded the level of their expectations. Fewer men *favoured* an increase in the number of women in leading positions than expected it.

The greatest discrepancies existed in the state-socialist countries, Poland and Czechoslovakia. (The sample also included respondents from Yugo-slavia, Finland, Holland, Norway, Spain and Japan.) In other words, great discrepancies between the attitudes of men and women concerning the female position in society exist in all modern industrial societies, but a far greater number of men who *do not favour* more women in the leading positions of authority seems to exist in the state-socialist countries. These attitudes have persisted in spite of the rhetorical emphasis on equality between men and women and public statements made from time to time by leading public figures on this issue.

To account for this prejudice, we have to look at individuals and their attitudes. Men's views about women's subordinate position in society stem from the past and from current experience. The survival of popular images of man's privileged position in society seems to be common to all contemporary societies, and, as such, cannot explain why so many more men in the state-socialist societies do not wish to see more women in leading social positions. Rather, the explanation must be that men have had particularly negative experiences in the context of markedly widespread women's employment. In the absence of adequate provision of public household and child-care facilities, and with the woman out at work full-time, many tasks connected with housework and child care have to be passed on to the man. The degree to which this sharing is required is naturally related to the rank, commitment and responsibility of the woman's economic or political position – the greater a woman's position of authority, the more it infringes on aspects of a man's personal life and freedom.

A good example of male attitudes was published in the party daily. *Rudé právo*, in February 1971. Describing an election meeting of a Communist Party group in a farm co-operative, a reporter noted that, while more than half of those present were women, not one of them had been nominated for the executive committee, not did they take part in the discussion.

> 'Oh, they know how to say what they think when something is really at stake,' I was assured by one of the newly elected officials. 'But nominate them for the committee? It's tough. Women get up early, they're always busy, and give them a function on top of it? We can't really ask that of them' (Scott, 1974: 15–16).

Such consideration may seem very appealing, the reporter continued, but it would be still more gallant of the men to give the women more help in the household and in caring for the children.

Such male prejudice constitutes an unwritten, but continuously effective social barrier against women's advancement in the social sphere of production and positions of power. The prejudice is reflected in public debates in the media, the continuing differentiations between occupations suitable for women, and the appointment of only very few women to leading positions (deemed 'suitable' for only exceptionally talented women!). This ideational climate influences the perceptions of the roles of both men and women. Moreover, owing to the double role they are playing, most women are objectively prevented from developing their working qualifications, or their development takes place at a slower rate. Subjectively, they are, to a certain degree, prepared by their socialisation and life-experience to accept this reality and to strive for leading positions less frequently than men, or even to refuse them on the grounds that they are unsuitable for women! For example very few women teachers *would like* to work in leading positions – only 4 per cent of women teachers in rural schools and 7 per cent in urban schools (Mrkosová, 1974).

More than two decades of state-socialist transformation have affected the traditional values concerning social roles of women less than one might expect. In fact, when we talk about values and attitudes towards women, we can identify a definite polarisation of opinions. The Marxist model, accentuating the activity of women in an outward direction, has not penetrated the masses, largely because it runs ahead of the material and spiritual conditions of contemporary Czechoslovakia. As a result, the traditional model, which sees the basic functions of women to be those of mother, wife and housekeeper, appears more attractive and continues to hold its own in the thinking of both men and women. A crisis in the model of the 'socialist' woman in Czechoslovakia became particularly acute in the late 1960s in the course of the stormy debates and polemics on the question of the effectiveness of women's employment. *Rudé právo*, the party daily, published a number of letters on the subject between October 1966 and February 1967. The debate was sparked off by an emotional letter from a woman living in a village, which was published under the heading, 'What Have You Got Against Us?'.

At the present time an employed woman is almost afraid to read the newspapers or listen to the radio or TV. It's not her life that's at stake, but her peace of mind . . .

The employed woman is the cause of the current economic difficulties, rising divorce rates, etc. At work, she is insufficiently productive, and does not show enough care or concern for her home and family . . . (H. Pražáková, *Rudé právo*, 28 September 1966).

The publication of this letter provoked a strong reaction. Various conflicting opinions were expressed.

We can't go on increasing expenditure on nurseries, after-school care, and nursery schools indefinitely. These social advantages are used by many families who could get along without them. Today, women themselves are calling for the defeminisation of some fields – schools, for example – because they themselves would benefit from this. Feminisation and the overemployment of women are concepts that are very close to each other (Dr Pernica, *Rudé právo*, 12 October 1966).

What can we expect from children whose upbringing has allowed them to play unsupervised in the streets from the age of ten onwards? (E. Vlásková, *Rudé právo*, 26 November 1966).

The movement for the emancipation of women was and is a just one. I think that it should be achieved slightly differently. Not by blindly imitating men, but by making allowances for what is specific to women, and assuring them that housework is just as important as work which is paid for (An anonymous reader from Istebne, *Rudé právo*, 26 October 1966).

That women belong to the kitchen is today no less reactionary than it was yesterday (Dr Šprynářová, *Rudé právo*, 19 October 1966).

The employment of women is actually a whole cluster of questions. Where, and in what jobs are too many women employed? What other occupations can we offer these women? What industries employ women in jobs for which they are not properly qualified? What qualifications should be demanded of them? How soon can jobs calling for unskilled female labour be phased out and what should replace them? How do we solve the problem of untrained women, with small children, working in dead-end jobs in order to help support their family?

Of course, as soon as we ask these questions, it becomes clear that with the exception of the last, they apply not only to women but equally to men. Why then are these questions only asked about women? (Dr Háková, *Rudé právo*, 8 December 1966).

There is also another solution. We can stick to the opinion that creative work is the meaning of life, but in the interests of society, only men will be considered as people in the full sense of the word. This solution seems very promising, because its adoption would represent the greatest saving . . .

If things go on like this, and any means are used to prevent the employment of women instead of society's creating favourable conditions for their work, socialism will lose all its attraction for me personally, and I shall be intensely sorry that two of my three children are girls (Tesařová, *Rudé právo*, 9 November 1966).

Some correspondents, both men and women, consistently defended the right of women to work, and its economic and humanitarian implications for the female personality. Others saw in women's employment only a means of whiling away time, justifiable only if it were financially necessary for the livelihood of the family. Some women expressed weariness and irritation with endless discussions, which led nowhere, because the state of affairs remained unaltered. Many readers wanted to see economic conditions such that the male income would be sufficient for the whole family, allowing the woman to stay at home and devote herself full-time to 'home-making' and child-rearing. Others attributed the current economic difficulties and stagnation (in the early 1960s) solely to the high rate of female employment. It was argued that woman's labour was too costly and unproductive (in terms of educational wastage, high operating costs of pre-school child facilities and loss of production resulting from frequent absence from work of mothers of small children, who tend to be frequently ill); that feminisation of certain sectors of the economy was harmful, because it was those sectors that experienced the greatest economic difficulties; that employed women were to blame for juvenile delinquency, etc.

Noting that they had published dozens of letters and had received many more, the editors of *Rudé právo* closed the discussion by publishing a lengthy interview with representatives of the State Planning Commission. It appeared under the title 'No New Policy' and its message was full employment. There would be a shortage of labour in the future as there had been in the past and woman power would be needed. Overemployment in particular instances and the closing of economically unprofitable enterprises were not women's questions, but questions which touched all workers. A 50 per cent increase in nursery-school places (for 100,000 children) and 25 per cent more kindergarten places (to cater for 400,000 children) were promised (*Rudé právo*, 8 February 1967; Scott, 1974: 130).

These assurances may have considerably alleviated the apprehensions of women. In fact, no restrictive measures against women's employment were taken, although some 'experts' have continued to see women's work as economically ineffective and inefficient (Kontšeková, 1974). Kontšeková emphasises, however, that women's economic activities are valuable in two respects: (1) as a contribution to society's and their family's living standards; and (2) as a means of developing the woman's personality. Thus, in determining the efficiency of women's work both the tangible, economic aspects and intangible, psychological factors are important. She agrees that in strictly economic terms, women's work-effectiveness and contribution to the economy are somewhat lower than those of men, chiefly because women are under-utilised.

Findings from a more recent survey on attitudes towards women's employment, conducted by the Research Institute for Culture and Public Opinion in Bratislava, reveal that the majority of women in Czechoslovakia work because of financial necessity rather than an internal need for self-realisation. However, very few respondents saw housewifery as a desirable occupation, either for themselves or for women in general. Moreover, many women have indicated that they want to be financially independent (Zukalová, 1975). There is good reason to believe that the concept of not being a dependent of one's husband is taking a very strong hold among Czechoslovak women, although Malá (1975) cautions that there are still significant differences among women of differing educational and occupational statuses.

Overall, in assessing the question of female economic participation, it seems fair to say that practice has been somewhat different from theoretical concepts, but that, in principle, those concepts can eventually be implemented if women's productive and reproductive roles are harmoniously integrated and related to social development. Women's lower pay is a result of female concentration in 'non-preferred' occupations (as against 'preferred' heavy industry and mining), lower skills, less professional education, refusal to work overtime or accept promotion, and absenteeism for child-care reasons. Let us turn now to a closer examination of maternity and child-care policies.

16 Child-Care: Individual Versus Collective

THE IDEOLOGY OF CHILD-CARE: ACTIVE CO-OPERATION BETWEEN THE FAMILY AND THE PARTY-STATE

An examination of the current family code (enacted in December 1963) reveals that 'the main social purpose of marriage is the foundation of the family and regular upbringing of children'.[1] We can also learn that both parents have equal rights and responsibilities towards their children,[2] although when it comes to a divorce, it is the mother rather than the father who is usually given the custody of the children. The law also clearly specifies the relationship between the family and society: the family is subordinated to society. Following Soviet ideas on the subject, the Czechoslovak state 'delegates' the responsibility for child-care to the family. As Article 4 of the 1963 Family Code put it:

> Parents are responsible to society for the all-round mental and physical development of their children, especially for their regular upbringing in such a way that the unity of interest of the family and society is consolidated.

The argument about the unity of the educational role of the family and society is then further developed and expanded. Paragraph 30 states:

> Bringing-up of children is taken care of by the inseparable unity of the family, the state and social organisations, especially the Czechoslovak Union of Youth and its Pioneer Organisation.

As another paragraph (no. 32) specifies that parents are legally (and ideologically) regarded as the primary agents for educating children, the law also states basic criteria of socialist education in order to avoid possible conflict of family and social goals, and to achieve the desired educational unity. These criteria are (Paragraph 31):

1. The foremost task of education is to promote the emotional, intellectual and ethical development of children in the spirit of the moral principles of the socialist society.

2. Upbringing must be conducted in such a way that children acquire wider and deeper education and responsible attitudes towards work, so that their consciousness and behaviour is penetrated by such moral principles as love for one's native country, friendship among the nations, protection of social property, subordination of personal interest to the interests of the community, voluntary and conscious adherence to the rules of socialist public life, respect for others, personal modesty, integrity and self-sacrifice.

Thus the upbringing of the new generation is primarily entrusted to the family, but the principles of socialist upbringing (which the party felt necessary to specify in the family code) are directed at the level of ideology towards ensuring that child-rearing conforms to the objectives of the party. The principle of subordination of personal to collective interests (as defined by the party) is particularly interesting, because it differs from the Western ideology of 'bourgeois individualism'. The mechanism through which the party-state ensures adherence to socialist principles of child care implies active co-operation between the family and other social institutions, such as public child-care facilities, the school, the national committees and the courts.

Although the law influences individual citizens, it cannot, of course, by itself create the desired socialist relationships within and outside family. In fact, as the law represents only the most institutionalised form of social relations, it may bear very little relation to what happens in practice. In other words, an examination of family law can tell us a great deal about the party's ideology of the family, but it is not very helpful if we are to evaluate social arrangements for child care which exist in practice. To determine the extent to which maternity and child care have become a social rather than an individual matter, we have to look at the availability of public child-care facilities and the extent of male participation in child care.

PUBLIC CHILD-CARE FACILITIES: DEBATES ABOUT THEIR USEFULNESS AND HARMFULNESS

The growth of public child-care facilities is definitely a post-war phenomenon that must be credited to the communist regime. In 1921, Bohemia had only 50 day-nurseries and Moravia only 20 such institutions. Slovakia had virtually none (Malá, 1925: 50). The expansion of crèches was so slow during the following three decades that, by 1937, Czechoslovakia had only 87 crèches with 1,286 places (Janouchová, 1973) and in 1946, day nurseries numbered 94. The capitalist economy and the Great Depression prevented investment in such 'unprofitable' undertakings; in additon, demand for nursery places was also lower because of the lower rate of employment of women with small children. The situation with regard to kindergartens was much better, although far from satisfactory. In 1921, there were 543 kindergartens in Bohemia and 418 in Moravia (Malá, 1925: 50). Their expansion was faster than that of crèches: in 1937, Czechoslovakia already had 2,713 kindergartens with 10,000 places (Janouchová, 1973). In 1948, the year of the communist seizure of power, there were 4,664 kindergartens. Yet even this rate of growth was very modest, when compared with the post-war development (see Tables 16.1 and 16.2)

Table 16.1 Crèches in Czechoslovakia

	1946	1948	1955	1964	1968	1972	1974*	1976
Number of crèches	94	268	1155	1526	1643	1613	1639	1732
Places in crèches	2542	6050	35024	59746	67382	66874	68691	73996
Places in enterprise crèches	–	–	5553	14851	17948	–	–	–

* In 1974 there were an additional 358 joint crèches-kindergartens, with 13,500 places.
Source: Dunovský, 1971; Brablcová and Kabrhelová, 1971: 191; *Čísla pro každého*, 1973: 257; *Statistická ročenka ČSSR*, 1974: 503; 1975: 547; 1977: 579.

Table 16.2 Kindergartens in Czechoslovakia

	1948/49	1960/61	1965/66	1970/71	1974/75	1976/77
Number	4664	6633	7569	8227	8871	9554
Classes	6107	9853	12568	14803	16794	18900
Children	205416	285863	330084	377593	440022	522066

Source: Kabrhelová and Brablcová, 1971: 191; *Statistická ročenka ČSSR*, 1972: 489; 1974: 490; 1975: 507; 1977: 537.

As the initial number of crèches was so small, their growth has been more spectacular than that of kindergartens, but a closer analysis of the data (Table 16.1) reveals that the most rapid expansion took place in the 1950s. The following decade witnessed a much more modest rate of growth of crèches, and between 1968 and 1974 the number actually declined. Why did this happen? Initially, in the early 1950s, there were no problems, at least for the authorities. The ideological and economic commitment to female labour-force participation nicely coincided with the socialist educational theories of that period, which emphasised that child care should take place mainly in collective institutions, beginning shortly after birth. The development of crèches was determined more by the needs of society and employed mothers than by the needs of individual children – it was simply assumed that collective upbringing would be beneficial for them too.

These views underwent a marked change in the 1960s. The harmful effects of an impersonal, institutional environment on the child's mental development, which had been pointed out by some paediatricians, psychologists and other specialists in the 1950s, began to be echoed in official circles. In 1960, Dr Langmeier addressed the Second National Congress of Psychiatry in Prague on sensory and emotional deprivation in childhood. Although there had been critical studies published before then, he summarised the shortcomings of collective care and clearly formulated for the first time the objections to the official ideology that man prospers in a collective under any circumstances. The Czechoslovak Paediatrics Society discussed similar problems at national conference in 1961. (Previous congresses had been devoted wholly to medical questions.)

While the specialists were very careful not to confuse day care in nurseries with the system of institutional care for abandoned and orphaned children, this distinction was ignored by the mass media, which changed the nature and emphasis of the problem. The analysis of the situation of children without families was unjustifiably broadened to include all children. A documentary film, *Children Without Love*, made by the director Kurt Goldberger in co-operation with two psychologists, Langmeier and Matějček, had a particularly significant impact in this respect. It compared the life of babies and toddlers in a model Czechoslovak children's home with that of a child from a secure family who spent a few hours a day in a nursery. It caught the hunger of institutionalised children for affection and physical contact with a sympathetic adult, and the extent of psychological deprivation when faced with the unfamiliar – in this case a huge teddy-bear – in contrast to the calm curiosity of a 'normal' child. Moreover, children in day nurseries were portrayed as growing restless by 4 o'clock in the afternoon, and wanting to go home. The film-makers also interviewed the director of a 5-day, 24-hour nursery. She regarded these institutions as an unfortunate necessity and hoped to see them reduced to a minimum. The film was shown in Parliament and was seen by the entire government (Scott, 1974: 175–9).

The mass media of the 1960s were thereafter filled with sharp exchanges of opinion about the usefulness or harmfulness of crèches, and the 'over-employment of women'. Suggestions advocating a return to the old system of housewives being solely responsible for child-rearing also emerged, but these were by and large rejected as unrealistic, both economically and ideologically, as we have seen in the previous chapter. One result of these debates was a review of the whole system of children's homes and the introduction during the next decade of various types of substitute family care in small homes and children's villages. An increased number of children were given out for adoption; and finally, in 1973, legislation re-instituting foster care was passed.

Another consequence was the decline of weekly and 24-hour nurseries. The Ministry of Health issued a firm statement that these were to be regarded as social institutions for emergency situations; that mothers (fathers were not mentioned) should work morning shifts so that their children could be in the nursery during the day; and that under no circumstances should nurseries be run on a shift basis, with children spending nights or days there depending on what hours there mothers were working (Scott, 1974: 179). Whereas in 1961 24-hour nurseries had formed 15 per cent of all crèches, by 1965 their proportion had declined to 5 per cent of the total and by 1968 to less than 3 per cent (Dunovský, 1971: 154). Day nurseries were also affected, as their numbers increased at a much slower rate than in the previous decade. The net growth for the period 1966–71 was only 1,033 places and the number of crèches actually declined.

The whole question of just what impact crèches do, in fact, have on children is complex and controversial. It is important to distinguish between the physical and mental aspects of children's development, because the effects of institutionalised child care are not necessarily the same in each of these spheres. Crèches in Czechoslovakia care for the children of employed mothers in the age category 6 months to 3 years. They are built and administered either by local authorities or by enterprises. One crèche normally caters for 50–60 children. It has three sections, one for infants, one for toddlers up to 18 months and one for toddlers from 18 months to 3 years. Each section has three or four paediatric nurses and about 20 children, which is a better ratio than in the USSR. The state health administration and its employees – part-time paediatricians, paediatric nurses and governesses – are responsible for the medical and educational care of the children. The standard of care is quite satisfactory, partly because the staffing is reasonable – one paediatric nurse to six or seven children – and partly because paediatric nurses are well qualified – they undergo a 4-year training programme in a health school and they also have to take additional courses in psychology and educational theory. This expertise has enabled paediatric nurses to approach child-rearing in a professional and comprehensive way. Various elements of crèche-pursued education – physical, rational, musical, artistic and emotional – aim at the child's full self realisation. The emphasis in physical education, for example, is on movement and specific exercises which prevent bad posture.

Because of this comprehensive approach, crèche-reared children have been found to grow and move faster than children reared entirely within the nuclear family, to speak earlier, to have more hygienic habits and to be more self-reliant in eating and dressing. Children in crèches have also been found to have a better and a more balanced diet than their family-based counterparts. On the other hand, crèches also have some undeniably negative effects on children's physical development. Because children are forcibly awakened (to reach crèches before their parents start work), they have been found to get less sleep than family-cared children whose sleep is not interrupted, and thus have appeared to be more fatigued (Polívková, 1974). This, of course, is a problem that can be solved relatively easily by a later start to the working day of one of the parents.

The main problem, a complete solution to which has not yet been found, is the frequency of illness, particularly diseases of the upper respiratory tract, among children of all age-categories who are reared in crèches. The incidence of infectious jaundice among crèche-reared children has been reported as being five to ten times more frequent than that of children living entirely in a family environment. Infants, that is, children younger than 18 months, are particularly susceptible to illness, and doctors have therefore recommended 18 months as the minimum age at which a child should become part of a group; most children, in fact, enter earlier (Dunovský, 1971: 154). However, the collective way of life and early entry are not the only factors responsible for the frequency of illness. Other, specifically medical factors, such as children's low immunity and the high accumulation of infectious factors, particularly viruses, against which no specific preventive protection or cure has yet ben developed, are equally to blame. Crèches fight against illness by emphasising fresh air and a correct diet, with adequate vitamins, and by maintaining a balanced daily routine.

Co-operation with parents is especially important, yet they are frequently unable to do all that is required of them. Insufficient convalescence of children returning to crèches after they have been ill has been singled out as another factor responsible for the recurrent illnesses of small children, but parents usually cannot afford to keep children at home for as long as they should, for the very reason for which they send their children to the crèches in the first place – they have have to go out to work. Children are away from their crèches, on average, for about 60 days a year, half of which is spent in illness, the rest on vacation (Dunovský, 1971: 154). One month of illness a year is quite high, as employers, eager to prove the lower productivity and 'wastage' of female education and employment, often point out. Although regulations do not specify who has to stay at home with sick children, it is usually the mother. She is, however, entitled only to 3 to 6 days leave at a time, which is often not sufficient for the child's full recovery. The frequency of this leave nevertheless adversely affects her professional performance. To date, the whole area of the care of sick children has been little investigated and no solution has as yet been proffered.

The mental and emotional development of children in crèches presents fewer problems for the children and their parents than do the medical aspects of their care, despite some research findings to the contrary.[3] Each child has its own neuropsychic chart, which shows all the basic characteristics of physical and mental development. As instruction in psychology and educational theory forms a prominent part of the training of paediatric nurses, they are better qualified to follow and compare children's physical, mental and emotional development than the children's mothers. Moreover, the latter tend to be so busy with their various household tasks that they have less time to devote to their children's education and stimulation. They tend to be less patient with the child and often stimulate him or her passively (for example, by television). Children reared entirely within the nuclear family also tend to suffer from lack of contact with other children.

Nevertheless, the child's initial experience of crèches can be quite traumatic. In fact, about 80 per cent of newly admitted children find it hard to adapt during the first 2–4 weeks. They tend to be restrained, aggressive or solitary, and may have difficulty in keeping clean and in feeding themselves. However, after the first 6 weeks, most children begin to behave naturally and seem to be happy in the crèche environment. Only about 10 per cent of children do not adjust to crèches and continue to suffer from various physical and mental disturbances (Polívková, 1974). For these children, family or micro-crèche care is probably a better alternative than large groups.

For the majority of children in crèches, however, initial difficulties may be minimised by a more gradual transition from the family to the crèche environment. To make the change less drastic and abrupt, parents can learn the crèche's daily regime beforehand and prepare the child accordingly. A number of short visits before the actual admission to the crèche can also be useful. Once in the crèche, children seem to suffer only if their daily stay is overextended. Most children spend 9 hours a day in crèches plus 1 hour for the journey, while doctors recommend a maximum of 6 hours (Dunovský, 1971: 154).

The conflict seems to be not between the home and the collective, but between the ideal day-care centre and the real one. In the view of Dr Hanuš Papoušek of the Institute for Mother and Child Care in Prague, the question of when best to transfer a child from all-day care in the family to part-time care in the nursery had not yet been thoroughly studied; current hypotheses have been based on nurseries as they were and not as they might be. Infants over 6 months old might be admitted for 4 hours a day and children over a year old for 6 hours. Experimental nurseries and collective care should be developed, and funds made available for this purpose (Scott, 1974: 180–1).

This raises another, and probably the most important question about day-care centres – their high cost. It has been estimated that, in Czechoslovakia, operating costs (including food) per place are 2½ times as high in crèches as in kindergartens. The cost per place in nurseries is equivalent to about 30 per cent of the average salary of employees of all grades (Fogarty, Rapoport and Rapoport, 1971:88). R. Hušek (1963) has calculated that a child's 3-year stay in a crèche costs the state more than the whole of the child's 9 years at school. In aggregate, such a high operating cost, borne largely by the state,[4] considerably lowers the economic effectiveness of employed mothers, especially those with lower qualifications and incomes and large families. Table 16.3, based on data collected in the 1960s, illustrates the overall cost of public child-care facilities in greater detail:

Table 16.3 Levels of operating costs of care of childen of one employed mother (in Kčs)

Number of children of one mother	Operating costs for children in:				
	crèches	kinder-gartens	school canteens	after-school care	Total
1	5720	–	–	–	5720
2	5720	1500	–	–	7220
3	5720	1500	340	550	8110
4	11440*	1500	340	550	13830

* Two children in a crèche
Source: Čap and Peltrámová, 1965:413.

We can see that the expense of operating pre-school child-care institutions is high indeed. In some cases (such as that of a mother with four children earning 1,000 Kčs monthly), the overall costs of crèche and kindergarten care exceed the economic value of the product which the employed mother creates for society by her labour in the social sphere of production. However, such a strictly economic argument is too instrumental and pragmatic: female equality and the nature of child care is a social and political matter in which more than the question of cost is involved. I would contend that child-rearing is not exclusively the woman's responsibility, but a social responsibility. If a society demands more children – the future generation of workers – then it has to pay for their upbringing, especially if there is individual demand for crèches.

Clearly, the growth of crèches has been too slow to satisfy women's demand for them. In 1961, 36 per cent of all economically active women were mothers with children under 3 years of age. By 1967, this proportion had reached 45 per cent (Dunovský, 1971: 154). Most of these women presumably needed places in crèches, which they were frequently unable to obtain. For example, in central Prague there were twice as many applications in 1965 as available places (Hilbertová, 1968: 17–21). At present, no more than 12 per cent of the child population is looked after in crèches, which is nowhere near the rate of employment of mothers of small children. The actual decline in the number of crèches in recent years (there were fewer crèches in 1972 than in 1966) suggests that a further expansion is not envisaged by the Czech authorities. The situation with regard to kindergartens is slightly better, as they have been given priority over crèches, but even they cater for only 50 per cent of all the children in the age-category of 3–6 years (Brablcová and Kabrhelová, 1971:92).

In comparative terms, the provision of day-care facilities in Czechoslovakia is worse than in the Soviet Union or the GDR, though superior to child-care arrangements in the West. What then, are the alternatives for women with pre-school children, who want to go out to work, either from financial necessity, or from a wish not to interrupt their careers, or because they want to break out of the isolation of the individual home?

CHILD-MINDING AND MICRO-CRÈCHES

One possibility is the use of child-minders. In the United Kingdom, child-minders care for more children than all local-authority and employer-run nurseries put together and are the main form of child care for children under two. However, only 30 per cent of parents using child-minders do so from choice, and a third of parents with children looked after in this way are dissatisfied with the care their children receive. Child-minders tend to be women already tied to the home by children, and a study by the Thomas Coran Research Unit discovered child-minders do not, on the whole, offer a warm, individualised relationship. A major criticism of this arrangement is that it exploits the minders, who are paid an average £8 per week. Such poor payment encourages them to take more and more children into their care. The Borough of Lambeth, in London, is running a pilot project with 12 salaried minders, who are paid about £2,000 a year, with further allowances for second and third children up to a maximum of three (Phillips, 1976).

A borough in Prague set up a similar experimental scheme, called 'micro-crèches', in 1964. Mothers of children older than 3 years undertook the care of three more (or fewer, if the children were in the age-group 1–3 years). The mothers were paid by the local authority, while the parents of the children contributed the same amount that they would have paid for a nursery. Similar schemes are now operated by some enterprises, such as the electronics factory, Tesla Pardubice, which set up a micro-crèche and paid mothers (fathers were not considered) for their work.

A Czech government resolution of August 1976 proposed that micro-crèches, each catering for three to five children, should be established by national committees, enterprises and co-operatives in the homes of child-minders or in suitably converted rooms and buildings. The Czech child-minder is required to undergo a short course in the education of young children, which is supervised by the district paediatrician and the district paediatric nurse. The salary varies according to the number of children cared for, including any of the minder's own under the age of 4. With three children to look after, the Czech child-minder is paid 1,450–1,700 Kčs monthly ($290–$340); with four children the salary goes up to 1,650–1,900 Kčs ($330– $380) and with five children, the salary amounts to 1,850–2,150 Kčs ($370– $430) per month ('Zásady vlády ČSR pro zřizování a provoz mikrojeslí', *Populační zprávy*, nos. 1–2, 1977).

However, is paid child-minding the best solution for working mothers and their children or does it simply amount to the politics of convenience? Researchers at the Thomas Coran Research Unit have argued that if child-minders were properly trained, housed, equipped and supervised, covered for illness and holidays and given pensions, they would cost as much as day nurseries. The main advantages of 'micro-crèches' seem to be the more individualised care for very young children or for those needing special attention, as well as the lowering of the frequency of children's illnesses. Nevertheless, minding can create new problems. Even where it is legal and supervised (and many child-minders in the West are not registered), isolation and depression, common among mothers, can be increased by the added burden of up to three extra children. It would be naive to assume that child-minding alone can fill the vacuum created by the dramatic increase in the number of mothers who work outside the home.

THE INSTITUTION OF 'GRANNIES'

Another alternative, used more widely in Eastern Europe than in the West, is to rely on grandmothers and other relatives. This extension of the maternal role to grandmothers is a subject much discussed in the popular press, but sociological literature has touched upon this phenomenon usually only in connection with the problem of day-care centres and their impact on children. Another approach is to study grandmothers, from the perspective of kinship, as a type of kin network of mutual assistance, not a type of extended family. This perspective was adopted by the State Population Commission in its 1962–4 nationwide survey on married women. The findings revealed that white-collar women, with higher education and income, were more likely than working-class women to seek the help of grandmothers.

To account for this class difference, we have to look at the rules which govern admission to crèches and kindergartens. Unmarried mothers and applicants with lower incomes and education are privileged – their children are more easily accepted in crèches. However, demand for assistance with child-care increases as the educational and income level rises, because professionally educated and qualified women are likely to value their economic and professional careers more than full-time motherhood. For example, of the 380 applicants for nursery places in central Prague in 1964, all were women with higher education and incomes. These mothers were lucky enough to be able to resort to micro-crèches, but most mothers are forced to rely on relatives. The formal reliance on relatives means that households of employed mothers are more often composed of three generations than households where women are not employed (Musil, 1971). This tendency was confirmed by later research findings. In the late 1960s, Vlasta Fišerová (1969: 456) conducted a nationwide survey on multigenerational households. She found that her sample contained a relatively large number of respondents who were living in three generational families (19 per cent of all respondents). Living with elderly parents was more frequent in Slovakia, in less-developed rural areas and in municipalities up to 1,000 inhabitants.

However, living together in a house does not in itself imply an integrated and mutually supporting wider family unit. For example, the nationwide sample of married women showed a relatively low frequency of relatives' participation in child care in farmers' extended families (Musil, 1971). The family pattern in which three generations live together seems to be more common among families where both spouses have a university education or where they are engaged in professional or skilled manual work; however, each generation tends to have its own budget and frequently cooks its own meals – hardly an ideal example of an extended family. This situation creates a special paradox and might lead to new kinds of tensions. Social involvement of relatives in child-rearing is higher among middle-class professional families, and yet mothers in these families are likely to disagree with their kin's (or, more specifically, their own mothers') views on children's upbringing more than women who are less educated and earn lower incomes.

Thus, the specific social and economic conditions in state-socialist Czechoslovakia – lack of public child-care facilities combined with a high rate of female employment – strengthen the family in a particular way, by emphasising the social functions and importance of kinship. However, this is likely to be a temporary phenomenon, because grandmothers constitute a diminishing source of labour. With higher levels of education and professional jobs, older women are likely to be reluctant to assist their sons and daughters full-time.

In conclusion, it should be noted that the family has remained the unit responsible for the main burden of upbringing. Current legislation protecting maternity and the extensive state assistance Czechoslovak women and their children receive are impressive when compared with that of many capitalist countries, but fall short of providing a satisfactory solution to the problem of integrating women's productive and reproductive roles. As we shall see in the next chapter, recent population policies have aimed at an integration that trims women's productive roles to allow them to play a larger role in the reproduction of labour power.

17 Pro-Natalist Population Policies[1]

The meaning of population policy is complex and ill-defined. Different governments treat their 'population problem' and its eventual consequences with varying degrees of urgency. One point which seems to be common to the rationale behind all population policies – despite some eugenic, nationalist or even racialist elements in the discussion – is that measures are generally a response to assumed future manpower requirements. Since the late 1960s, anti-natalist ideas have prevailed in many Western countries, largely because the natural increase of population has not been regarded as relevant to future manpower requirements; in large measure, the current advocacy of population control and zero growth appears as a response to the fear of shortage of resources brought on by the population explosion.

The converse tendency is found in official circles within the state-socialist countries of Eastern Europe, which have adopted pro-natalist policies. These are directly related to manpower requirements – there is a fear that there will be severe shortages of labour in the future caused by policies favouring quantitative rather than qualitative development of the labour force, the inability to import labour from elsewhere and a marked decline in the birthrate.[2] Czechoslovakia has been suffering from a chronic shortage of labour since the end of the Second World War. Initially, housewives who had not previously been employed provided the required reserve pool of labour, but this source has now practically run dry. As we noted in Chapter 15, the employment of women has reached its upper limit and cannot be extended any further. One alternative, the employment of foreign labour, is very restricted – only labour from countries within the COMECON bloc may be used. At present, Czechoslovakia assigns a number of construction projects, such as the building of roads and factories, to Polish and Yugoslav workers, but this 'solution' is unlikely to be a permanent one. With increasing levels of industrialisation, Poland and Yugoslavia are unlikely to be able to spare their current surplus of labour for much longer. It is for this reason that the rapid post-war decline in fertility in Czechoslovakia has been viewed with such alarm (see Table 17.1).

In the first decade after the war, the birthrate was relatively high, and little attention was therefore paid to population growth – the emphasis on

Women and State Socialism

Table 17.1 Birth rate in Czechoslovakia (%)

1937	16·3	1962	15·7	1968	14·9	1974	19·8
1945	19·5	1963	16·9	1969	15·5	1975	19·5
1948	23·4	1964	17·2	1970	15·9	1976	19·2
1955	20·3	1965	16·4	1971	16·5		
1960	15·9	1966	15·6	1972	17·3		
1961	15·8	1967	15·1	1973	18·8		

Sources: *Děti, naše budoucnost* 1971: 10; *Čisla každého*, 1973: 59; *Statisticka ročenka ČSSR*, 1975: 580; 1977: 21.

women's emancipation in terms of their participation in production was considered of greater social importance and significance. However, from 1952, the population situation began to worsen. This was the result of greatly increased opportunities for women in paid employment, as well as of other policies favouring a lower birthrate. These have resulted in rapid urbanisation, inadequate housing, insufficient investment in consumer goods and services, low wages and relatively free availability of abortion.

Most Czechoslovak women limit the number of their children because of material considerations. As in other East European countries, the majority of Czech families live in crowded housing conditions and each additional child takes up more room. The authorities have been aware of this problem for a long time but have not succeeded in finding a solution. For instance, the long-term plan for 1959–70 included measures to eliminate the housing shortage by constructing 1,200,000 new apartments, but only 981,000 (less than 82 per cent of the target) were built. Another plan for 1966–70 envisaged 460,000 new dwellings, but only 429,000 (93 per cent) were actually built (Šteker, 1971: 9). Even this figure may be an over-estimate, because apartments listed as finished are not, in fact, ready for immediate occupation. Nevertheless, there is some indication that the gap between supply and demand in housing is narrowing. Since 1970, the number of new housing units has greatly increased compared to previous years (see Table 17.2).

The high demands on physical and mental energy made daily by housework were discussed in Chapter 14. We should note, also, that the time and energy spent in laundering, washing by hand, ironing, mending and cooking obviously increase with the number of children. With so many women at work, the inadequacies of household services and aids have done nothing to help the decline in the birthrate. The arrival of the second child, and almost certainly of the third, tends to be postponed indefinitely.

However, the main consideration seems to be money. In the state-socialist societies, both spouses must have jobs if an adquate standard of living is to be secured, and children frequently bring financial hardship. Family allowances, even when progressive, do not constitute an adequate

Table 17.2 New dwellings in Czechoslovakia

Year	Loss of housing units	Newly constructed housing units	New housing units (including conversion of existing buildings)
1955	10385	48790	57105
1956	9762	62240	68993
1957	10748	60259	66545
1958	12075	50881	58550
1959	15045	66885	75028
1960	16613	73766	81325
1961	16162	86032	92505
1962	13776	85221	92469
1965	20201	77818	83146
1967	20601	79297	86521
1968	23000	86571	94171
1969	21605	85656	93907
1970	33706	112135	119353
1971	16410	107380	113540
1972	19338	116176	122403
1973	22765	118594	125195
1974	20849	128988	135426
1975	21928	144678	149255
1976	28225	132451	138302

Source: *Statistická ročenka ČSSR*, 1963: 146; 1973: 202; 1977: 210.

material compensation for the loss of income of one spouse, invariably the wife. The care of a child also interferes with a woman's professional career, especially, as we have seen, in view of the fact that the supply of day-care facilities has not kept pace with demand. Thus, when faced with the choice between a career and a child, a large number of women, not surprisingly, opt for employment. The problem facing pro-natalist policy-makers is therefore to find and implement ways of inducing women to have more children. This requires intervention in two broad areas: the welfare of the family on the one hand and procreation and fertility on the other.

FAMILY WELFARE AND FAMILY INCENTIVES

After the Second World War, the coalition government introduced a new system of family allowances and tax deductions. Demographic objectives do not seem to have been the principal reason for these measures. Family allowances and tax deductions were originally introduced in the name of greater social justice and equal opportunity and to affirm the responsibility of the state for the welfare of the family, especially for the family with a large number of children. For these reasons, family allowances were increased in 1947 and 1951, and again in 1953 when they were significantly raised and also made more progressive. The 1959 changes aimed explicitly at assisting large families, with substantial increases for third- and higher-order children. Reduced prices of consumer goods, including children's clothing and shoes, in the same year, and the introduction of free textbooks in the academic year 1960/1, were also intended to help larger families.

In 1962, after a decade during which the birthrate declined rapidly, the Twelfth Party Congress initiated measures extending paid maternity leave to 18 weeks, grading minimum retirement ages of women according to the number of children they had raised, and introducing rent rebates dependent upon the number of children in the family. As things now stand, women who have been employed for at least 25 years and who have reared 5 or more children are entitled to an old-age pension at 53. Mothers with 2, 3 or 4 children who have also been engaged in gainful employment for at least 25 years can retire at 55. Women with no children qualify for an old-age pension at 57, men at 60. Maternity is therefore recognised in real economic terms, but the 'benefits' and 'privileges' are rather small. In fact, at the level of ideology, these measures reinforce traditional views which do not separate child-bearing from child-rearing, and consider the bringing up of children as women's work.

The Twelfth Party Congress also set up a special population body, the State Population Commission. Its main terms of reference were as follows:

1. to evaluate the development of the demographic situation, to report to the government and appropriate bodies and to make recommendations for policy changes;
2. to undertake research on all problems connected with demographic development, especially correlations between demographic, economic, social and health factors, to examine the development of the individual functions of the family and relations between the family and society;
3. to prepare and contribute to the preparation of educational and political propaganda on questions relating to the socialist family and education for conscious parenthood;
4. to co-operate with all central bodies and all social organisations in developing education for conscious parenthood;
5. to follow up and evaluate all legislation from the point of view of increasing the living standards of families with children so that families with a greater number of children be given priority;
6. to monitor the results of the abortion law.

Education for parenthood seems to have been one of the most important tasks of this body. In 1963, the State Population Commission helped with the preparation of a serial entitled 'Family and Society', which was broadcast by Czechoslovak television during the spring and summer of 1963. A radio series entitled 'Intimate Conversations', broadcast during the same period, also followed the specific directives of the party to educate people, especially young people, in the 'correct' approach to questions of parenthood.

The State Population Commission also conducted a number of surveys on the social aspects of female employment, especially its relationship to a low birthrate. Following the recommendation of the commission, paid maternity leave was later extended from 18 to 22 weeks. A new measure, unpaid maternity leave for 1 year after childbirth, was also introduced on the commission's recommendation. This meant that Czechoslovak enterprises employing nursing mothers were obliged to keep their jobs open for a year if the mothers chose to look after their babies during this period.

However, these measures did not achieve their aim – an increase in fertility. The Thirteenth Party Congress had, therefore, an agenda similar to the previous one: much attention was devoted to unfavourable demographic development. As a result, maternity benefits were further improved: paid maternity leave was extended from 22 weeks to 26 weeks, and, for unmarried, widowed, divorced or otherwise unsupported mothers, to 35 weeks. Maternity leave for a period of up to 35 weeks was also granted to women who gave birth to two or more children at a time.

Ironically, 1968 witnessed the lowest birthrate since the war. But other pro-natalist measures followed. In 1970, unpaid maternity leave was extended for another year, up to the child's second birthday. At present, women in Czechoslovakia arc entitled to 3 years of unpaid maternity leave. Research conducted in 1969 showed that 52 per cent of women returned to work immediately after the expiration of paid maternity leave and an additional 37 per cent after a year of unpaid maternity leave (Havelka, 1972a: 30). Thus, more than half the sample did not take advantage of the provision for unpaid maternity leave. This confirms the need of both spouses to earn incomes, but it also reflects the changed status of Czechoslovak women outside the home. Women in professional jobs returned to work to retain their qualifications and because their work gave them satisfaction.

However, it would appear that the latest population measure, maternity allowances, has had the effect of providing a real family incentive. Introduced in July 1970, it provided for a monthly salary of 500 Kčs to be paid to all employed mothers for the care of their *second* child until its first birthday. Housewives became eligible for this allowance in January 1971, when its duration was also extended to 2 years. At the same time, assistance given at childbirth was doubled – from 1,000 Kčs to 2,000 Kčs. Although 500 Kčs is only about one-third of the average female monthly wage, the amount does seem to have acted as an incentive. Research findings indicate that about 90 per cent of all mothers take advantage of maternity allowances for 1 year and 75 per cent for 2 years (see Table 17.3). As was the case with unpaid maternity leave, mothers with higher educational attainments have taken less advantage of this opportunity than women with lower levels of education and income (Havelka, 1972a: 42; Janečková, 1976).

Table 17.3 Educational level of women granted maternity allowances in 1975 (%)

Educational Level	Length of time allowance received (months)				
	1–4	5–9	10–14	15–19	20–24
Basic	4	4	5	6	81
Basic with apprentiship	2	6	4	5	83
Secondary	3	7	6	7	77
University	2	14	8	13	63

Source: Janečková, 1976: 21

On the level of ideology, this latest measure represents recognition of motherhood as a socially necessary and economic activity, which has to be remunerated. Given that the maintenance of the population requires that a significant proportion of families have 2 or more children, motherhood has acquired a new 'professional' status. By upholding the level of reproduction, mothers become much more useful to society than has been traditionally admitted in socialist theory and practice. Nevertheless, a policy that fails to distinguish between child-bearing and child-rearing again reinforces the idea that child-rearing, like child-bearing, is women's work.

In June 1971, the State Population Commission, which recommended the maternity allowance scheme, became the Government Population Commission. As its composition was also changed, the change of title was more than a mere formality. The commission is no longer merely a governmental body, and now consists of representatives from various ministries and other state and voluntary organisations. The trades unions, the Socialist Union of Youth, and most importantly, the Czechoslovak Council of Women, are all represented. Women thus have at least formal representatives who can express their point of view on issues which are vital to their individual lives as child-bearers. Specialist research workers in various branches of medicine and social science are also involved.

The first discussions of the commission centred around problems similar to those that had been publicly discussed more than a decade earlier: the inadequacy of public household facilities, including their high prices and lengthy delivery; education for parenthood; child-care facilities; housing; and abortion. Education for parenthood seems to have been the main topic of discussion. An enlarged journal of the commission, *Populační zprávy*, nos. 4–5, 1972, published several articles dealing with this problem. The 'directives of the Government Population Commission on education for parenthood' also appeared in this issue.

The mass media were given the task of influencing public attitudes towards children in order to bring about the desired demographic changes. Young people, in particular, were to be converted from consumerism, and to this end the media were called upon to stress:

1. the irreplaceable value of children in making life fuller and richer;
2. deep and firm moral and emotional relationships, mutual love and respect between young men and women and between spouses;
3. the disadvantages suffered by only children;
4. that the ideal family was one with three children, a size sufficient for the children to interact, thus favouring their intellectual development;
5. health education for women and the dangers of abortion;
6. the need for real equality between the sexes, e.g. equal division of labour in housework;
7. improvement of living standards, by:
   a. expansion of social services for the care of children;
   b. improved supplies of children's goods;
   c. limitation of food preparation in the home, e.g. expansion of canteens and greater use of pre-cooked foods;
   d. increased output of labour-saving domestic appliances;
   e. improvement of working conditions for women, e.g. part-time work, shorter hours, etc.;
8. that conditions of life for families with children would steadily improve;
9. that unfavourable demographic developments would hamper economic development and thus have serious effects on living standards.

The first four points confirm the existence of a consumer consciousness among the majority of the population, particularly young people. Most young people prefer to acquire consumer goods, such as cars or weekend houses before having any children. The most prevalent family size seems to be one or two children. However, demographers and economic planners argue that this average, 1.9 children per family, needs to rise to 2.5 children in order to maintain the existing population size of between 14 and 15 million. Thus, the aim is a typical family size of two to three children, that is, many more young couples are required to have three or more children to reach this desired figure (Havelka, 1972a: 35). While in 1950, 16 per cent of all live births were third children, by 1970, this figure had dropped to 11.5 per cent. In 1973, there were fewer families with only 1 child, and more families with two children, but the proportion of families with three children remained constant. Moreover, there were fewer families with a larger number of children.

Thus, exhortation does not seem to be enough; some fiscal measures are required in addition. In January 1973, monthly family allowances were again increased. They remained the same for 1-child families (90 Kčs), but for two children they rose from 330 Kčs to 430 Kčs. For three children, the increase was from 680 Kčs to 880 Kčs, and for four or more children from 1,030 Kčs to 1,280 Kčs. These amounts represent a significant contribution to the family income, especially the increments for the third and fourth child. April 1973 saw the introduction of a new loan scheme with very low interest rates to help young married couples under 30 years of age to obtain or furnish a flat. Its value is up to 30,000 Kčs, to be repaid within 10 years. For the first child born after the signature of the contract and surviving to its first birthday 2,000 Kčs of the loan is cancelled, and for each subsequent child 4,000 Kčs (Pelikán, 1973). This is another effective incentive. The government is thus attempting to direct the demands of young couples from cars to children, and this strategy seems to be achieving the desired result – an increase in natality.

Since 1970, the birthrate has increased markedly (see Table 17.1). But, while family-incentive measures have been important, this relatively rapid increase has in part been due to a more favourable demographic composition: the many women born in the post-war 'baby boom' have now reached child-bearing age. It is estimated that this factor accounts for 20 per cent of the recent increase (Matěj Lúčan, Chairman of the Government Population Commission, in an interview published in *Děti a My* [Children and Us], no. 4, December 1974). An additional factor, although its impact is difficult to assess, has been a stricter application of the law on abortion.

ABORTION AND CONTRACEPTION

Policies on family planning are not only the most widely discussed, but also the most controversial aspects of population policy. This is not surprising because, in the absence of immigration, fertility is the main factor in population increase. Compared with the advanced industrial countries of the West, modern contraceptive methods have only relatively recently become available in Central and Eastern Europe. After the Second World War, Czechoslovakia inherited a network of voluntary, pre-marital, eugenic advice-centres. However, in the early 1950s, these were abolished and not replaced by other institutions. The change was largely due to the prevailing Stalinist ideology, which did not recognise genetics, and therefore considered such centres unnecessary. In the late 1950s and early 1960s, new pre-marital advice-centres were set up, but they were few in number and relatively inactive. Moreover, information about family planning was not included as part of their work. Instruction about contraceptive devices was limited to women undergoing abortion (rather too late for such advice) because such advice could only be given in the gynaecological departments of hospitals. Research in the late 1950s on problems connected with marriage, contraception and abortion confirmed that the dissemination of information about the availability and price of contraceptives was wholly inadequate (Srb, 1961).

In June 1964, the Ministry of Health arranged a special conference on contraception which recommended both oral and mechanical forms of contraception. In 1966, the ministry agreed to the production and widespread distribution of IUDs called 'DANA'. Besides being a girl's name, DANA's initials also stand for 'Good and Harmless Contraception' (*Dobrá a neškodná antikoncepce*). The efficiency of DANA is said to be between 94 and 96 per cent. A Czech-produced oral contraceptive, *Antigest*, became available in April 1966. However, it was expensive and in limited supply, so was mainly prescribed for women who had had more than two children or those who had already had an abortion (Dvořák, 1966). This situation is now changing – in the last few years, the use of oral contraceptives has spread to other sections of the female population, even to young single women. However, there was a shortage of the Pill in 1969 and I was informed about another shortage during my visit to Prague in December 1974. Pills imported recently from Yugoslavia (where they are produced under US licence) have somewhat alleviated the situation – although this may be short-lived, as the government finds them too expensive and is planning to stop their import.

Thus, in the main, only Czech-produced pills (which have more side-effects than Western-produced pills) and inter-uterine devices are currently available. Moreover, it appears that the general public is still ill-informed about contraception. It has been estimated that only 6 per cent of all women in the fertile age group use modern forms of contraception. *Coitus interruptus* is, therefore, still the most widely used method (Zelenková, 1970: 41). Research conducted by the State Population Commission in the 1960s on the sexual life of young married couples showed that more than a quarter of the men and half of the women in the sample considered their sex education insufficient or non-existent. Books, rather than the family or the school, seemed to be the main source of information. Knowledge of contraception was generally absent; the majority of women depended on the responsibility, experience and skill of their partners, both before and after marriage (Prokopec, 1966).

It was not until 1972 that the Ministry of Education announced that it was finally at work on a comprehensive new curriculum on 'education for parenthood', which would include sex education. Until then, sex education at school consisted of a single lecture to 14-year-olds in the eighth grade, given by the school doctor to boys and girls separately. There was a woeful lack of suitable literature for children and young people, and even for parents, on this subject. At the same time, the number of schoolgirls who became pregnant was increasing, and young people and their parents were regularly castigated in the mass media for their 'irresponsibility' and 'lax morals'. This situation is now changing and information on family planning is becoming more accessible than in the Soviet Union.

Nevertheless, Czechoslovakia, like the rest of Central and Eastern Europe, has a relatively long history of socially acceptable illegal and legal abortion. On the whole, it is considered neither sinful nor disgraceful to terminate an unwanted pregnancy. Abortion in hospitals was already permitted in 1920, but in 1936 a new interpretation of the relatively liberal law restricted it to cases where pregnancy or childbirth would directly endanger the life of the woman. Thus, until 1950, any form of individually induced abortion was a criminal offence (as it still is in West Germany). In 1954, restrictions on abortions were relaxed, but full legalisation occurred only at the end of 1957, following the lead of the Soviet Union in 1955.

The extent to which a woman has a legal right to determine the fate of her pregnancy is differently interpreted in the various state-socialist countries. Only in the Soviet Union and the German Democratic Republic is abortion available on request during the first 3 months of pregnancy, provided the woman has had no previous abortions during the immediately preceding 12 months. In Czechoslovakia, each woman seeking an abortion must first apply to a special abortion commission in her locality, which decides on her application. These commissions are composed of doctors, elected members of local national committees, representatives from the Population Commission, the trades unions and the Council of Women. The local abortion commissions are often very bureaucratic – it can easily happen that the required 12 week period passes before any decision is reached. They also frequently refuse to accept responsibility and refer applicants to higher bodies, thus prolonging the procedure. They are also often moralistic and sometimes even critical in their attitudes. 'Few members of the commission realise', wrote one mother of five children to a weekly magazine, 'what it means for a sensitive mother with human feelings to sit before them as in a pillory.' Another described her feelings in this way: 'The operation itself caused me no specific trouble but every time I think of the commission (and especially one of the woman members) I'm filled with panic and I can't bring myself to sleep with my husband' (Hájková and Tučková 1965; Scott, 1974: 145).

Other critics of the procedure have pointed out that it encourages hypocrisy. Because it may speed up the hearing before the commission if the woman claims to have conceived out of wedlock, she and her husband fabricate a lover. The commission, although it may suspect the story to be an invention, must still accept it. This procedure also encourages irresponsibility on the part of men. The woman is the one who decides whether she gives birth to a child or not. She makes the application; she must go before the interruption commission; she is the one who receives the moralistic lecture, is subjected to pressure to have the child, is reproached for getting herself 'into trouble'; and she is the one who pays the fee. The man has to 'worry' neither about conception nor about its after-effects, as all the responsibility for the future of the unborn child is put on the woman (Scott, 1974: 145).

However, on the whole, the commissions' attitude towards authorising abortions has been permissive, especially when the pregnant woman persists in her application. This lenient practice has been reflected in high abortion rates and the high ratio of abortions to births (see Table 17.4).

Abortions in Czechoslovakia may be performed on health as well as on other grounds. These include advanced age of the woman, a minimum family size of three children, loss or disablement of husband, breakdown of the marriage, financial hardship caused by an additional child, unmarried status, inadequate housing, rape, etc. Only 20 per cent of abortions are performed on health grounds. The rest, 80 per cent, are authorized for social reasons. In 1970, the most frequently stated and accepted social reasons were: three or more children (18 per cent), unmarried status (16 per cent) and inadequate housing (18 per cent). In Prague, this order was reversed: 33 per cent of applications for abortions were based on the grounds of unmarried status, and 16 per cent were due to inadequate housing or a large number of children (Havelka, 1972a: 34; Vaněk, 1971: 291).

The relative stagnation or even decline in the number of abortions performed on request, which occurred in 1963–5, was largely due to a new, stricter abortion law passed in December 1962. Abortion, which up to then had been free, was now changed for, at rates from 200 to 800 Kčs. The socio-economic family-incentive measures initiated by the Twelfth Party Congress probably also contributed to a lowering of the abortion rate. In the early 1970s, abortion commissions were officially urged to limit the number of positive responses to requests for abortion based on social reasons, so that fewer women were able to terminate their pregnancies. The recently introduced 'motherhood' incentives also played their part, along with the greater use of modern forms of contraception.

This latest restrictive and unfavourable official attitude to abortion clearly has to be viewed within the context of a declining birthrate. In 1967, 96,421 abortions on request were performed, so that there were 44 abortions per 100 live births. In 1969 there were more abortions than live births. Thus, given the low level of natality, and the fears associated with it, a relatively high abortion rate represents an additional loss of population. Moreover, abortion frequently has unfavourable after-effects.

When Czechoslovakia introduced legal abortion, it also introduced a statutory 1-year follow-up as a legal requirement. The results were appalling – 25 per cent of patients had chronic inflammatory disease leading to infertility or ectopic pregnancy and 5–10 per cent had incompetence of the cervix. Moreover, the relatively high incidence of late

Table 17.4 Abortions in Czechoslovakia

	1958	1959	1960	1961	1962	1963	1964	1965	1966	1967	1968	1969	1970	1971	1972	1973	1974	1975
Total	89076	105536	114602	120304	115908	99933	99211	105758	115807	121198	123822	127232	125074	122853	119630	111465	111356	111779
on request	61418	79131	88288	94306	89815	70546	70698	75591	90263	96421	99666	102797	99766	97271	91292	81233	83055	81671
spontaneous	27110	26662	26070	25847	25966	29245	28414	26098	25494	24722	24124	24410	25288	25559	28302	30194	30259	30075
others	548	343	244	151	127	142	99	69	50	55	32	25	20	23	36	38	42	33
Applications for abortions	69633	87327	96866	105029	100703	81995	79828	86589	97013	104166	108008	110334	107107	104647	98790	88085	90202	88665
Abortions per 1000 inhabitants	6·6	7·8	8·4	8·7	8·4	7·2	7·1	7·5	8·1	8·5	8·6	8·8	8·6	8·5	8·3	7·6	7·7	7·6
Abortions per 100 completed pregnancies	27·3	32·5	34·3	35·3	34·6	29·6	29·0	31·2	34·0	35·8	36·5	36·2	35·2	34·0	32·1	30·6	27·9	27·7
on request	19·0	24·5	26·5	31·7	26·8	20·9	20·6	23·5	26·5	28·5	29·4	29·2	28·1	26·9	24·4	22·3	20·4	20·3
spontaneous	8·3	8·0	7·8	7·6	7·7	8·7	8·3	7·7	7·5	7·3	7·1	6·9	7·1	7·1	7·5	8·3	7·4	7·5
Abortions per 100 live births	37·5	48·1	52·2	54·5	52·8	42·0	40·8	45·3	51·6	55·7	57·5	56·7	54·4	51·4	47·3	44·0	38·7	38·4
on request	–	–	–	–	40·9	29·6	29·0	34·1	40·2	44·3	46·6	45·8	43·3	40·7	36·1	32·1	28·3	28·1
spontaneous	11·4	11·9	11·9	11·7	11·8	12·3	11·7	11·2	11·4	11·4	11·2	10·9	11·0	10·7	11·2	11·9	10·3	10·3
Performed abortions per 100 applications	–	–	–	–	89·2	86·0	88·6	91·9	93·0	92·6	92·3	93·2	93·1	93·0	90·4	92·2	92·1	92·1

Source: Vývoj společnosti ČSSR v číslech, 1965: 30; *Statistická ročenka ČSSR,* 1963: 95; 1964: 102; 1965: 105; 1967: 94; 1969: 102; 1972: 99; 1974: 115; 1975: 121; 1977: 108.

complications became apparent only when a woman who had had one or more abortions decided to have a child or actually became pregnant. The incidence was substantially higher among young women and among those whose first pregnancy had been interrupted. A review of 5,000 abortions in Czechoslovakia showed that 17 per cent of women visiting fertility clinics had legal abortions in their case histories, while 53 per cent had had 'spontaneous abortions' with inflammatory complications. In fact, there is a suspicion that many 'spontaneous' abortions in hospital records have actually been self-inflicted, for, whenever the commission adopted a stricter attitude, the number of recorded 'spontaneous' abortions rose noticeably but dropped again when the commissions relaxed their stance (Scott, 1974: 147–8).

Czech demographers estimate that abortion and its after-effects account for 30–35 per cent of the annual decline of the birthrate (Havelka, 1972*a*: 34). However, as the birthrate had already started to decline in 1952, that is, between 5 and 7 years before full legalisation of abortion, the unfavourable demographic situation cannot be blamed solely on abortions. On the other hand, the liberalisation of abortion laws has certainly contributed substantially to the declining birthrate, since fertility began to decline much faster after abortions were legalised.

The reasons given by women seeking abortions show that economic factors are the most important in explaining the high incidence. The findings of a public-opinion survey on abortion procedure indicated that improvement of social and economic conditions (91 per cent), better knowledge of contraception (70 per cent), improvement of sexual morality and responsibility (61 per cent) and better education for parenthood would lower the high abortion rate (Vaněk, 1971: 294). Only 16 per cent of the sample considered existing knowledge and availability of contraception to be adequate. However, with improved knowledge and availability, the abortion rate is unlikely to rise again – since 1969, it has been consistently declining.

The long-term effect of the various pro-natalist measures is difficult to assess, since there are forces working in opposite directions. On the one hand, we have financial incentives and propaganda glorifying womanhood and motherhood. Celebrations of International Women's Day on March 8 are characterised by outbursts of enthusiasm for the 'great and noble work' women do as mothers-workers-citizens; the popular press prints articles on the 'mother-heroine' awards or suggests ways of being feminine and liberated at the same time. The mass media wonder how women manage to do so much, but, in general, accept that this should be the case. In the absence of active, grass-roots organisation, where the problems of everyday living which women share could be articulated and confronted, each woman faces her problems individually. The complacency of the media reinforces in women's minds the feeling that the *status quo* is both right and necessary. The popular press and the educational system assure her that everyone values femininity and motherhood above all other qualities. (Holt, 1976a).

While the factors working in this direction should not be dismissed, the factors working in the opposite direction are, in my opinion, more powerful. On a strictly economic level, the economy could not cope with the mass exodus of half of its labour force, even if women left to ensure greater labour resources in the future. It is also possible that Czechoslovakia may find that the cost involved in paying maternity allowances and supporting large families is too high and conflicts with other priorities, especially investment in the consumer industries. But the most important factor in the situation is to be sought in the considerable changes that have taken place in the position of women during the state-socialist transformation.

A high proportion of women have joined the labour force, resulting in significant changes in family structure and life patterns. Increasing numbers of women with post-secondary education and professional jobs work for the sake of working, and seem to be unwilling to sacrifice their careers for the sake of raising more children. The main problem facing mothers with small children in Czechoslovakia is where to place them during working hours once maternity leave is over. The plans drawn up in 1971 did not envisage such a 'population explosion' and accordingly did not expand the network of kindergartens sufficiently. Lack of these facilities will undoubtedly act against higher fertility. For these reasons, it is quite probable that when the age-composition of the population becomes less favourable (that is, with fewer women of child-bearing age), the birthrate will decline again. Women's reluctance to bear and raise more children will then force the government to shift its policies and seek other solutions to its economic problems.

18 Conclusion

In the foregoing chapters, we have seen that the USSR and Czechoslovakia are not, and never have been at any time in their histories, truly egalitarian societies. Despite the official commitment to sex equality and despite policies designed to emancipate women, in neither country have the communists created a society in which sexual inequality, any more than other forms and types of inequality,[1] is absent. What then are the implications of the Soviet and Czechoslovak experiences for the more general questions raised in the introduction to this book? How successful have the state-socialist societies been in implementing their ideology of equality, what has hindered them and what can we learn from their experiences about the 'optimal' conditions necessary for achieving ideological goals? What do the case studies tell us, in comparative terms, about the implications of policies affecting the sexual division of labour for broad social processes? Finally, what is the relevance of these cases for feminist ideology and practice in the West?

STATE SOCIALISM, EGALITARIAN IDEOLOGY AND SEX EQUALITY

There are significant differences among the various egalitarian goals pursued in the state-socialist societies. For instance, the goal of full income equality, unlike full sex equality, was never on the socialist agenda. It was not the original intention of the Bolsheviks to abolish the wage system nor to introduce equal distribution of commodities (as advocated by the anarchists), although declared policy initially aimed at considerable equalisation of incomes and living standards. This egalitarian policy was cut short and replaced under Stalin by a system of greater wage differentiation. Stalin's immediate justification for the change was the need to reduce labour mobility, to introduce incentives for the unskilled to become skilled and to attract workers to industries essential for rapid industrial growth.[2]

In other East European societies, wage differentials have followed a pattern similar to that in the Soviet Union. The socialist drive for income equalisation was strongest in the period immediately following the nationalisation of property and the seizure of political power (the period of 'revolutionary optimism' and 'idealism'); later, with the consolidation of power by the new elites, greater pay-differentials were introduced. According to Marxist theory, egalitarianism would only be attained with communism, when all would be rewarded 'according to their need', while, in the course of building transitional socialism, workers could be paid 'according to their work'. Consequently, workers who have skills requiring training and education, and/or who are in short supply, have tended to receive a greater financial reward. Not unlike the situation in the West, income inequality has been closely linked with the occupational structure, although decisions in the state-socialist societies about 'preferred' and 'non-preferred' occupations (in heavy industry and mining, as opposed to medicine or teaching) have been determined by the political elites.

In contrast to income equalisation, sex equality has been consistently taken for granted as a goal by the communists, as has their view of women playing the threefold role of mother (housewife)-worker-citizen; a counterpart to the woman's triple role has never been spelled out for men. However, there have been important shifts in emphasis within this triple role, particularly from work to motherhood, primarily in response to the declining birthrate. One can also detect a shift from the original revolutionary optimism and idealism regarding the position of women to a stance that recognises existing inequalities between men and women and even advocates measures that would increase them.

Practically all socialist works on the 'woman question' have been based on Engels's hypothesis that the emancipation of women would result from the abolition of private property (along with class-rule and exploitation), the productive employment of women (giving them a public social role and economic independence) and the socialisation of private domestic work and child care (which would give time for self-cultivation and public life). However, much of the literature has concentrated on the first two factors to the exclusion of the third. Stalinist writings, in particular, tended to equate formal legal equality with day-to-day practical equality, and to imply that a high level of labour participation by women was tantamount to complete liberation; the question of socialising housework was largely ignored. In other words, it was assumed that women's emancipation and equality were automatically guaranteed in a socialist economy with a high level of female participation. A recent article by J. Bauerová, a Czech sociologist, illustrates the bland question-begging of much of the state-socialist literature:

> For the first time in history, socialist societies broke through the barrier erected between men and women by class-antagonistic societies, religions of all kinds and bourgeois ideologies. In the socialist societies, women have the same opportunities as men as regards work, working and living conditions, education, housing, utilisation of culture and political activity (Bauerová, 1976:29).

This quotation also evokes a typical theme – 'what socialism has given to our women' – that implies that equality is a benevolent grant rather than a basic right.

Although Bauerová represents a continuation of the earlier tradition in the literature, some changes in official thinking about sex equality became apparent in at least some of the East European countries in the late 1960s. In Czechoslovakia, women's weeklies and the Central Committee of the Czechoslovak Union of Women were among the first to point out publicly the discrepancies between the ideal and legal positions on the one hand, and the real situation of women on the other. At about the same time (1967), the *Literaturnaya gazeta* in the USSR launched a broad discussion on motherhood, the *'double shifts'* of women and illegitimacy, and called for new legislation to regulate alimony payments.

The professed axioms of sex equality in the state-socialist societies are thus gradually giving way to the recognition of extensive sex inequality: illegal but real practices of discrimination in hiring, pay and promotion; concentration of female workers in low-paid jobs and 'non-preferred' occupations; lack of significant easing of domestic burdens; difficulties experienced by employed mothers of small children; conflict between maternal and work roles; a wide discrepancy in terms of quantity and quality of leisure for women and men; and the survival of traditional values of male supremacy.

These manifestations of sex inequality are not essentially different from those prevailing in Western liberal democracies, but they demonstrate that the state-socialist countries have only partially attained their declared goal of sex equality. To be sure, there have been impressive achievements. As one would expect, the authorities have eliminated legal inequality between men and women, obviously the easiest step to take. More significantly, they have succeeded in broadening the accepted scope of women's education and work and in creating social provisions for maternity and child care. The near-universal participation of women in paid economic activity, the high proportion of women in professional occupations, the length of paid and unpaid maternity leave and other maternity benefits (the state-socialist societies do not regard motherhood as a private matter), and the now-widespread provision of child-care facilities in working hours are the most visible privileges women in the state-socialist societies enjoy over those in the capitalist ones. However, as I have noted, the creation of equal opportunities in education and employment have led to a multiplication rather than a re-definition of female roles, as women have continued to remain responsible for most of the labour in the home.

Why has sex equality been achieved only partially? What has held the state-socialist countries back? I have argued in the foregoing chapters that the persistence of sex inequality can be attributed to: (1) the relatively low level of economic development at the time of the socialist revolution (although this factor does not apply to Czechoslovakia and East Germany); (2) the Stalinist policy of rapid industrialisation, giving marked priority to the expansion of capital-intensive sectors and consequent low priority to easing women's burden in the home; (3) the minimal restructuring of the family; (4) the survival and reinforcement of traditional values and attitudes of male supremacy; (5) the lack of educational campaigns aimed at breaking down sex-role stereotypes; and (6) the nature of the state-socialist power structure. As the first five factors have been discussed extensively in the foregoing chapters, I shall here concentrate on an issue neglected thus far – the nature of the communist power structure – and show how it is related to some of the other factors.

Conflicting interpretations of how power is structured in the state-socialist societies reveal the complexity of the problem involved. The debates about the power structure in Soviet-type societies centre around the applicability of concepts of 'ruling class', *'nomenklatura'* (control over personnel appointments), 'elites' and 'ruling bureaucracy' (or bureaucracies).[3] For present purposes, it is sufficient to discuss the communist power structure in terms of elites and bureaucracies. The concept of elites is very useful in the analysis of social stratification of any kind, be it stratification based on income, education, sex, prestige or power. In turn, the concept of bureaucracy highlights the growing number of those who make their living by administering the lives of other human beings.

There are important differences between communist bureaucracies and bureaucracies of the Western type. Because of the overlapping of political and organisational structures, communist bureaucracies are strongly opposed to all organisational improvements which might endanger the existing balance of power. Moreover, because of the full control of the party-state over the economy and the interpretation of official ideology, communist bureaucracies can enforce and pursue aims of their own and cover up all sorts of organisational inefficiencies, instead of trying to implement targets determined by social demands and goals.

Marxist ideology essentially performs a legitimising function for those in power, although in certain circumstances with diminishing returns – as witness the case of post-1968 Czechoslovakia. Thus far, the socialist regimes have tried to reconcile ideology and reality by justifying their basic policies in Marxist terms. For instance, the repressive morality canonised during the Stalinist period is said to express the objective requirements of the first phase of the building of socialism; this is, of course, a doubtful explanation, but it is a useful legitimation.

In view of these characteristics, bureaucratic rule in the state-socialist societies does not conform to the values of egalitarianism. Political criteria seem to be as important as (and often more important than) expertise and professional qualifications; as a result, favouritism, clique-forming and patronage are significant characteristics of personnel policies. This subtle network of bureaucratic relationships makes the life of the elites much more comfortable and much easier than that of ordinary citizens: those who have the administrative power, who occupy strategic positions in the system of distribution, and who have the opportunity to control the allocation of sought-after goods, can appropriate an unfair share of what society can produce (Hirszowicz, 1976).

Equity in treatment of *all* ordinary citizens is difficult to accomplish in this kind of political system, but women are further disadvantaged by the persistence of attitudes of male supremacy among the elites. At a general level, Mandel (1975) argues that the tenacity with which sex-role stereotypes are held reflects the relatively recent emergence of the Soviet Union (and by extension many other areas of Eastern Europe) from feudal, agrarian societies and peasant ways of thinking. However, while the influence of the past is important in determining behaviour, one cannot help wondering why such rigid attitudes persist in East Germany and Czechoslovakia, countries that have long been industrialised. Moreover, these attitudes show little sign of weakening as industrialisation proceeds in the Soviet Union and elsewhere. In fact, private family sex-role training can be counteracted by public action (witness the case of Sweden) but, in Eastern Europe, the media and educational institutions (and generally the state apparatus) have, in recent years, done much to foster some traditional concepts and to impart to them an aura of socialist respectability. For example, etiquette books instruct the woman how to play a role that is essentially one of passive femininity – she is to be assisted on to buses and into her coat by a man, and he is the one to ask for a dance and to pay for the entertainment. Furthermore, recent pro-natalist policies have continually reinforced the idea that child-rearing is women's work. State-socialist legislation contains no provision for paternity leave.

One important manifestation of these lingering prejudices and their official sanction can be seen in the hesitation in ruling party circles to promote women to positions of real authority – witness the negligible number of women on the top *nomenklatura* list. Indeed, one could even argue that access to positions of political and managerial leadership is more difficult for women in the state-socialist societies than it is in the capitalist ones: the 'male chauvinist' prejudices (or authoritarian calculations) of powerful and highly selective elites in the former are more effective in 'keeping women in their place' than are the comparable prejudices of elites in less-controlled societies. *General* employment opportunities and child-care arrangements are, of course, superior in Eastern Europe, but access to *top* positions for career women is probably easier in some countries in the West.

Given the few women in leading positions in Eastern Europe, there have been few opportunities for them to influence priorities in economic planning or policies relating to the material reward structure of society. As a result, women have been political bystanders in a situation in which the prevailing strategy for industrialisation has had complex implications for sex equality. On the one hand, the pattern of economic growth in Eastern Europe, based as it has been on a quantitative rather than a qualitative development of the labour force, has required a substantial increase in the employment of women. On the other hand, the heavy emphasis placed upon increasing stocks of capital goods has led to wage disparities between the 'preferred' industrial occupations, largely dominated by men, and the 'non-preferred' occupations in the basically feminised service sector. Moreover, this emphasis has meant that low priority has been given to easing women's domestic responsibilities (as they have been eased in the West) by the relatively greater commercial provision of such aids as labour-saving devices and convenience foods. Thus, with so many women in the labour force, the state-socialist societies have been in a better position than Western capitalist ones to use available female talent. However, in practice, full utilisation of women's labour power has been precluded because of discriminatory practices and the failure to relieve women of the exhaustion they suffer from having to fulfil the dual role of housewife and worker.

Women are the victims of a further contradiction between their roles in social production and the reproduction of labour power, which stems from the structure of political power. Underlying the doctrinal commitment to a labour-extensive and heavy-industrial strategy of economic growth is a reluctance on the part of top bureaucracies to advocate any shift in production priorities that might undermine the position of managers of heavy industry and the military. However, this strategy has led, among other things, to the exhaustion of the supply of labour – in Czechoslovakia, for example, virtually all individual farmers and housewives have been drawn into the labour force. As the possibility of importing labour from non-socialist countries is limited for ideological and political reasons, further extensive growth depends upon increased levels of natural replacement in the labour force. Hence, we have seen the emergence of pro-natalist policies to reverse rapidly declining birthrates. As a result, women have been placed under increasing cross-pressures between having more children and remaining full-time in the labour force.

The reluctance of decision-makers in the state-socialist societies to switch to a more intensive form of growth, involving the improvement of labour productivity and greater emphasis upon consumer goods and services, can therefore be attributed largely to the strong opposition of communist bureaucracies to organisational improvements that might endanger the existing balance of power. An 'optimal' achievement of sex equality requires a reversal of this condition. Until social life is more effectively controlled by individuals, the economic and social emancipation of women gives them only an equal share in other forms of inequality.

STATE POLICY, THE SEXUAL DIVISION OF LABOUR AND SOCIAL CHANGE: THE CASE OF POPULATION CONTROL

There are obviously many issues one could discuss in an examination of the broader implications of state policies relating to women and the sexual division of labour. I shall restrict myself to one question to which I think this study has a particular contribution to offer: population policy. What do the comparative experiences of the East European countries tell us about the extent to which there is a unified socialist approach to the problem of reproducing labour power in the context of the severe labour shortages foreseen in the future? What can we learn from the East European experience of pro-natalist population policies about the effectiveness of this sort of planning in inducing desired patterns of social change?

While all East European societies have a state-owned, more-or-less centrally controlled and planned economy, and a politically dominant communist party, they do not constitute a monolithic entity. Considerable differences exist in social and economic development, urbanisation, living standards, social habits, religion and other characteristics, all of which have influenced and continue to influence population trends in varying degrees. All of the COMECON countries, therefore, have their unique features as well as common ones. All face somewhat similar population situations as a result of the official commitment to the strategy of labour-extensive growth, the gradual exhaustion of the labour supply and the inability to import labour from elsewhere, characteristics to which we referred in the previous section. By increasing the opportunity structure for women in the social sphere of production, and by implementing other policies favouring a lower birthrate,[4] the state-socialist countries have created a virtual certainty of future labour shortages. In the USSR, the size of the 20–59 age-group will fall in the late 1980s, after a big rise in the 1970s and early 1980s. And there will be fewer labour reserves to draw from: in 1959, there were 18 million housewives outside the labour force, but, in 1970, only 6 million out of a total population of 250 million.

As a result, we have witnessed the emergence in Eastern Europe of pro-natalist population policies that attempt to reverse this declining birthrate and find ways of inducing women to have more children. However, while all East European countries are seeking to increase their birthrates, their policies in this respect have differed both in the areas of procreation and family welfare.

Compared with the advanced industrial countries of the West, modern contraceptive methods have only recently become available in Eastern Europe. Nevertheless, the region has a long history of socially acceptable illegal and legal abortions, and, on the whole, it is considered neither sinful nor disgraceful to terminate an unwanted pregnancy. However, the extent to which a woman has a legal right to terminate her pregnancy differs in the various socialist countries. Only in the Soviet Union and the GDR[5] is abortion available on request during the first 3 months of pregnancy, provided that the woman has had no previous abortions during the preceding 12 months. In Czechoslovakia, where it has recently become more difficult to obtain an abortion, each woman seeking one must submit her case for decision to a special abortion commission in her locality.

Thus far, only Rumania has made abortions illegal, although the Soviet Union had such a policy in the 1930s and 1940s. In Rumania, abortions were freely available until 1965, when four abortions took place for every live birth – the world's highest recorded figure. Abortion was made illegal in October 1966, and this measure was coupled with increased family allowances, taxes on childless adults, prolonged divorce procedures, and a cessation of official importation of contraceptive pills and inter-uterine devices (legislation not dissimilar to that in effect in the Soviet Union in the 1930s and 1940s). A dramatic rise in the birthrate followed, from 14.3 per 1,000 population in 1966 to 27.3 in 1967. But women gradually returned to traditional birth-control methods (*coitus interruptus* in particular), illegal abortions and smuggled contraceptives; by 1974, the rate was down to 20 per 1,000 population.

Family-allowance schemes in Eastern Europe have been broadly similar (favouring two to four children in a family), although the Soviet scheme seems to be effective only at the top end of the scale (eight or nine children in a family), and has therefore been less geared than those elsewhere to encouraging procreation. As regards maternity allowances, the state-socialist countries have differed. Monthly payments to mothers who wish to stay at home to raise a child during its first 3 years are now provided in Hungary, Czechoslovakia, Bulgaria and, most recently, the GDR, but not in Poland or the USSR, although, as we have noted, the Soviet Union has adopted such a policy in principle.

East Germany, which has the lowest birthrate in the entire communist world (10.8 per 1,000 population in 1975), has opted for expanded and improved child-care facilities rather than for fiscal incentives that would encourage individual forms of upbringing.[6] The GDR probably has the most highly developed system of child-care facilities in the world. In 1975, 82 per cent of all pre-school children and 45 per cent of children under 4 years old used public child-care facilities; 70 per cent of all pupils between the 1st and 4th grades attended after-school centres ('Populační politika v NDR', 1977).

Czechoslovakia, which is almost as prosperous, has very few such facilities – no more than 12 per cent of children under 4 years old are cared for in creches. Many influential Czech and Hungarian psychologists believe, unlike the Germans, that institutional care, even if only during the day, has detrimental effects on a child's physical, intellectual and emotional development, and that maternal upbringing in the early years is preferable. The policy-makers in these countries have also found public child-care facilities too expensive and consequently have opted for the cheaper alternative of maternity allowances.

How does one evaluate maternity allowances? Insofar as they represent an attempt to transform maternity into a paid social activity, these allowances give new social recognition and prestige to the role of the mother, thus expanding the opportunity for choice among women – but women only. Thus far, men in the state-socialist societies have not been given as much opportunity as women to spend time with their children. As far as I know, Sweden is the only country in the world that has adopted a policy of paternity leaves and allowances, thus altering the sexual division of labour with respect to child care.

When we look at the question of effectiveness, we can see that these policies have met with varying degrees of success. The birthrate has gone up most noticeably in Czechoslovakia (from 15.9 per 1,000 population in 1970 to 19.2 in 1976), and is now has one of the highest in Europe. The Hungarian birthrate, however, has risen only slightly – from 14.7 per 1,000 population in 1970 to 15.0 in 1974. Thus, the long-term effects of various pro-natalist measures are difficult to determine. It is quite possible that the birthrate might start to decline again in Czechoslovakia when the age-composition of the population changes. It is also possible that national governments may find that the cost involved in paying maternity allowances and supporting large families is too high compared to the value of the results. Furthermore, once birth-control methods are widely known and available, it is families, and above all women, who will decide how many children there shall be. The Five-Year Plan in Czechoslovakia did not envisage a 'population explosion' such as has occurred and as a result did not expand the network of crèches and kindergartens sufficiently. Many mothers who are finding it difficult to place their children in a kindergarten will certainly think twice before deciding to have another child.

It is therefore quite probable that without more concessions from the government and the male population, women will prove reluctant to co-operate with plans to bear and raise more children. While the state-socialist maternity laws and benefits are very impressive when compared with those of most capitalist countries, they fall short of providing any satisfactory solution to the problem of integrating women's productive and reproductive roles. The policies of East European governments have attempted an integration that trims women's productive roles to allow them to play a larger part in the reproduction of labour power, thus sustaining the sexual division of labour and jeopardising the considerable gains that women have made in social production and social life generally.

At this point, it is important to ask whether pro-natalist goals are compatible with those of feminism and, if so, what kind of supportive social-welfare policy is needed to encourage voluntary motherhood and sex equality.[7] Where a socialist country wants an increased birthrate, one strategy might involve providing 7-day, 24-hour nurseries; encouraging commune-living; implementing various schemes of community care; and ensuring equal participation of men in child-rearing. The case for child day-care centres would be made on the grounds that they freed both parents to take up paid employment, not merely women; nor should talk of 'dual roles and children' be confined to women. Only in these ways could such a population policy be reconciled with the goals of feminism.

SOCIALISM AND THE WOMEN'S MOVEMENT

In assessing the relevance of the socialist experience of feminism to the contemporary Women's Liberation Movement in the West, it is instructive to pursue the following questions. Do orthodox Marxist assumptions about women workers and their revolutionary potential need reexamination? Can we learn anything from the strategic conflict between an independent women's movement and a single revolutionary party of the working class? What have been the shortcomings of the socialist theory and practice of feminism, and to what extent can they be avoided?

Orthodox Marxism has considered gender differentiation less important than the division between social classes, as defined by their relationship to the means of production. This has meant that, at the level of strategy, the class struggle and the exploitation of the industrial worker have been seen as politically more significant than the specific oppression experienced by women. The socialist parties saw women as having revolutionary potential only when they entered the industrial labour force. This attitude was reflected at the organisational level, for few systematic attempts were made to mobilise the wives of industrial workers, although some socialists tried to do this individually in their personal relationships. For instance, G. Bareš, a Czech historian, noted that many Czech workers before and after the First World War gave their wives and girl-friends Bebel's book in the hope of politicising them and drawing them into the proletarian struggle (Bareš, 1962: 5; Scott, 1974: 57–8).

We need to know more, too, about the implications for political education of husband-wife relationships in working-class families. Traditionally, Marxist theory and strategy have had little to contribute to our understanding of the changing social relations of the family. Not only have housewives and their labour in the home been considered marginal to the socialist struggle, but so have other 'personal' concerns. While the East European Marxists have been right in emphasising the centrality of production, they have been wrong in assuming that the social relations of personal life can be transformed without conscious struggle. They appear to have erred in arguing that changes in the relationships of production would necessarily transform, as if by reflex, the sphere of private and family life (Zaretsky, n.d.: 73–4).

In addition, socialists have paid little attention either to the question of male prejudice against women or to discriminatory practices against women members of the party. Male hostility to women in the labour market and within the party has seldom been openly discussed in the socialist parties, although there have been occasional pronouncements on the need to combat male prejudice. The available evidence suggests that men have shown little interest in the issues that have concerned the socialist women's movement. These issues were seen as unimportant 'women's work', to be left entirely to the women members of the party.

As we have seen, the socialists and the communists initially opposed separate women's organisations. However, recognising the special needs of women and the need to develop their leadership capacities in all-female meetings, Zetkin argued for separate women's sections or departments within the party framework. She was thus suggesting that the idea of separatism does have certain positive values *vis-à-vis* the party's strategy towards women workers; enhancing women's support for social democracy and also, for women themselves, increasing their confidence and developing their leadership capacities. However, the special methods of agitation and organisation of women workers were to be stopped at the point where they disturbed the unity of the working class. Class oppression came first, sex oppression second.

The Bolsheviks were also opposed at first to a separate organisation for women workers. They believed that independent activity by women workers would undermine the party unity necessary for overthrowing capitalism (a view that remains current in many left-wing groups today). The Bolsheviks were compelled to revise their assumptions about the 'woman question' and a separate women's section when women workers began to demonstrate their political independence. The growing militancy of many Russian working women after 1910 challenged the Marxist practice of subordinating women's struggle to the class struggle and called into question the prevailing view that a separate female organisation was necessarily 'bourgeois'. In order not to lose the political support of women workers to the opponents of Bolshevism, the party was compelled to incorporate women's issues in its programme of agitation and to find ways of recruiting more women.

As a result, the Bolsheviks abandoned their initial opposition and established separate women's sections. These, however, remained subordinate to the party, its goals and strategy, and did not really function as continuing pressure groups having a voice in policy-making at all levels of the hierarchy. Furthermore, the party, rather than women themselves, set the tasks and goals of the liberating process. It was assumed that women would help themselves by helping the revolution, which meant implementing tasks set by the party – providing electoral assistance (in the case of the German SPD), recruiting women to the party, celebrating International Women's Day, publishing a women's paper and organising women's conferences.

The question of autonomy became crucial with the communist seizure of power. In Czechoslovakia, the establishment of socialism was used to legitimise the abolition of the women's section: in line with the orthodox Marxist argument that there is no distinct 'woman question', it was claimed that women were emancipated in a socialist society and that they, together with men, would express themselves through other organisations. As women's entry to social production was supposed to bring their full emancipation, the political activities of women were transferred to the mixed trades unions. However, this transition came about slowly.

The resolution of the Presidium of the Central Council of the Trades Unions, which laid down the principles of trade-union activity among women, was passed only in 1957. Female demands did not figure on the list of trade-union priorities until 1959, more than a decade after the communist victory, during which time women's share in the labour force had increased from 38 to 43 per cent. From the point of view of women, experiencing so many new problems and difficulties in their daily lives, there was certainly still a need for their own organisation!

Under pressure from the few women members of the Central Committee of the Communist Party and the Central Committee of the Union of Women, and in response to the debates about the problems of 'over-feminisation' and the 'social profitability of women's employment', the Czechoslovak Communist Party began in the mid-1960s to re-examine its attitude towards a women's organisation in a society that claimed to be socialist. A separate women's organisation was eventually established in 1967, but, with the brief exception of the 'Prague Spring', under the full control of the party. In all state-socialist societies, the ruling communist parties insist on a monopoly of power and doctrine, and a potentially autonomous political force would be regarded as a threat to this monopoly. An independent feminist movement of the current Western type therefore cannot legally emerge to campaign against male domination or for change in the sexual division of labour.

The advice centres run by the women's organisation in Czechoslovakia today do not, by and large, challenge existing sexual stereotypes and the division of labour. They rather suggest ways in which women can become more efficient in housekeeping, child care, solving marital problems, etc. – in short, ways in which they can cope better with their present overload. The existence of the 'double burden' of females is recognised, but accepted as being, by and large, inevitable. Discussions and proposals for change are conducted in terms of deficiencies in human nature, such as male resistance to housework, or of inefficiencies in the consumer sector of the economy, rather than in terms of structural, historical analysis. The traditional Marxist interpretation of female oppression, formulated by Engels, still constitutes the guideline. The need to go beyond Engels to develop a Marxist-feminist perspective incorporating analysis of such issues as domestic work, sexuality and emotionality, has not been given the recognition in Eastern Europe that it has in the West by Marxists associated with the Women's Liberation Movement.

As far as the general question of socialist women's organisation is concerned, the main historical problems seem to have been reaching women (who were neither in the mass militant nor political), integration of women's issues at the party level and the lack of influence of women on decision-making within the party. If the goals of feminism and socialism are to be reconciled, these problems have to be avoided. A women's section of a revolutionary socialist party today has to ensure that issues concerning women are seen by the party as integral to its overall programme, and to influence policy decisions to this effect at all levels of party hierarchy. If and when the party seizes state power, women's influence on decision-making has to extend to economic planning and the allocation of available resources to make sure that women's issues are not sacrificed to 'more important' male issues. In other words, there is a need for an autonomous Marxist-feminist power-base *before* a revolution, sharing in priority-allocation *after* it.

The experience of Eastern Europe clearly shows that a state-socialist transformation is insufficient to bring about the liberation of women. Women have entered the productive labour force in large numbers, yet still suffer from inequality – an important lesson for women socialists (and men too) who argue that the socialisation of the means of production is all that is required. Nevertheless, the cases we have studied do confirm the thesis that female participation in the labour force is a *pre-requisite* of emancipation, and that this participation strongly influences women's status in society.

My conclusion is that the liberation of women in any society involves, therefore, a dual process: entry into the national economy and relative withdrawal from the domestic economy. In Eastern Europe, for a variety of reasons, the two processes have not proceeded in a smooth and simultaneous way. Experience demonstrates that the burden of domestic work is not automatically lessened by nationalisation of the means of production, and confirms that structural changes must be accompanied by a *cultural revolution* aimed at the elimination of sex-role stereotypes. Only the equal sharing of domestic work by both spouses (or several adults in a communal setting) can lead to the elimination of excessive drudgery. It is hard to see how such a transformation can occur without a social and political climate supportive of both the socialisation of housework and child care and of new cultural dynamics governing male-female re-lationships. In the absence of such a climate, the development of which would appear to require many more women in positions of political authority, women in general can hardly hope to play equal roles in society.

Thus, one cannot but agree with the position taken by many socialist feminists in the West today that the struggle for women's liberation has its own specificity. It is related to the class struggle, but it is at the same time independent of it.

Notes

Chapter 1

1. However, there is an excellent new study published after this book went to press: Gail Warshofsky Lapidus, *Women in Soviet Society: Equality, Development and Social Change*, Los Angeles, University of California Press, 1978.
2. For an explanation of the difference between the social and the individual levels of analysis, see Galtung's discussion of the 'fallacy of the wrong level' (Galtung, 1967: 37–48).
3. The literature on biological and psychological sex differences is so vast that one can cite only few examples. Briefly, the sexes differ in the way they think, perceive, aspire, experience anxiety, daydream and play competitive games (Hochschild, 1973). Some studies document these differences; others try to explain them as due to hormones, chromosomes, internal organs, instinct or 'innate' psychological traits on the one hand, or upbringing on the other. The main debate is therefore between biological and socio-cultural explanations. The former is summarised by Hutt (1972) and Bardwick (1971), while the latter is supported by evidence on cultural variation by Mead (1948, 1950) and Weisstein (1971). The most comprehensive treatment of the nature of sexual differentiation has been written by Money and Erhardt (1972). Their multidisciplinary approach (they utilise genetics, embryology, endocrinology, psychology and anthropology) focuses on the interaction of hereditary endowment and environmental influence rather than on the old, rather outdated dichotomy of nature versus nurture. Their findings indicate that the difference between man and man, or woman and woman, can be as great as between man and woman.
4. There are no official Soviet statistics on the distribution of earnings and income, and it was only in the mid-1960s that the authorities resumed publication of data on average earnings. Only figures relating to average earnings in particular sectors and for state employees as a whole are published by the Soviet authorities. Since 1960 a number of monographs and papers on income distribution have appeared in the USSR, but they do not contain explicit figures and are restricted to indirect statistics and graphs. Indirect statistics refer to family budget surveys, income-distribution surveys, earning censuses and earning surveys; the graphical material contains histograms or polygons that represent the distribution of earnings or incomes for specific groups in particular years. Enough information is given in these monographs and papers to permit most of the available distributions to be reconstructed with reasonable accuracy. See Wiles and Markowski (1971), Wiles (1974, 1975) and McAuley (1977) for Western estimates of the Soviet distribution of earnings and income.

Chapter 2

1. One has to make an important distinction between sociology and anthropology, and the assertion certainly applies to sociology only. Social anthropology has studied sex roles extensively, as sex is the principal source of the division of labour in primitive societies. The most famous, if controversial studies are by Margaret Mead (1948, 1950). See also Douglas (1966: 140–58), Friedl (1975), Kessler (1976) and Reiter (1975).

2. For a criticism of this approach, see Acker (1973) and Oakley (1972b: ch. 1, esp. 8–14). See also Rossi (1969) and Berreman (1972), who discuss the ways in which sex-role differentiation differs from stratification based on race, ethnicity or religion.

3. See, for instance, the outline of Bell's and Vogel's influential reader entitled *A Modern Introduction to the Family* (1960). The possibility of 'strain' or conflict arising out of the existing sex-role differentiation is nowhere suggested.

4. See Komarovsky (1950), Mead (1950), Moore (1958), McKee and Sheriffs (1959), Friedan (1963), Rossi (1964), Gavron (1966) and Oakley (1974b).

5. For empirical evidence, consult Chesler (1971) and Gove and Tudor (1973).

6. See Klein and Myrdal (1956), J. M. and R. E. Pahl (1971) and R. and R. Rappoport (1971).

7. For a criticism of functionalism as a weak explanatory theory, see Hempel (1959) and Isajiw (1968).

8. See J. A. and O. Banks (1964a), Ehrlich (1971), Laws (1971), Middleton (1974) and Oakley (1974a: 156–85).

Chapter 3

1. For a sympathetic anthropological critique of Engels's analysis of the position of women in primitive societies of the remote past, see Leacock (1972), Sacks (1975) and Gough (1975). See also Delamont (1972) and Delmar (1976).

2. A distinction needs to be drawn between personal and private property. The former refers to individual items of consumption (dwelling, clothing and various consumer durables), while the latter refers to the individual ownership of the means of production, either directly, through a family firm, or indirectly, through numerous shares.

3. See Benston (1969), M. and J. Rowntree (1970), Morton (1970), Edwards (1971), Della Costa (1972), Harrison (1973), Secombe (1974, 1975), Coulson, Magas and Wainwright (1975) and Gardiner (1974, 1975).

4. See Part III.

5. This also applies to Western men and women and to much of Western feminist thought of that period. For an evaluation of the very strong puritan element in Western feminism, see J. and O. Banks (1964b: 107–13).

6. Since these views were expressed in a private conversation with Clara Zetkin (they were not intended for publication), one cannot be dogmatic about what Lenin would have said in public, had he decided to speak about sexuality. Zetkin cannot be considered a reliable source; she was elderly and, when she wrote her reminiscences, faction lines were already being drawn. Moreover, Lenin's downgrading of the importance of sexuality was time-specific: it referred to the revolutionary period in Russia and that of the expected revolution in Germany. One could be reasonably confident that he would

evaluate sexuality differently today. Both Lenin and Engels were open as regards the future.

7. The other East European countries, especially Hungary, differ in this respect. See, for instance, the works of Hegedus, Markus, Heller and Vajda (1976) which are now available in English.

8. For instance, all official Soviet biographies or references to Alexandra Kollontai emphasise her diplomatic career rather than her involvement in the women's movement. Her ideas on sexuality are either not mentioned at all, or disapproved of.

9. Marcuse's analysis in terms of 'repressive de-sublimation' might be applicable here. See Marcuse (1964, 1966).

Chapter 4

1. For radical feminism, the 'root' cause of the oppression of women is their ability to bear children. This is not just because maternity has been socially exploited to oppress women, but because *in itself* it is a brutal, painful experience. In Firestone's view, the 'ultimate' revolution, both ecological and feminist, is not just against a specific form of society (such as capitalism) but against Nature. Science and technology would conquer the trap of biology and eliminate, among other things, reproductive distinctions. Cybernation, test-tube babies and other technological advances would put an end to all painful and joyless labour, i.e., labour in the factory, child-bearing, making human living a 'real' possibility. While the basic premise of this perspective is rather utopian and oversimplified, Firestone's analysis does lead to some very pertinent insights: the shared oppression of women and children, the permeation of all cultures by a fundamental pattern of family relationships, the psychology of oppression and the various mystifications that surround women, pregnancy, 'being in love', etc (Mitchell, 1971: 87–9).

2. For a detailed analysis of the emotional and ideological changes in family life over the last 300 years, see Shorter (1975).

Chapter 5

1. The material presented in this chapter is a revised version of Heitlinger (1977*b*).

2. An extensive review of bourgeois feminism is outside the scope of this book. However, it is sufficient for our purposes to point out what it was that the bourgeois feminists were advocating and where they differed from the socialists. Western feminists were, as a rule, legalist and moderate upper-class ladies or middle-class professional women who sought to broaden existing 'male rights' into 'universal human rights'. They dedicated themselves to philanthropic activities, educational reforms and lobbying for the recognition of equality of rights and opportunities with men. In most cases the bourgeois feminists were interested in obtaining the same privileges as the men of their class and their demands did not go beyond the framework of capitalist society. For instance, the demand for equality in income ownership in marriage was aimed against the male's exclusive power of disposal over this income, while the socialists were fighting against the very existence of such income and the social privileges based upon it. The bourgeois feminists were unwilling to submerge the women's cause in the general cause of social or national liberation, while the socialists placed the freeing of women in the context of

freedom for all subjected social groups. The socialists also opposed the feminist attempt to unify women of all classes, on the grounds that it challenged the class allegiance of working women.

3. The analysis of the German SPD is based on secondary sources, especially Thönnessen (1973).

4. There is little evidence to show any concern with the question of female labour, that is, with the aspect of women's emancipation immediately affecting the workers in the period before 1863. See Thönnessen (1973: 13).

5. The International Working Men's Association, retrospectively to become known as the First International, was established in London in 1864. Although Marx was given the task of writing the inaugural address, there were only a few Marxists in the IWA at the start. Nonetheless, the supporters of the right of women to work eventually had their way and the organisation's congress in Geneva rejected the call for a ban on women's employment and supported special legislation protecting the 'weaker female organism' from working conditions harmful to it. The general reaction following the Franco-Prussian war and the defeat of the Paris Commune, as well as the renewed rift between the anarchists and the Marxists, compelled the First International to move its headquarters to the United States, where it was quietly disbanded in 1876. When the nearly 400 labour and socialist delegates from twenty countries founded the Second International in Paris in 1889 on the hundredth anniversary of the fall of the Bastille, the SPD, at that time the strongest party, and with the strongest Marxist orientation, became its acknowledged leader. See Thönnessen (1973: 21–4) and Scott (1974: 5–3).

6. In this respect, one could see a similarity between the Lasalleans and the campaign for wages for housework.

7. The anti-socialist laws were introduced by the chancellor, Bismarck, in 1878, when the SPD was already polling half a million votes and had elected August Bebel to the Reichstag. In spite of the emergency laws, the party continued to gain followers and after the laws were abrogated in 1890, it received a million and a half votes, one-fifth of the total. The rapid industrialisation which followed Germany's unification in 1871 was accompanied by the growth of the German proletariat and of its trade-union and political activities. The centre of the European working-class movement moved from France to Germany.

8. As was argued in Chapter 3, current archeological and anthropological data suggest that sex oppression pre-dates class oppression, although there is some evidence to support the argument that the position of women relative to men deteriorated with the advent of class societies and colonial conquest.

9. Quoted in Thönnessen (1973: 30).

10. Zetkinová (1961: 88–9). Czech translation from German original.

11. Bareš (1962: 5). Also quoted in Scott (1974: 57–8).

12. The distinction between bourgeois feminism and socialist feminism is an interesting one that would repay elaboration to explain some of the differences in the women's movement today.

13. Zetkin (1960), a Russian translation from the German. At the Gotha congress it was decided by a majority vote to print Zetkin's speech in the form of a pamphlet.

14. This system was set up at the SPD conference in Berlin in 1892. Although the Combination Laws forbade women to belong to political organisations, they

did not affect the activity of individuals, so that the laws could be circumvented by a network of individual representatives. For a more detailed description of this system, see Thönnessen (1973: 48–9).

15. All quotations reprinted from Thönnessen (1973: 66–7).

16. For a more detailed account of the feminist movement in Russia, see Selivanova (1923), Stites (1973) and Bobroff (1973).

17. For the official account of the conference, see Stasova (1958: 195, 219–20). An alternative interpretation is offered by Kollontai (1972b) in her autobiography and by Bobroff (1973). Bobroff used this episode to substantiate her thesis that the Bolsheviks were initially hostile to the 'woman question'. She does say that there were objections to working with a bourgeois group, but her argument is that the party saw any woman's work as deviation. She ignores the fact that the positions taken on the congress were ultimately determined by wider tactical considerations and not by considerations of sexual politics alone. The Russian Social Democratic Party was at that time divided into various groupings, basically over the question of the bourgeois or the socialist nature of the future revolution. The immediate question was how to react to the official establishment of the Duma (parliament). The Mensheviks were for participation in the assembly and for alliance with the leftist liberal parties; Lenin's Bolshevik group was for participation, but for maintaining social democratic autonomy. A group known as the 'Ultimatists' was in favour of participation only if it were of an uncompromising nature and another group, the *otzovists*, were against participation under any circumstances. In view of these strategic differences, it is hardly surprising that there was some hesitancy and confusion about how to respond to a major bourgeois conference. And since the St Petersburg Committee was at this time controlled by the Ultimatists, it is not surprising that the St Petersburg party apparatus did not make a very vigorous intervention on the issue of a bourgeois women's congress (Holt, 1976b). By failing to place conflicts in the overall political context of that period, Bobroff distorts their meaning and gives an inaccurate interpretation.

18. Halle (1938: 89) claims that in the winter of 1907–8, 300 women agitators, charged with the task of winning the proletarian women for the revolutionary class struggle, began agitating among textile workers, where most working women were concentrated.

19. Between 1901 and 1910, the number of women in the labour force increased by 18 per cent, while that of men increased by only 1.3 per cent (Bobroff, 1973: 550). Factory owners preferred to hire women because they were more docile, only rarely went on strike and could be paid less money. It would be interesting to know how men reacted to this situation and whether this particular hiring practice had been used successfully elsewhere.

20. Bobroff talks of the need for the Bolsheviks to have encouraged a mass women's movement and recognised its autonomy, but during the period under discussion the basis for a large-scale women's movement did not exist. The overwhelming majority of Russian women were 'backward' and politically conservative – their social location made this inevitable. On the other hand, one needs to point out that while the working-class women's movement was insignificant in proportion to the total female population, its political significance exceeded its numerical strength.

21. International congresses of the social democratic women's movement also used to take place in connection with the main 'male' congresses – a further

illustration of the auxiliary status of the socialist women's movement within the working-class movement as a whole.

22. The proceedings of the conference are published in *Otchet o pervoi mezhdunarodnoi konferencii kommunistok* (1921).

23. *Decisions of the Third Congress of the Communist International* (1921: 102).

24. The Czech Social Democratic Party was founded in 1878. Its first publication designed specifically for women, *Ženský list* (Women's Gazette) was launched in 1892. Like the SPD women's conferences, the first congress of Czech working-class women, which took place in Kolín in 1905, criticised the limitations of bourgeois feminism. The resolutions of the congress called for shortening of working hours, abolition of Sunday and night work, social insurance and protection of pregnant and nursing mothers. The Czech socialist women also attended the two women's congresses of the Second International. See Vaníčková (1971).

25. *Komunistka* played the same role within the CCP as *Die Gleichheit* did within the SPD.

26. The granting of female suffrage after the end of the First World War in most European countries took the wind out of the feminist sails, so to speak. The suffragettes felt things had been achieved and there was no longer a need for their activity. The decline in feminism meant that the communists had to worry less about feminist influence on working-class women than had their social democratic predecessors.

Chapter 6

1. While, in European Russia, female emancipation was a by-product of broader revolutionary schemes, women's liberation in Central Asia was a primary issue *par excellence*, an important catalyst for generating the revolutionary process itself. Muslim women in Central Asia were identified as a 'surrogate proletariat' and their oppression singled out by the Bolsheviks as the main structural weak point in the traditional, highly integrated Muslim order. As women were seen as particularly susceptible to militant revolutionary appeal, *Zhenotdel's* activities in Central Asia were much broader in scope than in Russia, more specialised, self-conscious and autonomous. For an excellent account of feminism and the Bolshevik strategies towards women in Central Asia between 1919 and 1929, see Massell (1974).

2. Not unlike consciousness-raising today! The chief aim of consciousness-raising groups in the West today is to make women more confident, less reluctant to speak and act in the presence of men, and to enable them to realise their full potential.

3. See Volkova (1975) for a content-analysis of Soviet women's magazines in the 1920s and today. While the 1920s' issues are full of information about the theory and practice of socialist women's movements at home and abroad, the current Soviet women's magazines tend to concentrate on mass entertainment, dress patterns, beauty advice, cooking recipes, guides to children's reading, poetry, short stories, interviews with public figures, colour photographs, etc. Politics does not figure prominently, although it is not entirely ignored.

4. The vast majority of both men and women were initially quite unsympathetic to feminism. Many women could neither understand nor accept any change

from their traditional way of life. For example, in Central Asia between 1924 and 1926, Muslim women did not respond as much as was expected. They did not unveil, they failed to vote or otherwise assert their newly proffered rights, they avoided contact with Soviet institutions, and they failed to bring their grievances to Soviet courts. Even if they attended a *Zhenotdel* – sponsored club, a handicraft or consumer's co-operative, or a literacy circle, they tended to retain their veils and shun communication, commitments and action that would in any way violate traditional taboos and provoke opprobrium from the community or kin group. Early recruits to feminism in Central Asia consisted largely of maltreated wives, wives of polygamous men, recent child brides, orphans, widows, divorcees and menial employees in well-to-do households, who were all to some extent marginal to the traditional society. However, despite the initial setbacks and great male opposition, *Zhenotdel's* attempt to organise native women met with a huge success. See Massell (1974).

5. Her speech was published in *Rabotnica*, no. 43, November 1929.
6. The exact date of the abolition of *Zhenotdel* is unknown. Rowbotham (1972) gives 1929, but this is at variance with the Russian sources. After all, Artiuchina gave her speech at the end of 1929. Massell (1974) does not give an exact date and Stites (1973: 473) claims that *Zhenotdel* was abolished in 1930 as part of the reorganisation of the Secretariat of the Central Committee. In this chapter, I have used the information given by Stites.
7. Major changes in the status of women were the result of the overall policies of the regime, which are discussed in 'Part III.

Chapter 7

1. An abridged version of this chapter was presented as a paper at the Ninth World Congress of Sociology, Uppsala, 14–19 August 1978.
2. The trades union works committees deal with workers' grievances concerning working conditions at offices and other enterprises. They investigate industrial accidents, occupational illnesses, causes of working disability, etc. and arrange for compensation. They welcome comments and suggestions with regard to a general improvement of hygiene and working conditions, such as provision of protective clothing or warm drinks, adjustment of working tools and facilities, etc.
3. This was officially acknowledged in an internal publication of the ideological section of the party's Central Committee, entitled *Figures, News, Articles: the Leninist Concept of the Woman Question and Topical Problems of the Women's Movement at Present*, Prague, 1970 (my translation).
4. This particular aspect of women's inequality will be discussed in Chapter 15.
5. To the best of my knowledge, women's absenteeism on the grounds of their children's sickness has not been substantially reduced to this date. Passing resolutions is one thing, their implementation quite another.
6. This issue will be discussed extensively in Chapter 12.
7. Examples will be presented in Chapter 12.
8. Small extracts from the action programme were published in *Vlasta*, no. 28, 10 July 1968. Since all official publications issued in 1968 have been removed from public and university libraries in Czechoslovakia, I have been unable to obtain a copy of the document. The 1968 issues of the women's magazine

Vlasta, which are used as the main source of information in this text, were obtained at the British Library.

9. In January 1969, like the rest of the country, the organisation became federal, with autonomous Czech and Slovak sections.

10. Jarmila Knoblochová at the session of the Central Committee of the Czech Union of Women on 6–7 May 1969, published in *Vlasta*, no. 20, 29 May 1969.

11. This document was prepared for the April 1974 Congress of the Czechoslovak Union of Women and was kindly made available to me by the CUW secretariat.

Chapter 8

1. Russian populists in the 19th century believed that Russia possessed in the peasant commune, the *mir*, a relic of a primitive state of harmony existing before man enslaved himself to such abstract products of his alienated reason as the state. They also believed the *mir*, if developed into conscious socialism, could provide the basis for a new age in which men would fulfil themselves as integral beings (Kelly, 1975).

2. Reich (1969: 212–34) describes youth communes in some detail, but his objectivity is rather doubtful. Wesson (1963) is more detached and scholarly, but the discussion of spontaneous youth communes is not his primary concern.

3. The idea of men doing the cooking was even more radical and as such unlikely even to have occurred to them!

4. It is significant that the Left opposition made no complaints or suggestions on this score during the 1920s and allowed the debate on the 1926 marriage code to pass without comment.

5. In failing to consider the possibility that housework could be also done by men, Ostrovskaya followed the general party line of concentrating not on the attitudes of men directly, but rather on those of women.

6. This policy is still pursued today – Soviet industrial and military power has been built largely at the expense of consumer industries and the standard of living, both of which are well below Western levels.

7. We have to bear in mind that the notion of the commune as an alternative to the family never represented more than a minority trend of 'leftist deviation' within the Bolshevik Party. There were certainly changes with respect to the family in the 1930s, but there was also basic continuity. The emphasis on strengthening the family was also a response to the massive problems that accumulated during and immediately after the civil war. There were 7 million homeless children in the 1920s, many of whom were turning to juvenile delinquency. The magnitude of the problem and the methods of dealing with it through children's colonies are discussed by Madison (1968: 39–41) and Fitzpatrick (1970: 229–30). Juvenile delinquency is discussed in Makarenko (1954) and Hazard (1953: 252–3). The complexity of that period and the reasons for changes in family policy are summarised in Geiger (1968: 43–106) and Bronfenbrenner (1968).

8. Increases in divorce rates have accompanied urbanisation, industrialisation and the relaxation of strict divorce laws in most countries. For example, following the 1968 changes in Canadian divorce regulations, the crude divorce rate jumped from 54.8 divorces per 100,000 population in 1968 to 124.2 the following year, and continued to rise until it reached 200.6 divorces per

100,000 in 1974. When divorces are expressed in relation to the population at risk (married women) the increases are equally dramatic, increasing from 248.6 divorces per 100,000 married women in 1968 to 854.9 in 1974 (Boyd, 1977).

Chapter 9

1. A study prepared by the Royal Commission on the Status of Women in Canada estimated that the work of housewives amounted to 11 per cent of the gross national product. An estimate made in the United States, based on a somewhat different method, imputed for 1965 a value of slightly more than 21 per cent of the gross national product to housewives. As in the West, Eastern European countries do not take the economic value of housework into consideration in their computation of their gross national products.

2. Even this figure is an overestimate, since it included dinners prepared in *all* public institutions, including those whose primary purpose is not public catering, such as hospitals, boarding-schools or prisons. As the latter are grouped together with restaurants, canteens, schools and holiday resorts, the final figure is distorted and overestimated (Kurganov, 1967: 221).

3. See Meissner, Humphreys, Meiss and Scheu (1975). Shopping and work involving food and clothes were divided into regular and irregular categories. Irregular work on food and clothes included canning, baking, sewing, mending, and fruit- and vegetable-pickling. Irregular purchases included shopping for clothes, household equipment, car, leisure goods, house or apartment, and commercial services. The corresponding regular housework items were cooking the daily meals, laundry and ironing, and shopping for groceries and toilet articles. Sundry services included pick-up and delivery of persons and things, the rare case of fetching a cleaner or gardener, household accounting, animal care, and work entailed by leisure activities. Repairs and maintenance involved work on appliances, cars, bicycles, boats and other leisure equipment, the yard garden (but not gardening proper). Building included major construction and remodelling.

4. The time-budget data and other survey material presented in this book should be treated cautiously. Unlike the Canadian survey, the meanings of Soviet surveys are often not at all clear and sometimes there are obvious mistakes in calculations (as in Table 9.6).

5. For a comparative cross-cultural analysis of the patterns of leisure distribution between men and women, see Szalai (1972).

Chapter 10

1. It is interesting to note that more men in the West are entering schoolteaching and graduate nursing. For instance, the percentage of female teachers in Canada declined from 73 per cent in 1951 to 71 per cent in 1961, and of graduate nurses from 98 per cent to 96 per cent. The relative changes in the sex-typing of these jobs represent real declines for women, since the female percentages dropped (albeit marginally) in the only two *professional* occupations that are significant for women workers in Canada. At the same time, the proportion of women grew by more than 10 per cent in two relatively low-skilled, low-paid occupations, janitors and sales clerks, and by 8 per cent in another, waitresses and bartenders (H. and P. Armstrong, 1975: 373).

2. Local soviets are fat less ceremonial than is generally believed, especially on locational decisions, zoning, environmental controls, etc. They are politically weak, but there is much 'politics' within them. See Hough (1969) and Taubman (1973).

Chapter 11

1. Mandel's reflection on men and prams and on women wanting to care for their children has to be treated with caution, since his reportage is too biased to constitute acceptable sociological evidence. What Mandel does not explain is the extent to which traditional attitudes on motherhood have been sustained and reinforced by educational institutions (starting in kindergarten), the media and 'experts'. For example, some Soviet sociologists have warned of the dangers of confusing children if sex-roles are not sufficiently emphasised in upbringing (Volkova, 1975).
2. The National Educational Research and Development Trust's review states that nine out of ten children in the United Kingdom receive no day care, despite reassuring official figures showing that in early 1976 almost one-third of children under 5 were using day-care provision. These figures are calculated by including nursery schools and pre-school play-groups in the day-care category, but these do not provide all day care. A Wednesday, term-time, 2-hour play-group bears little relation to the all-day, every-week needs of working parents and their children.
3. The debate on boarding-schools as institutions providing communal upbring-ing for all or most pupils was sparked off by Khrushchev's proposals for educational reforms at the 20th and 21st Party Congresses, and by Strumilin's article entitled 'Family and Community in the Society of the Future', published in *Novyi Mir* in 1960. The article provoked a strong response and opposition both from the public and the 'experts'. For a review of the debates on boarding-schools in the official media, see Dodge (1966: 87–9), Osborn (1970: 64–7), Matthews (1972: 273–4) and Jacoby (1974: 25, 34, 132). Osborn emphasises costs, while Jacoby reports that the majority of parents in cities were against boarding-schools.
4. For a more detailed account of the principal demographic features of Soviet society, see Dodge (1966: 5–31, 251–8) and Matthews (1972: 3–31).
5. One should point out that the French pro-natalist scheme is rather exceptional among the Western capitalist countries.

Chapter 12

1. The text of the decree is reproduced in Schlesinger (1949: 44).
2. Comparable data for the 1970s have not been published by the Soviet authorities.

Chapter 13

1. Article 32 of the 1963 family code states explicitly: 'The decisive agents in the upbringing of children are the parents.'
2. Czechoslovak protective legislation is comprehensive. It regulates overtime, night work (although there are exceptions for nurses and other occupations requiring night work), work underground, work safety and industrial hygiene. It also takes into account the general physiological needs of women, paying

special attention to pregnant women and nursing mothers, and including a detailed catalogue of jobs forbidden to pregnant women or women in general. The legislation is based on the concept that women are equal but biologically different and deserve special protection because of their maternal role.

3. For an excellent and extensive analysis of the events culminating in the 'Prague Spring' and the Soviet invasion, see Skilling (1976).

Chapter 14

1. Out of 14 million people in Czechoslovakia, 7 million are in the productive age category. Almost 80 per cent of these are employed.

2. Luisa Landová-Štychová was a leading member of the pre-war socialist women's movement, which might explain her commitment to socialised forms of living.

Chapter 15

1. The material presented in this chapter is a revised and updated version of Heitlinger (1977a).

2. For a more detailed discussion of part-time employment in the West, see *International Labour Review*, vol. 83, September and October 1963, 380–407, 490–517; Klein (1965); International Labour Office Report no. 8, *Equal Opportunity and Treatment for Women Workers*, 1975.

3. Statistics used in this section have been derived from Svoreňová-Királyova (1968), *Statistická ročenka ČSSR, 1953–77*, Šteker (1972), Bauerová (1974), Jančovičová (1974), Foret and Illner (1976).

4. The category 'judiciary and administration' is rather unclear, but one can assume that it refers largely to the legal profession.

5. By contrast, only two girls in ten go on to some sort of further training in the United Kingdom. The situation is different from that in Canada where the percentage of the female age-group attending school full-time rose from 21 per cent in 1941 to 44 per cent in 1971 – an impressive increase, although not as substantial as in Czechoslovakia.

6. Women are even worse off in the West in this respect. For example, the earnings-gap between male and female manual workers in the United Kingdom *widened* throughout the boom years of the 1950s and 1960s, as more and more women were drawn into the lowest-paid jobs. The ratios of women's to men's earnings were 59 in 1950, 51 in 1960, 50 in 1970, 52 in 1973, 56 in 1974 and 57 in 1975. Only in the last few years has the gap begun to close significantly, although it remains large. In 1975, women manual workers were still earning less, relatively to men, than in 1950. The Equal Pay Act was passed only in 1970 and employers were given 5 years to move towards equal pay. On the whole, they have used the 5 years to explore the many ways *around* the act.

7. Judging from Western experience, 'female jobs' have been consistently classified as less skilled and as worth less. For instance, 70 per cent of the jobs performed by women in the Norwegian clothing industry were classified in wage group 2, whereas the majority of jobs performed by men were classified in wage group 3. In the canning industry, 97 per cent of the labour force were working in jobs classified in group 1, the lowest group. Equal pay legislation (passed in Norway in 1959) is quite meaningless if women perform different

jobs (Vangsness, 1971). Canada has now adopted a principle of 'equal pay for work of equal value', but it remains to be seen how much difference this will make.

Chapter 16

1. See *Zákon o rodině ze dne 4. prosince, 1963*, c.94, Sb, article 1, on marriage, in Schiller (1964).
2. Ibid., article 4, on parents and children.
3. These studies were on children already deprived (coming from broken homes) and living in totally institutionalised environments – a very different situation from that of most children who return home from crèches each day. Moreover, research findings showing that children reared in collective institutions lag behind other children in their physical and mental development are typically associated with essentially conservative paediatrics, psychiatry and child psychology. These 'individual' sciences tend to operate within the confines of biological (as opposed to social) mechanisms. In comparison with the dynamics of social development, biological development proceeds at a snail's pace. It could be argued that this slow tempo of biological changes partly accounts for the relative rigidity and bias of the 'individual' biological sciences and for the tendency to see all the external pressures on the family, especially on the mother-child relationship, as fundamentally disturbing. Psychology, pediatrics, psychiatry, but also functionalist sociology tend – so to speak – to biologise this particular aspect of the family structure and consider it as unchanging.
4. The state (or in about 18 per cent of the cases, a large factory) pays all of the original investment in a nursery and meets five-sixths of the operating costs. Parents only pay 5–8 Kčs daily, which is, in fact, cheaper than if the child is kept at home, for children get all their meals in a crèche.

Chapter 17

1. The material presented in this chapter is a revised and updated version of Heitlinger (1976).
2. The question of the relationship between labour resources, female labour and the birthrate is discussed in greater detail in Chapters 4 and 18.

Chapter 18

1. For a discussion of other dimensions of inequality in the state-socialist societies, see Lane (1971).
2. For a historical examination of Soviet wages policy, see Bergson (1954), Kostin (1960) and Lane (1970, 1971).
3. These various approaches are discussed in Bell (1961), Lane (1970, 1971) and Nove (1975).
4. These include rapid urbanisation, inadequate provision of housing, insufficient investment in consumer goods and services, relatively free availability of abortion, and low wages.
5. The GDR legalised abortion only in 1972, some 15 years after the other East European countries.
6. However, the recent population measures, adopted in 1976 and 1977, indicate a significant shift in policy. The new benefits for employed mothers (not

applicable to fathers) include extension of pregnancy leave on full pay to 26 weeks from 18 weeks, cutting the 43-hour working week to 40 hours (with the same pay) for mothers of two or more children, payment of maternity allowances for two or more children until the child's first birthday at a minimum rate of 300 DM monthly ($156), and the continuation of a childbirth grant of 1,000 DM ($470) and generous family-allowance payments. At the same time, the government offered young couples interest-free loans of up to $4,700 to buy furniture and, in some cases, a house. If the loan recipients have a child within 8 years, the state reduces its repayment demands by $470. A second child within the period reduces the debt by a further $700, and a third clears it altogether. Official figures show that some 85,000 couples have taken advantage of the scheme. These measures have unleashed a tidal wave of births which doctors say has hopelessly flooded hospitals, and pushed the birthrate up to 13.3 per 1,000 population in 1977 – a significant increase over previous years, although the figure is still far behind the levels of other East European countries. The next lowest is Bulgaria with 16.6 per 1,000 population ('Populační politika v NDR', 1977; the *Toronto Globe and Mail*, 6 March 1978).

7. The social need for a higher birthrate must be recognised as a theoretical possibility for all societies; it is by no means restricted to the current East European debates about labour resources and declining birthrates.

Select Bibliography

A. THEORETICAL AND COMPARATIVE LITERATURE

Acker, Joan, 'Women and Social Stratification: A Case of Intellectual Sexism', *American Journal of Sociology*, vol. 78, no. 4 (Jan. 1973).

'An International Survey of Part-Time Employment', *International Labour Review*, vol. 83 (Sept. and Oct. 1963).

Ariès, Phillipe, *Centuries of Childhood* (London, 1962).

Armstrong, Hugh and Pat, 'The Segregated Participation of Women in the Canadian Labour Force, 1941–1971', *Canadian Review of Sociology and Anthropology*, vol. 12, no. 4 (Nov. 1975).

Banks, J. A. and O., 'Feminism and Social Change: A Case Study of a Social Movement', in Zollschan, George K., and Hirsch, Walter (eds.), *Explorations in Social Change* (London, 1964*a*).

Banks, J. A. and O., *Feminism and Family Planning in Victorian England* (Liverpool, 1964*b*).

Bardwick, Judith M., *Psychology of Women: A Study of Bio-Cultural Conflicts*, (New York, 1971).

Bártová, Eva, 'Několik informací o postavení žen v socialistických zemích', *Sociologický časopis*, vol. 12, no. 1 (1976*a*).

Bebel, August, *Woman and Socialism* (New York, 1904).

Bell, Norman W., and Vogel, Ezra F., *A Modern Introduction to the Family* (London, 1960).

Bennett, James E., and Loewe, Pierre M., *Women in Business: A Shocking Waste of Human Resources* (Toronto, 1975).

Benston, Margaret, 'Political Economy of Women's Liberation', *Monthly Review*, vol. 21, no. 4 (Sept. 1969).

Berreman, Gerald D., 'Race, Caste and Other Invidious Distinctions in Social Stratification', *Race*, vol. 13, no. 4 (Apr. 1972).

Board of Trade Report on the Census of Distribution and Other Services, 1966 (London, 1970).

Boyd, Monica, 'The Forgotten Minority: The Socioeconomic Status of Divorced and Separated Women', in Marchak, Patricia (ed.), *The Working Sexes*. Symposium papers on the effects of sex on women at work, delivered 15–16 October 1976 at the University of British Columbia, Vancouver (1977).

Chester, Phyllis, 'Women as Psychiatric and Psychotherapeutic Patients', *Journal of Marriage and the Family*, vol. 33, no. 4 (Nov. 1971).

Coulson, Margaret, 'A Contribution to the Discussion of the Family and the Oppression of Women under Capitalism.' Paper presented at the Women's Liberation Conference on the Family, Leeds, 1973.

Crisis: Women under Attack. Counter-Information Services Anti-Report no. 15 (London, 1976).

Dalla Costa, Mariarosa, *Women and the Subversion of the Community* (Bristol, 1972).

Davies, Ross, *Women and Work* (London, 1975).

Deckard, Barbara, *The Women's Movement: Political, Socioeconomic and Psychological Issues* (New York, 1975).

Delamont, Sara, 'Fallen Engels', *New Edinburgh Review*, no. 18 (1972).

Delmar, Rosalind, 'Looking Again at Engels's *Origin of the Family, Private Property and the State*', in Mitchell, Juliet, and Oakley, Ann (eds.), *The Rights and Wrongs of Women* (London, 1976).

Die Frau in der DDR: Fakten und Zahlen (Berlin, 1975).

Douglas, Mary, *Purity and Danger* (London, 1966).

Edwards, H., 'Housework and Exploitation: A Marxist Analysis', *The First Revolution: A Journal of Female Liberation* (July 1971).

Ehrlich, Carol, 'The Male Sociologist's Burden: The Place of Women in Marriage and Family Texts', *Journal of Marriage and the Family*, vol. 33, no. 3 (Aug. 1971).

Engels, Frederick, *Origin of the Family, Private Property and the State*. Edited, with an introduction, by Eleanor Burke Leacock (New York, 1972).

Equal Opportunity and Treatment for Women Workers. International Labour Office Report no. 8 (Geneva, 1975).

Firestone, Shulamith, *The Dialectic of Sex: The Case for Feminist Revolution* (London, 1972).

Friedan, Betty, *The Feminine Mystique* (New York, 1963).

Friedl, Ernestine, *Women and Men: An Anthropologist's View* (New York, 1975).

Galtung, J., *Theory and Methods of Social Research* (Oslo, 1967).

Gardiner, Jean, 'Political Economy of Domestic Labour in Capitalist Society.' Paper read to the 1974 British Sociological Association Conference in Aberdeen.

Gardiner, Jean, 'Women's Domestic Labour', *New Left Review*, no. 89, (Jan.–Feb. 1975).

Gavron, Hannah, *The Captive Wife* (London, 1966).

Giddens, Anthony, *The Class Structure of the Advanced Societies* (London, 1973).

Gough, Kathleen, 'The Origin of the Family', in Reiter, Rayna R. (ed.), *Toward an Anthropology of Women* (New York, 1975).

Gove, Walter R., 'The Relationship Between Sex Roles, Mental Illness and Marital Status', *Social Forces*, vol. 51 (Sept. 1972).

Gove, Walter R., and Tudor, Jeanette F., 'Sex Roles and Mental Illness', *American Journal of Sociology*, vol. 78, no. 4 (Jan. 1973).

Harris, Chris, 'Changing Conceptions of the Relation between Family and Societal Form in Western Society.' Paper read to the 1975 British Sociological Association Conference in Canterbury.

Harrison, John, 'The Political Economy of Housework', *Conference of Socialist Economists Bulletin* (Winter 1973).

Hedges, Janice Neipert, 'Women Workers and Manpower Demands in the 1970s', *Monthly Labour Review*, vol. 93, no. 6 (June 1970).

Hegedus, Andras, Markus, Maria, Heller, Agnes, and Vajda, Mihaly, *The Humanisation of Socialism: Writings of the Budapest* School (London, 1976).

Heitlinger, Alena, 'The Historical Development of Socialist Feminism', *Catalyst*, vol. 10–11 (Summer 1977*b*).

Heitlinger, Alena, 'Births in East Europe', *New Society*, vol. 33, no. 665 (3 July 1975).

Hempel, C. C., 'The Logic of Functional Analysis', in Gross, L. (ed.), *Symposium on Sociological Theory* (London, 1959).

Hobsbawm, E. J., 'Revolution is Puritan', *New Society* (22 May 1960).

Hochschild, Arlie Russell, 'A Review of Sex Role Research', *American Journal of Sociology*, vol. 78, no. 4 (Jan. 1973).

Hutt, Corrine, *Males and Females* (London, 1972).

Isajiw, W. W., *Causation and Functionalism in Sociology* (London, 1968).

Judek, Stanislaw, *Women in the Public Service: Their Utilization and Employment* (Ottawa, 1968).

Kessler, Evelyn S., *Women: An Anthropological View* (New York, 1976).

Klein, Viola, *Women Workers, Working Hours and Services: A Survey in 21 Countries* (Paris, 1965).

Klein, Viola, and Myrdal, Alva, *Women's Two Roles: Home and Work* (London, 1956).

Komarovsky, Mira, 'Functional Analysis of Sex Roles', *American Sociological Review*, no. 15 (Aug. 1950).

Laws, Judith Long, 'A Feminist Review of Marital Adjustment Literature: The Rape of Locke', *Journal of Marriage and the Family*, vol. 33, no. 3 (Aug. 1971).

Leacock, Eleanor Burke: *See* Engels, Frederick.

Mannheim, Karl, *Ideology and Utopia: An Introduction to the Sociology of Knowledge* (London, 1946).

Marcuse, Herbert, *One Dimensional Man*, (London, 1964).

Marcuse, Herbert, *Eros and Civilisation* (Boston, 1966).

McKee, John, and Sheriffs, Alex, 'Men's and Women's Beliefs, Ideals and Self-Conceptions', *American Journal of Sociology*, vol. 64 (Jan. 1959).

Mead, Margaret, *Sex and Temperament in Three Primitive Societies* (London, 1948).

Mead, Margaret, *Male and Female* (London, 1950).

Meissner, Martin, Humphreys, Elisabeth W., Meis, Scott M. and Scheu, William J, 'No Exit for Wives: Sexual Division of Labour and the

Cumulation of Household Demands', *Canadian Review of Sociology and Anthropology*, vol. 12, no. 4 (Nov. 1975).

Middleton, Chris, 'Sexual Inequality and Stratification Theory', in Parkin, F. (ed.), *The Social Analysis of Class Structure* (London, 1974).

Millett, Kate, *Sexual Politics* (London, 1971).

Mitchell, Juliet, *Woman's Estate* (London, 1971).

Money, John, and Ehrhardt, Anke A., *Man and Woman, Boy and Girl: The Differentiation and Dimorphism of Gender Identity from Conception to Maturity* (London, 1972).

Moore, Barrington, Jr., *Political Power and Social Theory* (Cambridge, Mass., 1958).

Morton, P., 'A Woman's Work is Never Done', *Leviathan*, vol. 2, no. 1 (Mar. 1970).

Oakley, Ann, *Housewife* (London, 1974*a*).

Oakley, Ann, *The Sociology of Housework* (London, 1974*b*).

Pahl, J. M. and R. E., *Managers and Their Wives* (London, 1971).

Parkin, Frank, *Class Inequality and Political Order: Social Stratification in Capitalist and Communist Societies* (London, 1971).

Parsons, Talcott, 'Age and Sex in the Social Stratification of the United States', *American Sociological Review*, vol. 7 (Oct. 1942).

Parsons, Talcott, and Bales, Robert, *Family, Socialisation and Interaction Process* (Glencoe, 1955).

Phillips, Melanie, 'What Kind of Child Care?' *New Society*, vol. 36, no. 711 (20 May 1976).

'Populační politika v NDR', *Populační zprávy*, nos. 1–2 (1977).

Rapoport, Rhona and Robert, *Dual-Career Families* (London, 1971).

Reiter, Rayna R, (ed.), *Toward an Anthropology of Women* (London, 1975).

Rossi, Alice, 'The Equality of Women: An Immodest Proposal', *Daedalus*, no. 93 (Spring 1964).

Rossi, Alice, 'Sex Equality: The Beginnings of an Ideology', *The Humanist*, vol. 29 (Sept.–Oct. 1969). Reprinted in Safilios Rothschild, Constantina (ed.), *Toward a Sociology of Women* (Lexington, Mass., 1972).

Rowntree, M. and J., 'More on the Political Economy of Women's Liberation', *Monthly Review* (Jan. 1970).

Sacks, Karen, 'Engels Revisited: Women, the Organisation of Production, and Private Property', in Reiter, Rayna R. (ed.), *Toward an Anthropology of Women* (London, 1975).

Secombe, Wally, 'The Housewife and Her Labour Under Capitalism', *New Left Review*, no. 83 (Jan.–Feb. 1974).

Secombe, Wally, 'Domestic Labour – A Reply', *New Left Review*, no. 94 (Nov.–Dec. 1975).

Shorter, Edward, *The Making of the Modern Family* (New York, 1975).

Szalai, A., *The Use of Time: Daily Activities of Urban and Suburban Population in Twelve Countries* (Paris, 1972).

Thönnessen, Werner, *The Emancipation of Women: The Rise and Decline of the*

Women's Movement in German Social Democracy, 1863–1933 (London, 1973).

Vangsness, Kari, 'Equal Pay in Norway', *International Labour Review*, vol. 103, no. 4 (Apr. 1971).

Weisstein, Naomi, 'Psychology Constructs the Female', in Gornick, Vivian, and Moran, Barbara K. (eds.), *Woman in Sexist Society: Studies in Power and Powerlessness* (New York, 1971).

Zaretsky, Eli, *Capitalism, the Family and Personal Life*, Canadian Dimension pamphlet (n.d).

Zetkin, Clara, *Socializm pridet k pobede s zhenshchinoi-proletarkoi*. Russian translation from the German of Zetkin's speech at the SPD 1896 Gotha Conference (Moscow, 1960).

Zetkinová, Klára, *Z dějin ženského proletářského hnutí v Německu*. Czech translation from German (Prague, 1961).

B. LITERATURE ON THE SOVIET UNION

Andryushchkyavichene, Ya., 'Zhenskyi trud i problema svobodnogo vremeni', *Problemy byta, braka i sem'i*, (Vilnius, 1970). Published by the Committee for Research on the Family of the Soviet Sociological Association.

Artemov, V. A., et al, *Statistika byudzhetov vremeni trudyashchiksya* (Moscow, 1967).

Artiuchina, A. V., 'V boevye kolony borcov za socializm', *Rabotnica*, no. 43 (Nov. 1929).

Artiuchina, A. V., et al, *Zhenshchiny v revolyucii* (Moscow, 1959).

Artiuchina, A. V., et al., '*Vsegda s Vami' – sbornik, posviashchenyi pyatidesyaletiyu zhurnala "Rabotnica"* (Moscow, 1964).

Arutyunyan, Yu., 'Sotsial'nye aspekty kul'tornogo rosta sel'skogo naseleniya', *Voprosy filosofii*, No. 9 (Sept. 1968).

Baikova, V. G., Duchal, A. S., Zemcov, A. A., *Svobodnoe vremya i vsestoronnee razvitie lichnosti* (Moscow, 1965).

Balabanoff, Angelica, *My Life as a Rebel* (London, 1938).

Barker, G. G., 'Women, Sex Roles and Soviet Society.' Paper presented at the Pendrell Hall Conference, Birmingham, 30 June–2 July 1972.

Bell, Daniel, 'Ten Theories in Search of Reality', in *The End of Ideology* (New York, 1961).

Belova, P. P., 'Reservy partii', in Artiuchina et al, *Uchastnitsy velikogo sozidaniya* (Moscow, 1962).

Berent, J, 'Some Demographic Aspects of Female Employment in Eastern Europe and the USSR', *International Labour Review*, vol. 101 (Jan.–June 1970).

Bergson, A., *The Structure of Soviet Wages: A Study in Socialist Economics* (Cambridge, Mass., 1954).

'Blonina, E.' (Innessa Armand), *Rabotnicy v Internacionale* (Moscow, 1920).

Bobroff, Anne, 'The Bolsheviks and Working Women, 1905–1920', *Soviet Studies*, vol. 26, no. 4 (Oct. 1973).

Bronfenbrenner, Urie, 'The Changing Soviet Family', in Brown, D. R. (ed.), *The Role and Status of Women in the Soviet Union* (New York, 1968).

Bronfenbrenner, Urie, *Two Worlds of Childhood: US and USSR* (New York, 1970).

Brown, D. R. (ed.), *The Role and Status of Women in the Soviet Union* (New York, 1968).

Bukharin, N. I., *Rabotnica k tebe nashe slovo*, Rabochie krestianskie listovki, no. 16 (Moscow, 1919).

Cohn, Helen Desfosses, 'Population Policy in the USSR', *Problems of Communism* (July–Aug. 1973).

Decisions of the Third Congress of the Communist International, Moscow, July 1921.

Dodge, Norton T., *Women in the Soviet Economy* (Baltimore, 1966).

Dodge, Norton T., 'The Role of Women in the Soviet Economy.' Paper presented at the NATO Colloquium on Economic Aspects of Daily Life in the USSR, Brussels, 29–31 January 1975.

Feifer, George, *Moscow Farewell* (New York, 1976).

Fitzpatrick, Sheila, *The Commissariat of the Enlightenment* (London, 1970).

Geiger, H. Kent, *The Family in Soviet Russia* (Cambridge, Mass., 1968).

Gordon, L. A., and Klopov, E. V., *Chelovek posle raboty: Sotsial'nye problemy byta vnerabochego vremeni rabochikh v krupnykh gorodach evropeiskoi chasti SSSR* (Moscow, 1972).

Gordon, L. A., and Rimashevskaya, N. M., *Pyatidnevnaya rabochaya nedelya i svobodnoe vremya trudyashchikhsya* (Moscow, 1972).

Grant, Nigel, 'The Role of Women in Soviet Society', *New Edinburgh Review*, no. 18 (1972).

Halle, Fanina, *Women in Soviet Russia* (London, 1932).

Halle Fanina, *Women in the Soviet East* (London, 1938).

Hazard, John N., *Law and Social Change in the USSR* (London, 1953).

Heer, David M., and Bryden, Judith G., 'Family Allowances and Fertility in the Soviet Union', *Soviet Studies*, vol. 18, no. 2 (Oct. 1966).

Heer, David M., 'The Childbearing Functions of the Soviet Family', in Brown, D. R. (ed.) *The Role and Status of Women in the Soviet Union* (New York, 1968).

Higgins, J. M. D., 'Notes on the Abortion Issue.' Paper presented at 'Women in Eastern Europe' Conference, Birmingham, 30 October 1976.

Hirszowicz, Maria, 'Is There a Ruling Class in the USSR? – A Comment', *Soviet Studies*, vol. 28, no. 2 (Apr. 1976).

Hollander, Paul, 'Family and Sex in the Soviet Union and the United States', *Survey*, vol. 19, no. 3 (88) (Summer 1973).

Holt, Alex, 'Women in the Soviet Union: Recent Change, Present Policies

224 *Women and State Socialism*

and Their Implications' (1976a). Paper presented at 'Women in Eastern Europe' Conference, Birmingham, 30 October 1976.

Holt, Alex, 'A Critique of Bolshevik Policy on Women' (1976b). Ibid.

Hough, Jerry, *The Soviet Prefects: The Local Party Organs in Industrial Decision-Making* (Cambridge, Mass., 1969).

Itogy vsesoyuznoi perepisi naseleniya 1970 goda, vol. 6, (Moscow, 1973).

Jacoby, Susan, *Inside Soviet Schools* (New York, 1974).

Juviler, Peter, 'Soviet Families', *Survey*, no. 60 (July 1966).

Kelly, Aileen, 'Revolutionary Women', *New York Review of Books* (17 July 1975).

Kharchev, A. G., *Brak i sem'ya v SSSR* (Moscow, 1964).

Kharchev, A., and Golod, S, *Professional'naya rabota zhenshchin i sem'ya* (Leningrad, 1971).

Kingsbury, Susan M., and Fairchild, Mildred, *Factory, Family and the Woman in the Soviet Union* (New York, 1935).

Knight, Hilary, 'Abortion Policy in the USSR between 1917 and 1936.' Paper presented at 'Women in Eastern Europe' Conference, Birmingham, 30 October 1976.

Kollontai, Alexandra, *Mezhdunardodnyi Den' Rabotnic* (Moscow, 1920a).

Kollontai, Alexandra, *Rabotnica mat'* (Moscow, 1920b).

Kollontai, Alexandra, *Za tri goda* (Moscow, 1920c).

Kollontai, Alexandra, *Trud zhenshchiny v evolyucii khoziastva* (Moscow, 1923).

Kollontai, Alexandra, *Communism and the Family* (London, 1971).

Kollontai, Alexandra, *Women Workers Struggle for Their Rights* (Bristol, 1971).

Kollontai, Alexandra, *Sexual Relations and the Class Struggle: Love and New Morality* (London, 1972a).

Kollantai, Alexandra, *Autobiography of a Sexually Emancipated Woman* (London, 1972b).

Kommunist (Feb. 1968); (Feb. 1972).

Kommunistka no. 7 (Dec. 1920).

Kontra, Martin, 'Sovětská ekonomická literatura o službách', *Politická ekonomie*, vol. 21, no. 9 (1973).

Kostin, L., *Wages in the USSR* (Moscow, 1960).

Kotlyar, A. E., and Turchaninova, S. Ya., *Zanyatost' zhenshchin v pro-izvodstve*. Statistiko-sociologicheskyi ocherk (Moscow, 1975).

Kozhevnikova, T., 'Extended-Day School', *Pravda* (1 March 1973). Translated in *CDSP*, vol. 25, no. 3 (1973).

Krupskaya, N. K., 'Krepkaya sovetskaya sem'ya', in Krupskaya, N. K. (ed.), *Zhenshchina strany sovetov – ravnopravnyi grazhdanin* (Moscow, 1938b).

Kryazhev, V. G., *Vnerabochee vremya i sfera obsluzhivania* (Moscow, 1966).

Kurganov, I. A., *Sem'ya v SSSR, 1917–1967* (New York, 1967).

Kurganov, I. A., *Zhenshchiny i kommunizm* (New York, 1968).

Kuznetsova, Larisa, 'Nasha ne po plechu', *Literaturnaya gazeta* (15 February 1967).

Kuznetsova, Larisa, 'Whose Job is the Kitchen?' *Literaturnaya gazeta* (12 July 1967. Translated in *CDSP*, vol. 19, no. 33 (6 September 1967).

Lane, David, *Politics and Society in the USSR* (London, 1970).

Lane, David, *The End of Inequality? Stratification under State Socialism* (London, 1971).

Lenin, V. I., *On the Emancipation of Women* (Moscow, 1965; first published in 1934).

Lennon, Lotta, 'Women in the USSR', *Problems of Communism* (Aug. 1971).

Libedinskaya, L., 'Freedom from the Kitchen', *Literaturnaya gazeta* (22 February 1967). Translated in *CDSP*, vol. 19, no. 15 (3 May 1967).

Lipset, Seymour Martin, and Dobson, Richard B., 'Social Stratification and Sociology in the Soviet Union', *Survey*, vol. 19, no. 3 (88) (Summer 1973).

Mace, David Robert and Vera, *The Soviet Family* (London, 1964).

Macura, Milos, 'Population Policies in Socialist Countries of Europe', *Population Studies*, vol. 28, no. 3 (Nov. 1974).

Madison, Bernice Q., *Social Welfare in the Soviet Union* (Stanford, 1968).

Makarenko, A. S., *A Book for Parents*. Translated by Rober Daglish (Moscow, 1954).

Mandel, William M., *Soviet Women* (New York, 1975).

Massell, Gregory J., *The Surrogate Proletariat: Moslem Women and Re-volutionary Strategies in Soviet Central Asia, 1919–1929* (Princeton, 1974).

Matthews, Mervyn, *Class and Society in Soviet Russia* (London, 1972).

McAuley, Alastair, 'The Distribution of Earnings and Incomes in the Soviet Union', *Soviet Studies*, vol. 29, no. 2 (Apr. 1977).

Mishkinsky, Moshe, 'The Jewish Labour Movement and European Socialism', in Ben Sasson, H. H., and Ettinger, S. (eds.), *Jewish Society Through the Ages* (London, 1971).

Narodnoe Khoziastvo SSSR v 1970–1976g (Moscow).

Narodnoe Khoziastvo SSSR za 60 let. Yubileinyi statisticheskiy ezhegodnik (Moscow, 1977).

Narodnoe obrazovanie, nauka i kultura v SSSR (Moscow, 1971).

Nove, A., 'Is There a Ruling Class in the USSR?', *Soviet Studies*, vol. 27, no. 4 (Oct. 1975).

Osborn, Robert, *Soviet Social Policies: Welfare, Equality and Community* (Homewood, Illinois, 1970).

Otchet o pervoi mezhdunarodnoi konferencii kommunistok (Moscow, 1921).

Otchet otdela CKRKP po rabote sredi zhenshchiny za god raboty (Moscow, 1921).

Panova, N. V., 'Voprosy truda i byta zhenshchiny', in *Problemy byta, braka i sem'yi* (Vilnius, 1970).

Petrosyan, G. S., *Vnerabochee vremya trudyashchikhsya v SSSR* (Moscow, 1965).

Pimenova, V. N., *Svobodnoe vremya v sotsialisticheskom obshchestve* (Moscow, 1971).

Popova, Nina, *Women in the Land of Socialism* (Moscow, 1949).

Programma i ustav KP SSSR (Moscow, 1964).

Rabotnica, no. 6 (1924); Jan. 1974; Feb. 1974.

Reich, Wilhem, *The Sexual Revolution* (London, 1961).

Riasanovsky, Nicholas V., *A History of Russia* (New York, 1963).

Rigby, Thomas Harold, *Communist Party Membership in the USSR, 1917–1967* (Princeton, 1968).

Rigby, Thomas Harold, 'Soviet Communist Party Membership under Brezhnev', *Soviet Studies*, vol. 28, no. 3 (July 1976).

Rowbotham, Sheila, *Women, Resistance and Revolution* (London, 1972).

Rubinstein, Alvin (ed.), *Communist Political Systems* (Englewood Cliffs, 1966).

Sadvokasova, A., 'Nekotorye sotsial'no-gigienicheskie aspekty izuchenia aborta', *Sovetskoe zdravookhranenie*, no. 3 (1963).

Sadvokasova, A., *Sotsial'no-gigienicheskie aspekty regulirovaniya razmerov sem'yi* (Moscow, 1969).

St. George, George, *Our Soviet Sisters* (London, 1973).

Samoilova, K. N., *Organizacionnye zadachi otdelov rabotnic* (Moscow, 1920a).

Samoilova, K. N., *Rabotnicy v Rossiskoi Revolyucii* (Moscow, 1920b).

Samoilova, K. N., *Krest'ianka i Sovetskaya vlast'* (Moscow, 1921).

Schlesinger, Rudolf, *Changing Attitudes in Soviet Russia: The Family in the USSR* (London, 1949).

Selivanova, Nina Nikolaevna, *Russia's Women* (New York, 1923).

Serebrenikov, G. N., *The Position of Women in the USSR* (London, 1937).

Sidel, Ruth, *Women and Child Care in China* (New York, 1972).

Slesarev, G. A., 'Voprosy organizacii truda i byta zhenshchin i razshirennoe vosproizvodstvo naseleniya', *Sotsial'nye issledovaniya* (1965).

Smith, Jessica, *Woman in Soviet Russia* (New York, 1928).

Sonin, M. Ya., *Aktual'nye problemy ispol'zovaniya rabochei sily v SSSR* (Moscow, 1965).

SSSR v cifrakh v 1974 g (Moscow, 1975).

Stasova, E. (ed.), *Slavnye bolshevichki* (Moscow, 1958).

Stites, Richard, 'Women's Liberation Movements in Russia, 1900–1930', *Canadian-American Slavic Studies*, vol. 7, no. 4 (Winter, 1973).

Strumilin, S. G., 'Natsional'nyi dochod v SSSR', *Planovoe khoziastvo*, no. 8 (1926).

Tarasova, E., 'Pod znamenem bolshevikov', in Artiuchina *et al.*, *Zhenshchiny v revolyucii* (Moscow, 1959).

Taubman, William, *The View from Lenin Hills: Soviet Youth in Ferment* (New York, 1967).

Taubman, William, *Governing Soviet Cities: Bureaucratic Policies and Urban Development in the USSR* (London, 1973).

Trotsky, Leon, *Problems of Life* (London, 1924).

Trud v SSSR (Moscow, 1968).

Velichkene, I., 'Trud i zdorovie zhenshchiny-rabotnicy', in *Problemy byta, braka i sem'i* (Vilnius, 1970).

Verbenko, A. A. *et al.*, *Aborty i protivozachatochnye sredstvo* (Moscow, 1968).

Vestnik statistiki, 1969/1, 1970/1, 1972/5, 1974/7, 1975/1, 1977/1, 1978/1.

Vinokurov, A. (ed.), *Sotsial'noe obespechenie v Sovetskoi Rossii* (Moscow, 1919).

Volkova, Tamara, *A Woman's Place in the USSR*. IMG Pamphlet, Series 'Communism versus Stalinism' (London, 1975).

Warshovsky Lapidus, Gail, 'The Women of the Soviet Union', *The Center Magazine*, vol. 7, no. 3 (May–June 1974).

Weaver, Kitty, *Lenin's Grandchildren: Pre-School Education in the Soviet Union* (New York, 1971).

Wesson, R. G., *Soviet Communes* (New Brunswick, 1963).

Wiles, Peter, *Distribution of Income: East and West* (Amsterdam, 1974).

Wiles, Peter, 'Recent Data on Soviet Income Distribution', *Survey*, vol. 21, no. 3 (96) (Summer 1975).

Wiles, P., and Markowski, S., 'Income Distribution under Communism and Capitalism', *Soviet Studies*, vol. 22, nos. 3 and 4 (Jan. and Apr. 1971).

Women in the Soviet Union: Statistical Returns 1970.

Yankova, Z. A., 'O bytovykh rolyakh rabotauyshchei zhenshchiny', in *Problemy byta, braka i sem'i* (Vilnius, 1970a).

Yankova, Z. A., 'O semeno-bytovykh rolyakh rabotauyshchei zhenshchiny', *Sotsial'nye issledovaniya*, no. 4 (1970b).

Yunina, Lyubov, 'Tol'ko Romeo', *Literaturnaya gazeta* (12 May 1971). Translated and abstracted in *Sociological Abstracts*, vol. 20, no. 5 (1972), Area 1900.

Yurkevich, N. G., *Sovetskaya sem'ya* (Minsk, 1970).

Zagumennykh, M., and Gaidukov, D., 'Kak postroit' rabotu zhensektorov pri sovetakh', *Rabotnica*, no. 34 (Dec. 1932).

Zanin, V. I., 'Byuzhet rabochego vremeni', *Sotsial'nye issledovaniya*, no. 6 (1970).

Zetkin, Clara, 'My Recollections of Lenin', in Lenin, V. I., *On the Emancipation of Women* (Moscow, 1934).

Zhenshchiny (i deti) v SSSR, 1937, 1961, 1963, 1969, 1975, 1977.

Zhenshchiny mira v bor'be za sotsial'nyi progress. Published by the Soviet Women's Committee (Moscow, 1972).

Zueva, E., *Zhenshchina v Sovetskoi Rossii* (Moscow, 1925).

C. LITERATURE ON CZECHOSLOVAKIA

Bareš, Gustav, Introduction to Bebel's *Žena a socialismus* (Prague, 1962).

Bártová, Eva, 'Postoje k problému ženy a rodiny', *Sociologický časopis*, vol. 8, no. 1 (1972).

Bártová, Eva, 'Žena a rodina v zrcadle společenského výzkumu v ČSSR', *Sociologický časopis*, vol. 9, no. 2 (1973).

Bártová, Eva, 'Několik informací o postavení žen v socialistických zemích', *Sociologický časopis*, vol. 12, no. 1 (1976*a*).

Bártová, Eva, 'Historický vývoj politické participace žen', *Sociologický časopis*, vol. 12, no. 1 (1976*b*).

Baštýř, Ivo, 'Rozbor rozdílu v úrovni odměňování mužů a žen v ČSSR', *Politická ekonomie*, vol. 19, no. 9 (1971).

Bauerová, Jaroslava, 'Rodinná problematika vedoucích pracovnic', *Sociologický časopis*, vol. 6, no. 5 (1970).

Bauerová, Jaroslava, *Zaměstnaná žena a rodina* (Prague, 1974).

Bauerová, Jaroslava, 'Marxismus-leninsmus a ženská otázka', *Sociologický časopis*, vol. 12, no. 1 (1976).

Bauerová, Jaroslava *et al.*, *Problémy zaměstnaných žen* (Pardubice, 1971).

Bezouška, Jiří and Vytlačil, Josef: 'Šetření o využití času obyvatelstva v ČSSR', *Demografie*, vol. 5, no. 4 (Oct. 1963).

Blucha, Jiří, 'Kvalifikace žen ve strojírenství', *Zprávy státní populační komise*, no. 1 (1966).

Brablcová, Vlasta, 'Modifikace efektu některých služeb vnitřní ekonomické činnosti', *Zprávy státní populačni komise* (1967).

Brablcová, Vlasta, and Kabrhelová, Marie, 'Konkrétni fakta a cifry o postaveni žen v socialistickém Československu', in Holečková, Božena (ed.), *Ženy v boji za socialismus* (Prague, 1971).

Brejchová, Jiřina, *50 let velike cesty* (Prague, 1960).

Brejchová, Jiřina, *Trade Unions and Employed Women in Czechoslovakia* (Prague, 1967).

Brejchová, J., Holečková, B., and Košnařová, V., *Postavení žen v ČSSR* (Prague, 1962).

Burešová, Marta, *Women in the Czechoslovak Co-operative Movement* (Prague, 1966).

Čáp, Václav and Peltrámová, Šárka, 'Problémy efektivnosti zařazování žen z domácnosti do pracovního procesu', *Politická ekonomie*, vol. 13, (May 1965).

Čech, Vladimír and Jukl, Eduard, 'Nevyužitý zdroj studia ženské otázky', *Sociologický časopis*, vol. 12, no. 1 (1976).

Čísla, aktuality, statě. Leninské pojetí ženské otázky a aktuální problémy ženského hnutí v současné době. Published by the ideological section of the Central Committee of the Czechoslovak Communist Party (Prague, 1970).

Čísla pro každého, 1973 (Prague, 1973).

Děti, naše budoucnost. A pamphlet published by the Central Committee of the National Front ČSSR with the collaboration of the Government Population Commission, June 1972.

Dix, Carol, 'Birth Rights', *The Guardian* (6 February 1975).

Dunovský, Jiří, 'Mateřství zaměstnaných žen a problémy péče o jejich děti v nejvtlejším věku', *Sociologický časopis*, vol. 7, no. 2 (1971).

Dvořák, Karel, 'Perorální antikoncepce v Československu', *Zprávy státní populační komise*, no. 5 (Oct. 1966).

Encyklopedie moderní ženy (Prague, 1964).

Fišerová, Vlasta, 'Rodina v sociální struktuře společnosti', in Machonin, Pavel & Co., (eds.), *Československá společnost: Sociologická analýza sociální stratifikace* (Bratislava, 1969).

Fogarty, Michael P., Rapoport, Rhona, and Rapoport, Robert N., *Sex, Career and Family* (including an international review of women's roles) (London, 1971).

Foret, Miroslav, and Illner, Michal, 'Vývoj zaměstnanosti žen v ČSSR 1954–1973 ve světě vybraných statistických ukazatelů', *Sociologický časopis*, vol. 12, no. 1 (1976).

Frejková, Eva, 'K postavení žen v socialistické společnosti', *Politická ekonomie*, vol. 13, no. 7 (1965).

Fukalová, D., *Ekonomická aktivita žen v ČSSR*. Unpublished dissertation (Prague/Ostrava, 1967).

Háková Libuše, 'Prosazovat marxistickou koncepci ženské otázky', *Zpravodaj*, vol. 1, no. 1 (Sept. 1967).

Háková, Libuše, 'Úvaha a podněty k chápání společenských funkcí ženy', *Sociologický časopis*, vol. 6, no. 5 (1970).

Háková, Libuše, and Svarovská, Anna, 'Socialismus a ženy', *Nová Mysl*, no. 3 (1961).

Hájková, Věra, and Tučková, Anna, 'Pranýř nebo pomoc?', *Kulturní tvorba* (17 June 1965).

Hamerník, Emilian, 'Postavení ženy v rodině za socialismu', *Sociologický časopis*, vol. 12, no. 1 (1976).

Havelka, Jaroslav, 'Hlavni směry naší populační politiky', in *Děti, naše budoucnost* (Prague, June 1972*a*).

Havelka, Jaroslav, 'Vládní populační komise zahájila činnost', *Populační zprávy*, no. 3 (1972*b*).

Havelka, Jaroslav, 'K aktuálním otázkám naší populační politiky', *Sociální politika*, no. 3 (May 1974).

Heitlinger, Alena, 'Pro-Natalist Population Policy in Czechoslovakia', *Population Studies*, vol. 30, no. 1 (March 1976).

Heitlinger, Alena, 'Women's Labour Participation in Czechoslovakia since World War II', in Marchak, Patricia (ed.), *The Working Sexes*. Symposium papers on the effects of sex on women at work delivered October 16–19, 1976, at the University of British Columbia, Vancouver (1977*a*).

Heitlinger, Alena, 'The Historical Development of European Socialist Feminism', *Catalyst*, nos. 10–11 (Summer 1977*b*).

Hilbertová, Slavie, 'Nové formy jeselské péče', *Zprávy státní populační komise*, no. 3 (1968).

Hinnerová, Jiřina, 'Malé rodinné školy', *Populační zprávy*, nos. 1–2 (1973).

Holečková, Božena (ed.), *Ženy v boji za socialismus* (Prague, 1971).

Hušek, R., 'Od jeslí až na vysokou školu', *Hospodářské noviny*, no. 29 (1963).

Jančovičová, Jolana, 'Problematika ženy v lékarskom povolání na Slovensku', *Sociologia*, vol. 6, no. 5 (1974).

Janečková, L., 'Šetření o mateřském příspěvku', *Populační zprávy*, nos. 4–6 (1976).

Janouchová, Blanka, 'Zabota o zhenshchine v CSSR', *Demosta*, vol. 6, no. 1 (1973).

Kadlecová, Z., 'Žena současnosti', *Sociální politika*, no. 2 (Mar. 1974).

Kaliberková, Jaroslava, 'Žena, ekonomický problém', *Hospodářské noviny*, nos. 49–50 (1968).

Kallmünzerová, M., 'K práci poslankyň národních výborů', *Sociální politika*, no. 2 (Feb. 1972).

Kerner, Antonín, 'Společenská dělba práce a rozvoj služeb', *Politická ekonomie*, vol. 21, no. 9 (1973).

Köhler-Wagnerova, Alena, *Die Frau im Socialismus – Beispiel ČSSR* (Hamburg, 1974).

Kohout, Jaroslav, and Kolář, Jaroslav, 'Komplexní sociologický výzkum v Tesla Pardubice', *Sociologický časopis*, vol. 2, no. 4 (1966).

Kontšeková, Ol'ga, *Ekonomické činitele a dôsledky ekonomickej aktivity žien.* Unpublished dissertation (Bratislava, 1968).

Kontšeková, Ol'ga, 'Ekonomická efektivnost' práce žien', *Sociologia*, vol. 6, no. 5 (1974).

Košnierik, J., 'Rodinná a populační politika nabývá v přítomné době stále většího významu', in *Děti, naše budoucnost* (Prague, June 1972).

Kuba, R., 'Zaměstnanost žien a rozmist'ovanie dorostu', *Plánované hospodářství*, no. 4 (1964).

Landová-Štychová, Luisa, 'Rodiče velmi potřebují děti', *Plamen*, no. 2 (1961).

Malá, Anna, *O výdělečné práci žen* (Prague, 1925).

Malá, Emilia, 'K dynamike kúlturnej úrovně žien v pomienkach socialistickej spoločnosti', *Sociologia*, vol. 7, no. 5 (1975).

Matějček, Julius, 'Nová úprava dětských dávek', *Sociálni politika*, no. 2 (March 1973).

Mínění žen o zaměstnání, domácnosti a rodině (Prague, 1972).

Mrkosová, Milada, 'Z výzkumu pracovních podmínek a společenské aktivity učitelek základních škol', *Sociologia*, vol. 6, no. 5 (1974).

Musil, Jiří, 'Some Aspects of Social Organization of the Contemporary Czechoslovak Family', *Journal of Marriage and the Family*, vol. 33, no. 1 (Feb. 1971).

Němcová, Jarmila, 'Postoje k ekonomické činnosti žen', *Demografie*, vol. 13, no. 1 (1971).

Nentvicková, Božena, and Janderová, Miroslava, 'Mzdy mužů a žen v průmyslových podnicích', *Populační zprávy*, vol. 1, no. 1 (1971).

Obsahové zaměření činnosti Československeho svazu žen a politicko-organizační zabezpečeni sjezdu (CSSZ.CSZ.SZZ). A cyclostyled internal publication of the Czechoslovak Union of Women (Prague, 1972).

Osnova referátu k volbám výboru žen (Prague, 1954).

Pelikán, Josef, 'Půjčky se státním příspěvkem mladým manželům', *Odbořář*, no. 8 (Apr. 1973).

Polívková, Viktorie, 'Jesle ano, ne?', *Děti a My*, vol. 4, no. 4 (1974).

Právní postavení žen v našem stàtě. (A stenographic report from the seminar on The Legal Position of Women in our State, at Castle Žihovost, Jihlava, 23–24 November, 1967), Jihlava (1968).

Prokopec, Jiří, 'Zpráva o průzkumu manželských vztahů: Sexuální život mladých městských manželství', *Zprávy státní populační komise*, no. 4 (1966).

Radvanová, Senta, 'Zaměstnaná žena v rodině a domácnosti', *Nová Mysl*, no. 12 (1963).

Radvanová, Senta, *Žena a právo* (Prague, 1971).

Rudé právo, 28 Sept.; 12, 19, 26 Oct.; 9 Nov.; 8 Dec. 1966; 8 Feb. 1967; 1 Feb. 1971.

Růžičková, Marie, 'Poslání a úkoly komisí žen ZV ROH', *Odbořář*, no. 25 (Dec. 1974).

Sagara, Dušan, and Mach, František, 'Profesionalizácia prace žien v socialistickom pol'nohospodarstve', *Sociologia*, vol. 6, no. 5 (1974).

Schiller, Milan, *Zákon o rodině* (Prague, 1964).

Schüller, Vratislav, and Stupková, Eva, 'Sociální problematika umělého přerušení těhotenství a možnosti jejího studia', *Demografie*, vol. 9, no. 3 (1967).

Scott, Hilda, *Does Socialism Liberate Women? Experiences from Eastern Europe* (Boston, 1974).

Selucky, Radoslav, *Czechoslovakia: The Plan that Failed* (London, 1970).

Šesták, Vojtěch, 'Demografický vývoj v ČSSR a nutnost jeho ovlivňování', *Děti, naše budoucnost* (Prague, June 1972).

Skilling, Gordon H., *Czechoslovakia's Interrupted Revolution* (Princeton, 1976).

Smutná, Jiřina, 'Postavení ženy v dnešní společnosti', *Zpravodaj*, vol. 1, no. 1 (1967).

Srb, Vladimír, 'K dalšímu zvyšování zaměstnanosti žen v ČSSR', *Zprávy státní populační komise*, no. 5 (Nov. 1964).

Srb, Vladimír, 'Kvalifikace a pracovní podmínky žen nově vstupujících do zaměstnání, *Demografie*, vol. 8, no. 1 (1966).

Srb, Kučera and Vysušilová, 'Průzkum manželství, antikoncepce a potratu', *Demografie*, vol. 1, nos. 1 and 4 (1961).

Statistická ročenka ČSSR (1953–77).

'Status Státní Populační Komise', *Zprávy státní populačni komise*, nos. 1 and 4 (1963).

Šteker, Antonín, 'Bytová výstavba v roce 1970', *Populační zprávy*, vol. 1, no. 1 (1971).

232 *Women and State Socialism*

Šteker, Antonin, 'O zaměstnanosti žen', *Sociální politika*, no. 2, (Feb. 1972).

Štetinova, D., 'Girls' Clubs Competing', *Československý svět*, vol. 29, no. 20 (Oct. 1974).

Svoreňová-Királyová, Blanka, *Žena 20. století ve svělě práce. Pohled na zaměstnanou ženu v moderním svělě* (Prague, 1968).

Tomášek, Pavel, 'Dělba práce v domácnosti a předpoklady socialistického způsobu života', *Sociologia*, vo. 7, no.3, (1975).

Tomášek, Přemysl, 'Referát o současných problémech zaměstnaných žen', *Současné problémy zaměstnaných žen*. Pamphlet published by the Czech Union of Women (Prague, 1968).

Typovská, Ludmila, 'Poznatky z výzkumu sexuálních postojů studentů', in Vítek, Karel (ed.), *Lékařské, právní, sociologicko-psychologické, sexuálně-psychologické a pedagogické otázky manželského soužití* (Olomouc, 1976).

Vaněk, Antonín, *Přízonaky krize manželské rodiny* (Prague, 1971).

Vaníčková, Bohuslava, 'Tak bojovaly . . .', in Holečková, Božena (ed.), *Ženy v boji za socialismus* (Prague, 1971).

Večerník, Jiří, and Vítečkova, Jana, 'Změny v některých podmínkách a rysech způsobu života pracujících žen v ČSSR', *Sociologický časopis*, vol. 12, no. 1 (1976).

Vítek, Karel, 'Manželská harmonie a disharmonie', in Vítek, Karel (ed.), *Lékařské, právní, sociologicko-psychologické, sexuálně-psychologické a pedagogické otázky manželského soužití* (Olomouc, 1976).

Vlasta, 20 July 1966; 11 June 1967; 6 and 19 July 1967; 24 Apr. 1968; 22 May 1968; 10 July 1968; 29 May 1969.

Vojta, Miroslav, 'Náměty na zlepšení práce interupčních komisí', *Zprávy státní populační komise*, no. 2 (1968).

Votruba, Bohumil, 'Druhá směna zaměstnaných žen', *Odborář*, no. 1, January 1973.

Vybavenost domácností ČSSR některými předměty dlouhodobé spotřeby (Prague, 1973).

Vývoj společnosti v číslech (Prague, 1965).

Working Women in Czechoslovakia (Prague, 1975).

Wynnyczuk, Vladimír, 'Nové cesty k uvolnění denního programu zaměstnané ženy', *Zprávy státní populačni komise*, no. 3 (1962).

'Zásady vlády ČSR pro zřizování a provoz mikrojeslí', *Populační zprávy*, nos. 1–2 (1977).

Zelenková, Marta, 'Poradenství na poli plánovaného rodičovství', *Zprávy populační komise*, no. 4 (1970).

Žižková, Jana, 'K otázkám dloudobého vývoje zaměstnanosti žen', *Demografie*, vol. 14, no. 3 (1972).

Zukalova, Ol'ga, 'K problematike motivácií ekonomickej aktivity žien v našej spoločnosti', in *Žena a rodina v socialistickej spoločnosti*. Collection of papers given at a scientific conference in Bratislava, 15–19 December 1975. Published by the Slovak Union of Women.

Index

Figures in *italic* indicate a table

Family (contd.)
analysis, 9–12, 28–9, 30, 206n, 216n; in USSR, 79, 80–5, 126–7, 130, 212n; state intervention in, 29–31, 73–4, 80–5, 117–21, 126–7, 130, 135–7, 166–7, 179–84; strengthening of, 73–4, 84–5, 179–84; see also Child care, Family allowances, Family code, Family planning, Housework, Pro-natalism
Family allowances: in Czechoslovakia, 179–84; in Eastern Europe, 198; in USSR, 118–21
Family code: in Czechoslovakia, 135–7, 166–7, 214n, 216n; in USSR, 62, 80, 123, 212n
Family incentives, see Pro-natalism
Family planning, 29–31, 119; in Czechoslovakia, 179, 199; in USSR, 20, 95, 122–9; see also Abortion, Contraception, Pro-natalism
Family size: in Czechoslovakia, 178–9, 182, 183–4; in Eastern Europe, 29–30, 119; in USSR, 20, 95, 119
Fathers, see Husbands, Sexual division of labour
Feifer, G., 22
Feminity, see Sex-role stereotypes
Feminisation, 12, 102, 149, 157, 163
Feminised occupations, 12, 70, 79, 99, 102, 148, 151, 163, 196, 215n; see also Medicine, Teaching
Feminism: and socialism, 5, 35–76, 82, 192, 200–4, 207n–8n, 209n, 210n, 211n; bourgeois, 37, 39, 42–4, 46–8, 54, 60, 206n, 207n–8n, 209n, 210n; puritan, 206n; radical, 28, 207n; see also Emancipation of women, Sex equality, Women's liberation, Women's organisations
Fertility, see Birth-rates, Pro-natalism
Finland, 101, 161
Firestone, S., 28, 207n
First Congress of Peasant and Working Women, 56
First International, 36, 208n
First International Congress of Women Workers, 51, 210n
First World War, 47, 50, 98, 123, 135

Five-Year Plans: in Czechoslovakia, 142, 199; in USSR, 60, 61, 62, 120, 147
Fourier, C., 81
Fourth Czechoslovak Trades Unions Congress, 66
France, 98, 109–10, 119, 214n
Friedan, B., 89, 139
Functionalism, see Structural-functionalism

Gavron, H., 11
German Democratic Republic (GDR), 3, 147, 151, 194, 195, 198
German Social Democratic Party (SPD), 5, 35–42, 48–9, 50, 61, 147, 202, 208n, 210n
Giddens, A., 14
Girls' Clubs, 73
Golod, S. I., 22
Government Population Commission, 182, 183
Grandmothers: in Czechoslovakia, 175–6; in USSR, 112, 116
Great Britain, 50, 86, 87, 88, 99, 101, 110, 113, 117, 144, 149–50, 214n, 215n
Gypsy women, 69

Halle, F., 209n
Health services: and abortion, 124–8, 185, 187–9; and contraception, 124, 185; in Czechoslovakia, 62, 67, 75, 185, 187–9, 211n; in USSR, 58, 60, 109, 123–8; see also Children's diseases, Medicine
Heavy industry, see Economic growth
Holiday camps, 116–17
Holland, 50, 161
Homosexuality, 21–2
House-communes, 80–5, 200, 202
Household services: and socialist feminism, 56, 139, 203; co-ordination of, 89–90; in Czechoslovakia, 25–6; 138–43, 161, 178, 182; in Great Britain, 86–7; in USSR, 17, 81, 86–7, 89; productivity of, 25–6; see also Consumer goods and services, Housework, Public catering